T0322186

Home Is Where We Start

Home Is Where We Start

Growing Up in the Fallout of the Utopian Dream

SUSANNA CROSSMAN

FIG TREE
an imprint of
PENGUIN BOOKS

FIG TREE

UK | USA | Canada | Ireland | Australia
India | New Zealand | South Africa

Fig Tree is part of the Penguin Random House group of companies
whose addresses can be found at global.penguinrandomhouse.com.

First published 2024
001

Set in 13.5/16pt Garamond MT Std
Typeset by Jouve (UK), Milton Keynes
Printed and bound in Great Britain by Clays Ltd, Elcograf S.p.A.

The authorized representative in the EEA is Penguin Random House Ireland,
Morrison Chambers, 32 Nassau Street, Dublin D02 YH68

A CIP catalogue record for this book is available from the British Library

ISBN: 978–0–241–65090–5

www.greenpenguin.co.uk

Penguin Random House is committed to a sustainable future for our business, our readers and our planet. This book is made from Forest Stewardship Council® certified paper.

To A and our three daughters

'Home is where one starts from . . .
In my end is my beginning.'
T. S. Eliot, *Four Quartets*

'There is no place like home.'
Dorothy Gale, *The Wizard of Oz*

Contents

CONTENTS

Prologue: Secret Lives

'If you want to keep a secret,
you must also hide it from yourself.'
George Orwell, *1984*

At the community, if all my days are rolled into one, they start here: Alison is back from milking the cows, the early morning shift. She opens my bedroom door. 'Time to get up.' I slip from under warm covers into sharp air, and a chill hits my face, feet, legs, chest and arms. It's always cold in the house. I run to my sink and stick my head in freezing water. My sink is always kept full of water, and no one ever pulls out the plug. This sink-water thing is something I invented. It is hard to endure and sometimes almost impossible, but for my system to work my head must be underwater. Eyes tightly shut. It is a homemade alarm. Gripping the sink and holding my breath, I slowly count: *One. Two. Three. Four. Five. Six. Seven. Eight. Nine. Ten.* Gasping, I lift my head. Face dripping, I check the vine. It has sneaked in through the top of my sash window. Green stalks and leaves are sprouting inside. A plant is growing in my bedroom, and I tell no one, just like no one knows about my alarm. The vine sketches a green pattern on my ceiling, the motif of a secret life.

In the corridor, my big sister Claire pushes me. She's always pushing. In the distance, I hear Alison waking my brother, and then humming the song 'We Shall Not Be Moved'. This song is from marches against nuclear bombs. The words mean we protest, and Alison is often singing and protesting because the fabric of society is falling apart, but as it crumbles we rise into a shining light. She's our mum, even though you can't say 'mum' in the community. I yank open our Unit door.

On the wooden staircase, by a banister curve, I meet Brandy. 'Hi,' she says. 'Hi,' I reply. We walk down thirty monumental steps. Handrails parallel the pitch of the flight. The banisters are long and dangerous. Liquorice brown. Smooth and warm. It is so high, we are banned from sliding down. You could kill yourself. But we slide.

I am nearly nine, and recently Charles and Diana got married at St Paul's Cathedral. More than 750 million people watched the wedding on TV. It was in the papers, and we are against it, but we watched it anyway. Diana's dress was a frothy white river of fabric, and her doe-like eyes peeped from beneath her veil. It was beautiful, but I know marriage is a patriarchal institution, a capitalist trap, a snare. You can read about it in *Spare Rib*, or if you ask community members, someone will tell you marriage is legalized rape. It is a construction, and that means it's not natural, and is part of the social reproduction of gender roles and women's unpaid domestic labour.

This is theory, and it means different things when it is given to an Adult or to a Kid. But I've been living in the community for a couple of years. The norms have become normal, and because I am an individual, I can speak the truth and express myself.

'Saskia's going to make ground muesli.' Brandy twitches her freckled nose. Her blond bunches bounce, and I see they are unbalanced. One is higher than the other, but I don't tell her, because sometimes Brandy kicks. Then we fight, and usually she wins. 'Ace idea,' I say. The Kids always make their own breakfasts. Knives heavy against our growing hands, we grip handles, saw bread, smear margarine, scoop lumps of oily peanut butter from white plastic catering-size vats. From the fridge, we grab large brown plastic jugs. Inside, the raw milk from our cows is topped with heavy cream. Precariously, we tip milk into brown glass mugs, trying to avoid the inch of yellow. If the cream gets in the cup, it is sludge inside your mouth. Paste coats your tongue.

Downstairs in the Kitchen, Brandy says, 'I'll go and get the muesli.' She slips into the unlit storeroom, where the Adults go, among the stockpiles of coal-black currants, apricots, sacks of chickpeas, rice, lentils, sunflower seeds, and cardboard boxes filled with wrinkled prunes, dark as midnight. Our diet is organic before the word exists and food is ordered in bulk from health food co-ops. We eat vegetables from our garden. We are self-sufficient and it is good for the planet. Meat, dairy and eggs come from our smallholding. Along a corridor, there is an industrial cold room. It closes with a clunk and refrigerates wheels of black-wax-coated cheddar cheese. 'Here we are,' Brandy says, moments later. In her hands is a large bowl filled with oats, currants and hazelnuts. It is scented like sawdust and something sweet.

Saskia waits by the coffee grinder. 'Hurry up. Give me the bowl, Brandy. Let's do it.' Saskia is our boss for now, though Jason comes in at a close second alongside Michael, and Troy is a candidate when he's around. Troy is Sunshine's big brother, and Sunshine is my friend. We are the Kids, and we have leaders even though we are all equal.

Saskia tips the heap of muesli into the grinder, and flips the switch: 'Yes!' The coffee grinder turns, and we whizz into the roles the Adults give us. Alone, we must cut, chop, slice, cook, wash and boil. Diving deep into the making of life, we are undoing the notion of childhood because they say it was invented like the nuclear family. A small blade rotates fast as light, crushing and pulverizing everything into dust. Tina puts her hands over her ears. Saskia laughs.

'You are skill,' Claire tells Saskia.

'Here you go.' Saskia hands Claire the first bowl. As the machine is small, we must wait for our powder: Troy, Michael, Jason, Sunshine, Brandy, Jake, Rainbow, Tina and me. When it is ready, I smother mine with milk. It is a miracle recipe, invented by a Kid. Standing by the coffee grinder, I cram it in my mouth, surrounded by the others. One to ten and back again.

Our gang has changed. Little Harry has gone; his mummy had bulging eyes, and talked too loudly. Often, she cried, and once she pulled me into a corner, weeping and whispering, 'They are all plotting to get me.' The Adults said, 'She has to go.' Nobody mentioned the words 'mental illness' or 'crazy', but she is one of the only members who will ever be asked to leave. Though she didn't hurt anyone, it was best for everyone. John (the Australian) and Dee (the Ghanaian) have taken their three children, Andrew, Merrilyn and Clementine, to live in the Australian outback. Apparently, David says, 'The two girls are going *fucking* wild!' David the Adult and ex-heroin addict is my best friend, but I am careful who I tell about this now. Community rules are different to those outside, and playground bullying singed my skin last year. But David still says he will marry me. The twins, Charlotte and Sarah, have moved down to Devon to live with their dad. They left after the girls found a razor in the communal bathroom. They tried to shave their little faces, and cut their skin into ribbons of red.

Over my fifteen years in the house, dozens of Adults and Kids will live in the community. People appear and stay for a few days, eighteen months, or years. When they arrive, we are joined at the hip, fused like metals, welded into bonds: we eat, sleep and live collectively. The house becomes their home, and in the woods, inside their Units, or outside on the front lawn, where crocuses are planted in a 'Ban the Bomb' peace sign, they learn our language and 'way of life'. New members talk about rejecting 'the mainstream' and 'disrupting conditioning'. They are libertarians, and that means they think children are fundamentally good and, if left to their own devices, will bloom. The Adults cuddle us, shout at us, cook us food and hold our hands. Then, one day, there is a random crack. A snap. People leave. There is a constant fracturing, and they say, 'We are like family,' and then vanish in a puff of smoke. It is a magician's trick gone wrong, for nothing else appears, and once people leave, I rarely see them again. Men, women and children flitter through our lives.

Brandy's stepdad, Thomas, enters the Kitchen. A roll-up dangling from the side of his mouth, blond curly hair standing on end, dirty jeans and an orange shirt, the sleeves rolled up to his elbows. 'Bloody hurry up. It is time to go to school.' We chuck our dirty bowls into a sink and run outside, ragged and undone. I am wearing Sunshine's new purple coat. Her grandma sent it through the post. Mine is lost, and Sunshine is homeschooled and doesn't need it today. We often share clothes, and I zip her coat to my chin.

Outside, our van is parked at the top of a slope, balanced on gravel. We crowd behind it. We do this every morning: push the van down the hill to start the motor. In the winter, our small fingers stick to the freezing metal. You must be careful; you can leave skin behind. In the summer, the metal is boiling hot. Our VW van is always broken. It is a communal vehicle. We use this word, 'vehicle', and we don't say 'car'. The community has another vehicle, a black London taxicab, but we don't all fit inside. Kids have to crouch on the floor. One day, Violet, Michael and Saskia's mum, drives me to Glastonbury Festival in the cab. Violet is an artist, and on the journey she tells me about the pictures she paints of purple vaginas, dinner parties, and a woman called Judy Chicago. At Glastonbury, people take photos and think we are a band. But when you travel in the black cab you must avoid the folding seats, because if you sit there, you are back to front, and will get carsick and puke. Everyone shares the two communal vehicles, and Thomas, Bill, David and

Lawrence spend hours repairing them. Hands black with grease, they crouch in the garage pit and swear. They maintain the van. But, often, we're late for school, and occasionally we have to walk.

'Don't shove me.' Brandy is trying to get near to the middle; she pushes her little sister Tina out of the way. The side is bad; it is more difficult to push, and you can fall in the gravel. Violet comes to help. 'Get a move on, kids.' Violet's black hair is stuck to her forehead; the strands line up, counting the morning minutes. She's wearing a long floating dress and wellington boots. We place our hands on the van. Thomas shouts, 'One, two, three, go,' and turns the ignition on. Our arms are outstretched, and we run forward, working as a crew. I pray to Lardy: *Make the van start. Make the van start.* Lardy is a god I invented, mixing 'Lord' and 'Lady' so I'm not being sexist. Even if religion is wrong – because, Tripti says, 'Marx believes it is the opium of the people' – I still pray. The van goes down the slope, and the Volkswagen chugs, the engine rumbling like a distant storm. Praise Lardy! Thomas brakes and Violet dashes forward, almost trips over her dress and yanks the side door open. We race to get inside.

'Get a fucking move on,' Thomas shouts. We must go before the engine dies, before the van breaks down again and the rage and swearing start. When the Adults swear and shout I can feel myself shrinking, and then I am outside of everything, and it is like I am watching and maybe I am not there. In the back of the van, I am quiet. Thomas is German, and speaks in sentences, straight and clunky like railway lines. He knows about agriculture, and he frightens me.

The road to school goes past hamlets and farms. We

should go to the local town school, but the Adults don't agree with the ethos. 'Ethos' is another communal word, and it describes what you believe in, and something called 'social behaviour'.

As we drive round a bend, Tina bumps into Saskia. Saskia elbows Tina, 'You're a div.' Tina answers, 'I am not.' Saskia elbows Tina again, and this time she hits Tina's stomach, and Tina starts to wail. Saskia gives her the finger. 'Swivel on it.' Saskia is nearly twelve and she is 'wicked', meaning great. She has crimped hair, and says she is a punk. Last month, in London, she bought 'gear' from Kensington Market – zipped black trousers and red Doc Martens boots. Afterwards, Saskia says, she went to an Edwardian theatre, now a punk disco, saw George Michael and Paula Yates, and drank vodka. Saskia has been hanging out with Derek, who is very old, and she is learning his punk style.

Recently, Derek had a party at the community. Hundreds of punks invaded the house and climbed the stone steps, in a trash fire carnival of beauty. They strode through the double doors, made-up and cut-out. It wasn't planned but they gatecrashed, and they were like aristocrats in ties and plastic, some dressed in school uniforms. In the Lounge, Sunshine and I watched them lift their heads and look through the stained-glass windows. We saw the angles of their chins and I thought they were beautiful. They carried the spirit of Judy Nylon, because Judy says punks are rocks too big for the frame, and Derek says this means breaking the rules. One of the Adults called them 'fucking bastards'.

The party caused a scandal. At the Friday Meeting, Thomas stroked his blond beard and said, 'They don't take things seriously, these punks. They are not political, not suitable for the house.' Someone added, 'It must never happen again.' A woman snorted, 'Did you see that dreadful make-up!' We don't approve of make-up at the community, because bodies must be bare, like boy bodies, like machines. The punks did not fit in with the ethos.

In the van, Tina starts to complain. 'Thomas, Saskia says I'm divvy, and she hit me and hurt me, and –' Saskia glares and Tina stops speaking. Eyes fixed on the road, Thomas replies, using the words the Adults always say: 'Deal with it yourself. Sort it out, Tina.' In the community, autonomy is better than dependency. It is not good to ask for help, even if you're five. Tina sniffles and holds a quivering finger up to Saskia. 'Swivel round it,' she whispers. We all laugh because we have escaped the square box of family life. Now, we are curved, zigzags, doodles on a piece of paper. Yet the direction we are going in is not clear.

Ten minutes later, the van drops us off at the village green, a circle of lawn. In the late spring, nasturtiums fill flowerbeds. Orange. Yellow. Black and red. We fall from the van, skip and jump towards the church, and the graveyard we must cross to reach our school. The Kid group separates. We enter the outside world.

Nearly four decades later, I am with my half-brother, Alex, in New York. I am here for a fortnight, teaching classes on clinical art therapy, bodies, and mental health. On campus, I talk about non-verbal communication, touch, and proxemics. 'Where you come from, and your life experience,' I tell the students, 'influences how you move your body, whether you speak quietly or loudly. Culture impacts how close we stand next to other people. If you were born in India, a New York suburb or in Nigeria, you will not sensorially perceive the world the same way – the questions of intimacy and separation. Our cultural upbringing shapes us; not only our values, but our senses and our bodies. Part of how we become who we are begins the day we are born.' Students ask questions and take notes.

Alex and I are chatting about my lectures, and about families and home, and I am describing our new granite house in France. We've just moved in with our three daughters, roses bloom in the walled garden, and in late June ox-eye daisies grow high. He's telling me of his excitement about getting his first apartment. Alex is much younger than me. The subject of the community is brought up.

'Where was it? What was it called? How many people lived there?' he says. Normally I am good at changing the subject when people enquire about the community. But Alex has never asked me this before, and as he has just set up home himself, his questions are timely. On his sofa, I am abruptly lost for words. For years, I visited my dad and his second wife's children in their middle-class home. During these monthly visits, I read bedtime stories to Alex and his brothers and sisters, distributed biscuits and crisps to their friends. Later, I picked them up from teenage discos. Our homes were separated by a couple of hours in a car. Yet, I realize, my siblings never came to the community. Why did no one bring them? Why was our experiment closed? Thoughts arrive in my mind, one after the other, forming a toppling stack.

Alex doesn't know this, but from when I was six years old, journalists would frame the same questions he's just asked, always aiming for something like: 'Do you love or hate your home?' Now, the answers are more complicated. For as I have grown older, I have realized that, unlike other people I've met, my stay in the community was not simply a short adventure, followed by a period of life with parents in a normal home. The community was the only childhood I knew. Do I begin with the larger or the smaller picture? Do I tell him how we got there, or why we stayed? Explain what life was like in the seventies for divorced women? Detail the Cold War, and our parents' generation's fantasy about socialism, the Iron Curtain and what was on the other side? Should I tell him about the Thatcher era, riots, and the burn for change?

These questions and their complicated answers seem even more relevant in our dystopian age, as our world feels trapped in ecological and social despair, and people seek out new solutions, a better society.

Yet what if he asks me how it shaped me – this ideal home? Everyone wants the 'exclusive' on paradise. For utopias are a form of heaven. As German philosopher Ernst Bloch wrote, 'Utopian unconditionality comes from the Bible and the idea of the kingdom, and the latter remained the apse of every New Moral World.' Can I describe the glorious buzz of revolution, alongside the isolation, the trauma, the shame? What happens to children when we try to abolish the family and replace it with an institution? And can I explain that we should be able to criticize the damage caused by revolutions while retaining a belief in the power of change?

I picture the community inside a glass snow globe. This tiny world fits in the palm of my hand, every faraway detail is magnified, the horror and beauty enclosed in curves. Usually, I keep this snow globe and my childhood hidden. But as we talk I realize this miniature world can be seen with fresh eyes. I think of a colleague of mine, who studies archaeology and emails me photographs of ancient Italian statues from Pompeii. He writes, 'It can take a lifetime of painstaking research to assess the meanings of a single vase. Solitary pieces transform our vision of history. It is not about the object but unearthing the habits and beliefs of the past.'

Later that evening, I wonder if I can become an archaeologist, and scientifically measure the community's dimensions, examine the world from which it came. An objective just-out-of-reachness might help me fathom this place. I think of Erving Goffman and Michel Foucault, and their work analysing power in insular social establishments – prisons, psychiatric hospitals, and religious retreats, estranged from the outside world. Goffman's interest stemmed from their nature as 'forcing houses for changing persons: each is a natural experiment on what can be done to the self'. As I fall asleep, I think about what it means to be the mismatched fabrication of someone's dream. If, as pioneering psychiatrist Donald Winnicott believed, home is where we begin, what is a home, and how did mine start?

1. The Utopian House

'Life without utopia is suffocating, for the multitude at least: threatened otherwise with petrifaction, the world must have a new madness.'
Emil Cioran, *History and Utopia*

'For our house is our corner of the world. As has often been said, it is our first universe, a real cosmos in every sense of the word.'
Gaston Bachelard, *The Poetics of Space*

A lot of what happens starts with words and numbers. It is July and we have packed up our house. We are what is called a Single Parent Family and we live at No. 5, by the park. It is 1978, being a Single Parent Family is not good, and we are the only children like this in our classes at school. When No. 5 was bought, there were five of us: three girls, Mum, and Dad. Then, our sister died and there were four of us left. Two sisters and two parents. Then my brother came, and we were five again. Then Dad left, and we returned to the number four. These are the sums of our family, the adding-on and the taking-away.

We are leaving this house because, in the past year, Mum has been going to meetings in Liverpool, London and

Manchester. At these meetings, the three of us play in corridors with kids from other Single Parent Families. Often, we wait for days and years, while Mum and the adults talk about 'class oppression' and 'marriage being a sacrifice'. We are told to be quiet when a woman cries, because divorce is a disaster when 'women aren't allowed bank accounts, just because they have vaginas!' Mum tells stories of dancing on double-decker buses, and other people shout 'Women's Lib!' Everyone has long hair and they cheer about the strikes by undertakers, firemen and bakers. At these meetings, the adults argue about: 'sexist language', 'the New Left', 'imperialism', and 'progressive education and the disruption of sexual repression'. One time, a big boy grabs my wrist and twists the skin in two directions. 'This is a Chinese burn. You have to scream when it hurts.' Now and then, we are given sandwiches or lukewarm soup, and ask Mum where we can go to wee.

In the meetings, a man called Alfredo stands tall. He is the leader, and they discuss communes, communities and communism. These words begin with the letter C. This letter is curved like the moon. If you turn it on its back, it can swing like a cradle, but if you push a cradle too hard it will topple and fall. Alfredo talks about budgets, capital and properties. One day, they decide members will contribute, 'and we'll buy the mansion together and make our commune!' – and everyone roars with joy. Sometimes, I long for our home, our quiet street, for Dad who has left us, for my books and my bed.

Today, it is time to go. Piles of boxes sit by a borrowed car. We're leaving No. 5, our climbing frame and our garden behind, and we're going to live in the mansion. No. 5 was our home, a four-bedroomed house. We had guinea pigs in a cage named Victoria and Albert. The back fence was the end of our universe, a dotted line to cut around with a sharp pair of scissors. As we drive away, No. 5 gets smaller and smaller. We slide on the sweaty back seat of the car for hours.

'We're here,' Mum says later, when we arrive. Wheels rattle over what she calls a 'cattle grid'. The tyres on the metal bars make a clunk, clunk, clunk. She turns to face us, and we shout, 'Hooray!' Slowly, we head down a snaking drive, and the car twists on tarmac curls. Fields stretch out either side of us, and barbed wire encloses cows. At the bottom of the drive, Mum pulls open the car doors, and we fly outside, landing on a gravelled courtyard. A giant house rises up like a fairy castle, so big we cannot see where it begins or ends.

We are broken husks sticky from the car, from the packed-up life we left behind. Yesterday is trickling away like sand. We do not see it going but it disappears. Here is the dream Mum has talked about for months, in the meetings and on the telephone – 'The commune . . . no, I mean the community' – and we scramble up stone steps and land at a door. She grabs a camera. 'Let's take a photo. It is the beginning of a new world.'

We are ordered by age and size: my sister, me and our brother grip a cast-iron balustrade. In the camera frame, we blur, sharpen and are blurred again: a trio of kid monkeys with flares and wonky fringes. We dangle in untethered hope. Claire pinches my leg, I moan, our brother laughs.

We yank open the double entrance doors and step over the threshold. Arrival is the point when the boat reaches the shore. The figurehead of our family is meeting the land.

At this moment, on the roof, ancient Furies and Fates lay bets. They are mumbling from on high, hissing prophecies and spinning the wheel of our destiny. From the tilt of this beginning, we turn a page. But I do not look up; I cannot hear. I am six, and I am running into my future. The double doors slam shut behind us. We stay inside for fifteen years.

As historian Anna Neima describes in her book *The Utopians: Six Attempts to Build the Perfect Society*, 'utopias are a kind of social dreaming', attempts to invent a 'perfect' world. Utopians will not necessarily use the label themselves, but the term 'utopia' describes an imagined legal, social and politically ideal place. Historically, in Western philosophy, the seeds of utopian thought were sowed in aspects of Renaissance and Enlightenment philosophy, the belief in rebirth and in humans (alongside or without God) having the power to make change and progress. The word first occurred in Thomas More's sixteenth-century work depicting an exemplary fictional society, cut off from the outside world and reminiscent of monastic life. Importantly, More's utopia was situated on an island.

Utopias are different to revolutionary movements, which grab society, turn it inside out and upside down, making everything and everyone change. Instead, utopias withdraw and isolate to create perfection, articulating a vision of society transformed. Imagined worlds made real, utopias have inspired a literary tradition. In Nadine Gordimer's novel *Burger's Daughter*, set in the political environment of the 1970s, a man argues in relation to communist utopias: 'If people would forget about utopia! When rationalism destroyed heaven and decided to set it up here on earth, that most terrible of all goals entered human ambition. It was clear there'd be no end to what people would be made to suffer for it.'

It is summer when we arrive in our utopia. Sun charges through our days. It lights the grubby back stairs and the cracked scullery sinks where tired maids once washed dishes. It sends rays through the one hundred grimy sash windows, and around an eighteenth-century monumental staircase. When we wake up the first mornings, the light casts shadows where old people were spoon-fed, slept and died – because before we got here this house was an old people's home. The sun has lit this mansion for centuries, bringing each day and carrying in each night. French philosopher Gaston Bachelard wrote that the principal benefit of any house is that 'the house shelters daydreaming, the house protects the dreamer, the house allows one to dream in peace'. That summer, the house is being dreamt, and we move from the 'we' of a family to a 'we' that is collective. There is rupture and upheaval, cutting and pasting.

Those first weeks, there are meetings about everything. The world must be made up: the house, the people, the language. To begin with, the adults talk constantly about the word 'space'. It is a word they like, and they have Space Meetings about rooms and names. 'What shall we do with this space?' a woman says, when she goes to find her inner child in the Kitchen. 'We need to make things happen here.' 'The house,' a red-haired man insists to a listening, eager crowd, 'is an egalitarian cake to be sliced into equal parts.' Architecture, they say, 'is an instrument of change'. When I listen, the words drift around. I am not always sure what they mean.

'We must radicalize domestic space,' an Indian woman, Tripti, declares at another gathering, 'to control irrational and potentially subversive domestic behaviours.' Mum is taking notes when another woman shouts above the rest that the Bolsheviks abolished private life, and the house shouldn't be a fortress, an enclosed domestic sphere, because 'everything "private" is politically dangerous!' Crouched between a stranger's legs during a discussion about washing up, I overhear Alfredo explain we should be 'inspired by Soviet housing experiments to abolish the family'. Everyone must have equal space, communal appliances, and a theoretically equal amount of air to breathe.

Later, I will read how ancient Roman inhabitants built the tiled *domus* complete with house gods, while land-locked Iranians brought gardens inside via carpets with intricate flower designs. The mundane act of how domestic space is organized translates our relationship with the world outside. In the community, the young South African journalists, earnest academics, British feminists, American ecologists, German teachers, Indian musicians, Dutch scientists, wannabe therapists and American dropouts are 'baby boomers'. They want more out of their lives and their homes than their parents' generation; they are running from the horror, doom and gloom of war, breaking free from the cage of domesticity. They want something else.

Soon it is agreed that all the ground floor – kitchen, lounge, yoga room, dining room, laundry, toilets and storerooms – will be communal; the second and third floors will be divided into communal bathrooms and private living spaces. These are to be called 'Units' and we are allocated a Unit on the second floor. 'Unit' is the word invented by the adults to describe the place where each family lives. Walker, a blond Dutch woman who is a maths teacher, explains, 'A Unit is an independent component of a larger whole.' She says we are like atoms, the tiniest particles, inside a Unit, and her words make me feel like the house is big and I am very small, which is exciting but worrying.

Our first Unit, just off the second-floor landing, has bedrooms for my sister, brother and me, and a run-down bathroom (with no hot water). Inside our Unit, each of our rooms connects to a long corridor. Inside each bedroom is a sink left over from the old people's home. At the end of the corridor is where Mum sleeps. Her bedroom is also our living room; as well as a bed and a sofa there's a table with a kettle, and in the corner a fridge. Like in Soviet experimental architecture, this is a modular space for living and sleeping, and different activities can happen here. Inside Mum's room are a forest of spider plants and a white and green duvet cover, coloured like frost on grass. On her shelves are feminist novels, paperbacks by the anti-family psychiatrist R. D. Laing, and a dark red set of miniature Beatrix Potter stories with watercolours of Peter Rabbit. Later, I will see Mum's book collection as a mirror of her character: both radical and deeply old-fashioned. She insists on politeness: 'please' and 'thank you'.

Along from our corridor are other Units, and a communal bathroom. Turn right or left and we are interconnected. A man tells us we're 'like bees in a hive'.

The definition of home entails geography, architecture and people, but also involves emotions. In my work as a clinical arts therapist, when a new patient group comes together we often begin by working on 'home'. 'Imagine your house,' I say, and we draw and paint fantastic make-believe buildings, and link our homes together with invented trees, bending roads and paths. We sketch the environment we would like around our homes: parks and libraries, shops and swimming pools.

It is an exercise in topophilia, a term coined by geographer Yi-Fu Tuan to describe the affective bond with our environment that creates 'a sense of place'. To 'feel at home' is an emotional state. I hand out pieces of paper to the patient group: 'Write down five words that evoke a feeling of home for you.' The words 'security', 'comfort', 'belonging' and 'nest' are repeated time after time. Homes house humans. This exercise aims to elicit an individual and shared feeling of home. In Old English the roots of the word 'home' take us to a gathering of souls.

In seventies Britain, home design is brutalist, and during this decade 4,500 tower blocks are built. Space is functional.

Mum and the adults talk about this: space can be designed. In the community, doors are everywhere, not a single one is locked, and I never own a key. As the first days pass, Claire and I run with the other kids. It is like a space endlessly opening, and we are carried through it on a river of light. A gang of us push through double doors, heavy fire doors, and wooden doors with stained-glass windows leading through to what they call an 'atrium'. In socks, we skid along old lino floors, slipping and sliding. The adults move stuff in and take stuff out.

'Can you give us a hand please?' says a nervous, sweaty white British woman pushing a mechanical bed. She says her name is Firefly, and she's being helped by Tripti, who is dressed in dungarees. Claire comes, and the three of us push and Tripti pulls, saying, 'It's going to be radical here. Kids and adults working as equals, "boulder-pushing". The hill is patriarchy. The boulder is sisterhood.' Tripti yanks the bed. 'It is tabula rasa! In this home, everything will change!' She catches my eye, and I feel the tremulous power of her dream. Every day on the news they show us where nuclear bombs could land – either we change or we die.

Tripti begins talking to Thomas. He is ticking a list on a clipboard. Beside him are mountains of old bedding and boxes. Everything smells. 'What are you doing?' Claire asks.

'Clearing up! Alfredo is finishing the Space Meeting. He says we need to get everything out that cannot be reused.' Thomas flicks my nose, and it hurts. He points at a mattress streaked with yellow and nods to Tripti. 'These are stained, but as Alfredo says you cannot be bourgeois about dirt. We can use them in our Units.'

'We're going back to zero, reconnecting with nature. Why worry about being clean when you're free?' Tripti grins.

'What's this?' Claire grabs a metal bowl. She holds it to her face, and in the concave reflection, our bodies elongate, unrecognizable. Claire puts the bowl on my head.

Thomas points. 'That's a bedpan. It was for the old people to *shit* in.' He emphasizes the word.

'Yuck!' I throw the bedpan to the floor. It clangs like a bell. I've never heard anyone say 'shit' before.

'Shit head. You're a shit head!' Claire shouts.

'Am not. You're a shit head!' I run after her, but I trip over the boxes, fall on the floor, and above me Thomas mutters, 'Fucking kids!' It feels like a good time to run away.

'Hey kids. Be cool!' Alfredo arrives dressed in a kaftan; he looks like he could fly. He drifts around the house, like a winged thing, a fairy.

'Alfredo,' says Thomas, 'I need to talk to you about scheduling the Chicken Meeting.'

But Alfredo is not listening to the word 'scheduling', and he lifts his cheesecloth arm. 'Let's do a radical gesture. Kids, follow me!'

Alfredo is a Founding Member. To be a Founding Member means he was at the beginning and did a thing called 'recruiting members'. Often, Alfredo has a pipe in his mouth, and clouds puff from a blackened hole. He is what is known as a Marxist. In the meetings, Alfredo weaves our dreams together, thread after thread, to create a new domestic world. He gathers the words from the adults' paperbacks on socialism, leaflets on kibbutzim, yoga, rebirthing, ecology and feminism, and articles from magazines like *Good Housekeeping*, one entitled 'WHAT ARE WE FIGHTING FOR?', about the fact that 'our most respected newspaper runs a column entitled Women's Appointments' as though women and men can't do the same jobs. There are flyers on London libertarian 'free schools' and photocopied journals where printed words say: 'Marriage should be abolished'; 'Wages for housework'. Alfredo is a spirit tailor, wielding the loom of our lives. He is like a jug filled with all our revolutionary wishes. Recently, in a meeting, he held up a book, and read out loud: 'Marianne Faithfull says that a hundred years ago, a person in a flying saucer looking down would have seen a dark planet. Now they see a whole planet that is lit, great cities lit up . . . we live in light now . . .'

H. G. Wells described utopias as shadows of light thrown by darkness. The light unfolds and refolds lives. Utopias tend to follow devastating periods, as they are an attempt to look forward and imagine a better world. This was the case for the utopian communes that proliferated in America after the Civil War, such as the anti-slavery Oneida Community. Later, in the twentieth century, each of the two waves of utopian experiments followed the horrors of a major world war and had different aims. The post-World War I utopian movements attempted to change society, but the post-World War II boomer generation – my mother's generation – of utopias was more individually based. Author Jenny Diski, who also grew up in this radical environment, provocatively wrote that Margaret Thatcher's famous dictum 'there is no such thing as society' was merely an extension of the hippy ethic of individual liberation.

As Claire and I gaze at him, Alfredo looks at the wall. His eyes are suddenly sad. Then, he lifts his arm and clenches his fist. We imitate him and raise our arms. This is a radical gesture, and we shout 'Power to the People'.

In the hallway, a little girl slides down the wooden banister. It is Sunshine and she is with Brandy. Alfredo says, 'Follow me.' 'Yoo-hoo,' Claire screams, and we run after Alfredo, Brandy and Sunshine, through a white panelled door. Alfredo slams the door shut. 'We're going to call this space the Yoga Room.'

Inside, it is empty and bright. White walls, wood, and light. We can be like astronauts and walk on the moon, because people can go to space. The floor is covered in what is called 'parquet'. A varnished puzzle made from a zillion rectangles of wood. Alfredo takes off his shoes and slides across the slippery floor. 'Come on, kids. Explore!' Claire, Sunshine, Brandy and I put our feet down. Soon, we are skidding, and it feels like the world is expanding, and sunlight shines through sash windows opening onto a green lawn, our fields and the woods, a verdurous sea.

Earlier, Alfredo called the outside of the house 'the Estate', and yesterday Sunshine pulled my hand, dragged me out of a meeting and took me round. In the garden, a topless, white woman was doing yoga, her nipples like purple wine gums. There was also a brown man with no clothes on, and his willy dangled as he whispered, 'Salute the sun.' I wanted to stare at the willy, but when we giggled, the man yelled, 'Bloody kids!' Then we became horses in an ancient apple orchard, cantered past sequoias tall as the sky and into the woods, where beetles advanced under umbrella-shaped flowers, crawling under rotting logs. The Estate is thirty-one acres, a number to remember. These figures and words measure our world. The number of rooms is sixty; the length of the drive is one-quarter of a mile. The drive separates us from the world outside.

'Yoo-hoo!' Claire slides past me. Fast as a big sister, she is always bigger than me. She once locked a teacher in a cupboard. She is bright, naughty and funny, and our dad's favourite even though he does not live here. She is his favourite, even if he's gone. In the Yoga Room, I stand still and then run. I am different to Claire. They took me to have tests for what is called 'gifted children' because I am always talking, saying long words, and taught myself to read before I was four. After the tests, Mum smiled and said, 'You are clever but not a genius,' and I think this means don't make a fuss, even if I understand everything at school before everyone else. I am also sickly, and have a squinting eye. Every winter, I cough so hard I cannot breathe because I once nearly died of pneumonia. On the parquet, my foot connects to the ground – and, arms outstretched, I pretend I am Evel Knievel jumping across the Snake River Canyon on a motorbike.

Then, I collide with Claire, crash to the floor, and start to cry. When we get up, Sunshine, Brandy and Alfredo have gone. Opening the door, I run out along the corridor, out onto the front lawn, calling 'Mum!' In front of the house, Claire is by my side, but all the adults have disappeared. The space is getting bigger and bigger; it stretches out to the frayed edges of the woods, through to the outbuildings, the dark corners of cellars, and up to the lofty attics. It elongates, expands up through the clouds to where nuclear bombs fly and space rockets zoom, and we are alone, tiny dots, waiting.

In the community, more meetings are held; and that summer our home and 'way of life' are designed. Our house is utopian and revolutionary, and that means politics sticks its fingers into the intimacy of our lives. In a meeting, a tall American woman with thick dark hair stands up, dressed in a shirt, jeans, and a belt with a silver buckle. Barbara says, 'Language is a mechanism of male supremacy. We must change it!'

Influenced by the adults' hodgepodge of textbook utopias, we undergo linguistic enculturation. It is strange to say new things, but it feels powerful when new words are in my mouth, like: 'consensus' (how decisions are made), 'non-income sharing' (how money works), 'self-sufficiency' (how we grow vegetables and will have animals) and 'radical education' (about the kids). The word 'commune' is forbidden now. 'We must always say "community",' Barbara says. 'Community is more serious.' Our image to the outside world is controlled, and our house swings between hippiedom and the New Left, flower power and puritanical Marxism.

In our community, Mum must also now be called Alison,

freeing her from the patriarchy. In the language of the community, she is renamed, and at first it feels funny to say her first name. But many of the adults, mainly women, also change their names. They put Cynthia, Mary and Doreen in the rubbish bin, and call themselves Walker, Firefly and Eagle. Eagle tells me, 'I am called Eagle because the Eagle eats the seed, the Eagle shits the seed. The Eagle is the seed.'

Under the roof, and in the thirty-one acres, we are now 'individuals', yet two distinct social groups are formed. One group is created by the other. Mum becomes one of the Adults, a powerhouse in dungarees. The other social group is the Kids. Over dinner, which we now eat in the Dining Room, Barbara tells us, 'We must explode the nuclear family. It's a comfortable concentration camp.' Meals are eaten on eight rectangular tables, each surrounded by eight wooden chairs. Mealtimes are busy: fifty people, thirteen families, single people – mainly men – and what they call 'multiple parenting'. People sit wherever they want, Adults next to Kids, nobody sits with their family. Thomas has cooked burnt potatoes and kidney bean stew, served in four industrial metal dishes. He waggles his finger in my face. 'The notion of family is old-fashioned and oppressive.' His partner, Walker, takes a plate from inside the hot cupboard and serves herself, adding, 'We can reinvent thousands of years of human history. Reformulate the numbers of human groups and start again.' Tripti joins in and she begins saying things about how anyone can replace the parental figure. 'Imprinting' is what animals do. Birds, coming out of their eggs, will follow and become attached to the first moving object. In the community, there are a lot of words like this.

There are three children in our family when we arrive: Claire, our brother and me. In the house, at the beginning, there are eighteen Kids aged between two and ten. Sometimes, we have Kids' Tea, and are given sausages and beans and we argue and joke. It is fun but you have to be tough to survive. Even now, I can list the Kids' names: Sunshine (who is my age) and her big brother Troy live with us on and off, so Eagle, their mum, can go to ashrams and stand on her head. There is freckled Brandy – also my age – and her half-sister Tina; a small silent boy called Harry with sticking-up black hair; and little Helen (Firefly's kid), another only child. Jason and Rainbow travel with Barbara, their mum, between the US and the community, and have sweets called Tootsie Rolls that their American grandpa hides inside their bags. Andrew, Merrilyn and Clem are half-Australian and half-Ghanaian. There are the Canadian twin sisters, Charlotte and Sarah, who one day hide behind a tree in the woods and put felt-tip pens inside their winkles. Finally, there is Michael and his elder sister Saskia, and us three. Punk Derek is too old, and does not play with us. Later, tons of babies are born in the house: Florence, Hanif, Betsy and others, and more. Nearly all of us are from Single Parent Families. But, when the Adults arrive, they often hitch up with someone new and we scramble between these different men and women. 'Oh look, it's the Kids,' they say when they see us: a mass, a gang, a horde.

We run free, and that first summer, as the Adults install

the house, the Kids explore. Each hot, dry morning is a present to be unwrapped. Barbara shows us the counter-cultural manifesto *Play Power* by Richard Neville and says, 'When you play, adults should not intervene.' Bedraggled and free, we climb trees, build camps, fight and wrestle. Right from the start, it is rough, and I am not good at this, the punching and pushing. But a Kids' group is invented, a pecking order, and some things are valued and others are not. Books are worthless but cartwheels count for gold.

Brandy is my new friend. Neat and blond, she can flip upside down. I always fall. We are both six. Her family is hard. Mine is soft and we are vulnerable. Both Brandy's parents, Walker and her stepdad Thomas, are on the Dole and shout in meetings. The Dole is good because it beats the system and puts you at the top.

On the front lawn, the Kids play British Bulldog. I must get across the grass, Brandy and I run fast, and she gets there, but red-headed Jason catches me and he pushes me hard. I fall. This game is banned in British schools but the boys like it best because it is a Kid war without rules. My breath is cut short. Jason holds me down, and it hurts. He calls me posh even though his granddad owns a yacht. I have tears in my eyes, and Brandy looks at me, and I know she's urging me to get up but Mum comes running. 'You shouldn't do that,' Mum says. Her voice is anxious when she tries to protect us. That summer she will try again and again. Jason smiles at her mockingly; he lets go of my wrist and walks back to his base, laughing.

Mum is left standing because Jason's mum is Barbara, and Barbara is more powerful than Mum. Barbara rises early, digs the garden, and organizes Friday Meetings. Her father – Jason's grandpa – works on Wall Street, and he is a bastard who, Barbara tells Eagle, 'buys our plane tickets fucking business-class'. Barbara has the beautifully carved tongue of a snake. In the order of the community, she is a queen and Jason is a prince. Alison is possibly a bishop, and I am a runt. Alison and the three of us carry the weight of loss and our dead sister. In the community, parents' power affects Kids' power. We are all equal, and power is invisible, but power makes superheroes. It gives strength and force, like the sun. As Jason leaves, Alison sighs and goes back to the Kitchen to make a roast dinner, peel one hundred potatoes, and line the sky with hope.

Jason walks back towards me. 'You need your mummy, don't you? You can't stand up for yourself!' He laughs, and his laughter travels across the lawn, climbs up the front of the house. It gets louder and louder.

I stammer, 'I don't need Mummy – I mean Alison.' The Kids surround me and begin chanting, 'Mummy! Mummy!' and Brandy joins in, and my face goes red. Jason is triumphant, a god of war. I have lost. Needing a mum is weak, and I realize the community is stronger than me, stronger than all the things I knew before. It has broken time and place, thrown the past away. We are lucky. It has blown history up with a bomb.

'Kids are equal to Adults,' I begin to spout precociously to anyone who will listen, and I make sure I never say 'Mum' and even tease Sunshine when she uses that word. Slowly, Alison stops trying to defend us, and I am relieved because I know that in the community a parent can't protect you even if they try. Tripti tells me, 'You're equal to me. Kids deserve rights!' and I drink up her words, get drunk on this potion.

From now on, I am a Kid, and this means not needing a parent. We form a utopian platoon, eating, playing, sleeping, sharing clothes and shoes, bullying and fighting. Sometimes, the Adults wash us together. Line us up naked and laughing in a bath. We are neighbours, best friends, enemies, cousins, family, brothers and sisters. We are none of these words and we are all of them and none of this is defined.

A few years ago, my partner A and I moved into our stone Breton house. Having left a seaside flat, we were helped by twenty friends to carry boxes of books, my shoes, hefty wardrobes and more than seventeen different pans. The stone house was a blessing in a strange time. Following eighteen months of being treated for colon cancer, my older sister Claire had recently died. In the spring, I had given birth to a wonderful, unexpected third daughter. In this new home, in the first months, our dreams concerned survival, but also the kind of joy born out of grief, a knowledge of fleeting time. That first evening, in our new walled garden, we lifted our glasses to the sky, grateful for the kindness of our friends.

Later, A and I discussed bank loans, budgets, fought over paint colours (A is more adventurous and I like neutrals), moved furniture, and debated which bedrooms – according to character and age – we thought our three daughters should occupy. A had renovated a beautiful office space for me, where I could write beneath the eaves. In this new life, we became five instead of four, and in the new habitat, set up a home.

The word 'habitat' leads us to 'habit', and any home has a rhythm, and a domestic micro-culture with a language, rituals and jokes. Today, we keep certain rituals we spontaneously established in that first year, like using a milk jug and fine china for Saturday breakfasts, just for the sense of luxury. Sometimes, A and I have meetings, check our diaries (he uses Google and I prefer paper), talk about the mundane and our dreams. We knit things together, argue, and occasionally pull stuff apart. Our home is very different to the one I grew up in, and recently, I said to him, 'One of the things I find hardest about my childhood, aside from the trauma, is knowing I'll never know what it is like to be a child in the small, quiet safeness of a home.' He replied, 'Sometimes, I notice certain very odd things about your behaviour and I realize it is because of your upbringing. It sounds strange but it is like you're missing something, like you've lost a limb.'

In the rhythm of the community, every Friday evening is now Friday Meeting time. In the living room, we sit in a circle. Mostly it is Adults, but I am on the floor, curled into Lawrence's long legs. Lawrence is Barbara's boyfriend, and just back from an Israeli kibbutz. He has a soft dark beard and plays a wooden pipe. The Adults are following the Agenda, and that means a list of things. Alfredo wrote the Agenda but got called away to Liverpool. Alfredo often says, 'I am the people,' repeating Robespierre's cry from the French Revolution. He ignites fires, and shepherds the herds. But Barbara says, 'Alfredo is not committed enough to communal life.' Alison is Acting Secretary, and reads out loud: 'The first item on the Agenda is the Cooking Rota.'

The Cooking Rota must always be decided first. People 'sign in' or 'sign out' for cooking and meals, writing their names on a chart. Signing in to anything is important because it shows you commit. Once this has been decided, Alison moves on to the second item. Firefly, Helen's mum, has suggested having horses. 'I feel it could be great for the Kids.'

Tripti moves her body into the circle. She is pregnant, and her stomach draws a perfect curve. She says, 'We've just got here. We need to focus on changing the world, not bourgeois horse-riding.'

Lawrence says, 'Too right. The Kids shouldn't be riding horses. I didn't move here to perpetuate the system.'

Thomas barks, 'Next thing the Kids will be members of the ruling class, hunting foxes.' It is obvious to Thomas – and to everyone – that these are things we are against. Horses are establishment, like royalty and the nuclear family: mummy, daddy and two-point-four children. Capitalism presses people into this mould. But we are making something else.

Eagle inhales, practising yogic breathing. 'We need to examine feelings.'

Firefly twists her hands in her lap. Sweat stains her T-shirt's armpits. Cigarette in hand, Barbara stands up, shouting, 'This is a consensus process. We all must agree to every decision taken and we don't and won't ever agree to horses!' She smiles at Lawrence; he strokes my forehead. Looking up, I see Tripti nodding enthusiastically. My head is next to Barbara's heavy, round sandals. She told me earlier these were handmade by an American women's collective. Her feet charge towards the final word. 'Horses won't happen, and they are totally irrelevant to the community.' Barbara pauses, and then concludes. She is good at conclusions. 'Firefly, you're lost in the fantasy of the mainstream life!'

Firefly bursts into tears, and rushes from the room. Nobody moves. I wonder if I should follow her. I look up at the Adults and their arguments plant themselves in my skin. Despite what they call 'consensus', I begin to notice that certain voices rule the roost. Power is grabbed by the domineering, the scary, by those who claim to do the most communal work and are on the Dole. Group dynamics create a de facto elite, like the Eastern Bloc *nomenklatura* or the Western Establishment. There is an informal and unspoken, yet steely, hierarchy.

Pushing sheets of long blond hair behind her ears, Walker frowns. 'What's next on the Agenda?' Her hair is irresistible, it hangs like gossamer, and I like it when she draws me Venn diagrams and talks about logic and inductive research. She has told me I am a hypothesis for a new life, but I am not sure I understand.

'The boiler,' Alison says, interrupting my thoughts. Everyone groans. Thomas declares, 'We have to be pragmatic.' Alison takes notes, using the shorthand from her secretarial training.

'Talking about the bloody boiler is symbolic of the

patriarchy,' Barbara says. Thomas shouts, 'That is too easy, our consensus policy states –' Barbara interrupts, 'Your consensus policy is another patriarchal concept.' She winks at Tripti. Tripti nods.

Later, they will admit Thomas was right, for in winter the house is freezing. For years, we sleep in hats, scarves and gloves. The toilet water freezes over. I have terrible coughs. The boiler is only good for cooking meringues, placing baking trays on tepid basement pipes. After hours, the egg whites harden.

'Is anyone making tea?' Lawrence yawns. Eagle says softly, 'I'll have lime flower.' She's cross-legged on the floor, doesn't believe in chairs. Tripti jokes, 'Fucking lime flower is bourgeois.' Eagle giggles and Alison stops writing and I go and help her make drinks. As we walk out, Barbara says, 'Firefly has a lot to learn.'

Tripti shrugs. 'Anyway, it was a pointless discussion. We all decided we were against the horses yesterday.'

Soon, Alison walks back in carrying a tray. The drinks are in dark brown glass mugs. They seem indestructible. But when they break, they shatter into shards. Hundreds and thousands of minuscule pieces spread into an endless broken-glass brown sea. Someone always gets hurt.

I grew up in utopia. Now, in France, at my desk beneath the eaves, at the top of a page, I write these six letters down: u-t-o-p-i-a. In the house, the Adults didn't use this word frequently, preferring the label 'community' – and much later, the vague term 'intentional community'. Over the years, I have understood that I didn't grow up in a cult, but a utopian experiment, a bird born from multiple eggs, a revolution inside a bubble. On revolution, Trotsky offered, 'Man will make it his purpose to master his own feelings, to raise his instincts to the height of consciousness . . . and thereby to raise himself to a new plane, to create a higher biological type, or, if you please, a superman.' When I was six years old, I arrived in this Promised Land.

My partner A was brought up in a suburb. His British Jewish parents began work at fourteen. A hairdresser and a tailor, they escaped Holocaust stories and poverty, and managed to get a big house, a beige three-piece suite, yearly holidays on cruises, and two sons with scholarships to attend private school. Recently, he described his suburban upbringing as a kind of free-market Thatcherite utopia. Everyone trapped in highly mortgaged individual houses with geraniums outside, keeping up with the neighbours, forgetting the past and obeying the terror of being 'nice'.

Within minutes of my first visit to their house, over tea and homemade cake, my partner's Jewish mother had covered questions of my upbringing and my parents' divorce. Inside, I was furious at her intrusiveness. Over the years, I would learn this house could be warm and loving, yet intensely claustrophobic and conservative. Carpets were constantly hoovered, surfaces bleach-sprayed and wiped. Yet, unexpectedly, this suburban Anglo-Jewish house became my longest experience of a traditional family home. When my in-laws asked about the community, I always responded, 'Oh, it was really quite normal,' and shut the conversation down.

Utopias create confusion and fantasy. Once, a therapist,

attempting to understand, asked me to draw him a plan of the house, outbuildings and land. The exercise took several sheets of paper, to include the house's three floors, the gardens and the woods, and to explain each location's function, linguistic appellation, and the various events that happened there. I even added the detail of the barbed wire and the cows, the curling drive, the doors that separated our universe from the outside. 'Look! This was the community,' I said when I had finished, and it was clearer to him then, and he understood. One usually imagines the word 'utopia' coming from the Greek word for 'good', but it comes from Latin and means 'nowhere'.

As that summer draws to a close, the Adults have more meetings, write Agendas about maintenance, the roof, sewage and chicken shit. Having discarded tights, dresses, make-up, shirts, ties, ironed trousers, hairdryers, perfume and shaved faces, in meetings they sit cross-legged, or sprawl on old sofas. They place dirty shoes on furniture, and do not often wash or brush their hair. The Adults learn quickly, for – as research like Steve Duck's on similarities shows – when we are placed within any new environment, our need for group conformity and compliance means we rapidly adopt group behaviour and new non-verbal communication.

Validated by the collective, the Adults copy and reproduce, move and meet as one. As the Adults homogenize, sometimes they decide the Kids should have meetings too.

'I need to talk to you all.' Barbara pushes us into the Kids' Room. The Adults have decided this is our room.

Inside are a pile of old blankets and a settee, foam leaking from a ripped arm. We rarely play here.

Barbara barricades the door. 'Today, you have to decide what you want.' We giggle and jostle, unsure why we are here. She shouts, 'It's not a joke.' I stop laughing. Barbara can be weird. I want to give her the right answer.

Recently, she took me into the Kitchen and pointed to a freshly plucked chicken. 'This is a dead bird. You need to know how this stuff works. These are intestines.' Barbara stuck her fingers into pink tubes, held them to my face, and her fingers travelled towards a hole. 'We shouldn't pretend just because you're a Kid. This is the anus. Shit happens.'

In the Kids' Room, Barbara puts us in a circle. 'Today, you get to decide about this community, your life. I've fought for civil rights, and now I fight for children's liberation. You have the power to become anything, rather than being protected and controlled by Adults. You aren't going to be bank managers or shave your legs. You are free from intervention, manipulation. What do *you* want?'

We search for the correct reaction. For despite this being freedom, there is right and wrong. When you grow up in a utopia, the perfect world requires perfection, and this means the renunciation of self for the sake of a greater power. Later I'll discover that every Judaeo-Christian revolution, be it French or Russian, has meant sacrifice. Bodies must be laid on the table. Don't mention money, telly, *Dallas*, dresses, God, central heating or discos. Don't say you want Barbies, to be pretty, fall in love or get a job. Do not be ambitious. 'You are so lucky, and free,' the Adults tell us, and yet there are great expectations. Kids must veer between pastoral Lucy in the Sky with Diamonds and rigorous Workers' Rights. If we were buildings, we would be a blend of fantasy sci-fi constructions and functional, brutalist concrete tower blocks.

Saskia says, 'I think people should be free.' Barbara smiles. I say, 'I think there should be the same rules for women and men.' Barbara grins. Claire says, 'Maybe we should get horses!' Barbara looks her up and down and I am afraid. Claire is always outspoken, will crack a joke. Barbara reflects. We all breathe in. She says, 'It's good, Claire, you speak your mind.' We all breathe out. Michael shouts, 'They should ban the Queen. All she does every day is ride around in a carriage.'

Barbara laughs, and we all start laughing. We Kids laugh as loud as we can, open our mouths showing teeth and tongues. We laugh like this on the lawn, shouting at army planes in the sky, laughing at Miss World, the idea of women staying at home, the thought of anyone wanting to make money, or a Kid wanting a mum.

Barbara keeps us in the room for over an hour. Before releasing us, she exclaims, 'You are lucky. You're not daughters or sons, shackled to the horror of the nuclear family. You are Rousseau's revolutionary Kids, born good, left wild. You are pioneers.' Barbara force-feeds us these words like we are foie-gras geese. When she opens the door, we run out of the room, wearing golden masks, radiating free light. We are Kid gods.

The word 'home' sits uncomfortably with the community. Like the wrong piece of a jigsaw puzzle, however hard I press it will not fit. Home and the community are not synonyms. In French, one of the synonyms for 'home' is *foyer*, the hearth. This word comes from *focus* in Latin: it is the place where all rays meet, the centre of fire. The home is a place that shelters, nourishes, and concentrates flames. I think about making – or unmaking – a home. Does habit make a home? How do humans feel at home?

In the Breton house where I live with my family, we have created a home. With my three daughters and A, I have discovered a place where we kindle our fires and protect the flames. As a home, the community emerges as both too big and too small; like Alice in the rabbit hole, it flips from mouse to giant. Even now, our bewildering utopian house enthrals me. It overwhelms, and then – seemingly from nowhere – a caress mutates into a slap, the tickle is a punch, and it strips me, flips me, kicks me to the floor. 'Beautiful Kids,' the house whispers, smiling sweetly. 'Fucking Kids.'

2. A Riddle

> 'Nurture, nature – in ways too complex to lead to scientific or cultural consensus they are in it together, and each word may mean a thousand things. Bubbling in the witches' brew aren't only genes and environment . . . (what else?) chance.'
>
> Maria Tumarkin, *Axiomatic*

> 'Life is so constructed that the event does not, cannot, will not, match the expectation.'
>
> Charlotte Brontë, *Villette*

Each time I have been pregnant, my partner and I chose not to know the sex of our child before birth. During pregnancy, I spoke to 'Baby', holding whispered one-sided conversations. 'How are you, Baby?' 'Baby, we are fine.' 'I love you.' Each child grew inside me, in a chamber like an anchorhold, the medieval Christian recluse cells attached to churches' exterior walls. The baby was in a dwelling place attached to me, where a riddle of nine months was composed. As trimesters passed, brain, backbones and spinal cords developed, buds transformed into arms and legs, but who was this baby? What would they become?

Much was already decided, for each baby carried the

history of A's family and my own. His Jewish diaspora. My British roots. Our family illnesses. Eye colours. His unruly black hair. My easily sunburnt white skin. His seemingly innate capacity – as the grandson of a taxi driver – to instantly memorize a route. My ability to regularly get lost on my five-minute journey home. Our babies' cells, their foundations, were programmed right from the start, and recent epigenetic theory even postulates that we can genetically transmit trauma from past generations, passing on forms of PTSD. For nine months, our babies were a living, moving architecture, a house built from DNA.

In the community, day after day, we learnt how we were manipulated by the patriarchy and capitalism. When I was little, I understood we were shaped, and not to take this for granted, because it meant we could be shaped a different way. In line with thinkers such as John Locke and behaviouralist John Watson, we were brought up to believe the mind begins as a blank slate. Everything was determined by experience. Away from the family trap of dependency, we could invent new life.

Yet our communal veneration of new social structures was not an anomaly but part of a post-war Western movement. At the time, radical reviews, such as *Power to Women*, spelt out this 'Crisis of Power': 'Prices are a crisis . . . Bringing up children is a crisis. Depending on a man is crisis.' The turmoil spilt into the mainstream, and in the well-respected BBC Reith Lectures, Edmund Leach claimed: 'The family, with its narrow privacy and tawdry secrets, is the source of all our discontents.' He encouraged bringing up children in 'something like an Israeli kibbutz perhaps or a Chinese commune'.

Recently, I spoke to a close friend in France. He participated in the 1968 Paris student revolt, and told me, 'I was ready to move into a commune. Everyone shared that fantasy. But very few people made the jump!' I pictured the barricades across busy Parisian streets and contrasted it with a utopia blocked off from the outside world. He made me realize that, despite the global longing for social change, going to live in a commune in the 1970s was still very rare. As Hannah Arendt wrote, 'Revolutions are the only political events which confront us directly and inevitably with the problem of beginning.' Aristotle said answers are situated at the start, and to respond to questions we must rewind. This is the riddle of our experimental life in utopia: What was the defining element which meant my family took the leap? How did we get there, and why did we stay?

At first, life advances in a logical fashion. My parents meet in the mid-1960s. She is a secretary. He's studying History at Oxford University. Like many future community members, they are middle-class. One day, a horse enters the house where she lives, and I picture its hooves clattering in the hall. She goes on a diet where she only eats apples, stripping the fruit down to the core. He rides a motorbike, and she sits in the sidecar. They have ruffled fringes, wear polo-necks and take black-and-white photographs of each other's unlined faces beneath English autumnal trees. On his motorbike, he travels to Czechoslovakia to work on communist farms and is followed by spies. She wants to follow her father and join the air force. Instead, she spends her days taking shorthand notes. He is left-wing, rebelling against a wealthy, religious upbringing. He, she tells me later, passes this politics on to her. They are baby boomers, have lived through post-war rationing, but their world is expanding. Young people want more, and they get engaged.

Their military and missionary parents tell them, 'You are too young. Far too young.'

My parents marry. In one wedding photo, he wears a rakish top hat. Slim as an elf, she is dressed in a plain white gown. On her cropped dark hair is a half-moon ivory hat. She slips into the wedding car, no make-up, heels or frills. This will never change. In another photo, the bride and groom are pictured with her parents. My granddad stands upright, in an RAF uniform. (I will only ever meet him a handful of times.) He is a wing commander, an East End boy made good, who started in the Royal Air Force as a mechanic and rose up the ranks to balance at the top. They say he once sewed matching clothes for his three daughters, and became a red-nosed gin-drinker who liked operetta. A highly organized man, he used to hang a ping-pong ball on a string from his garage ceiling, so he knew precisely where to park his car.

In the wedding picture, my grandma wears a black-feathered hat. She is a red-headed half-Belgian with broad tennis-playing shoulders. In World War II she drove ambulances. She enjoys cocktails, and speaks a smattering of European languages: *bonjour*, *hola*, *guten Tag*. Until she was four, my mother lived on a military base in Germany, so she calls her mother Mutti, and we will call her Mutti too.

This calling our grandmother our mother will add to our linguistic family confusion.

My father's parents are also in the wedding photographs. His soft-faced mother, Bella, stands next to his father. The vicar wears a clerical collar and a smile. This couple come from a long line of High Court judges, Church of England bishops, missionaries to Africa, factory owners and philanthropists. Highly intelligent, Bella was one of the first women to go to Oxford, and her brother was a famous left-wing politician. The word 'privilege' springs to mind – there are links to aristocracy, the first Quakers, a cousin who invited Gandhi to her house for tea.

Both families were comfortable financially. But I never experienced any financial stability as a child. Later I discovered sociologist Pierre Bourdieu and his distinction between cultural and economic capital. In my communal upbringing there was constant economic poverty, but we were surrounded by intellectual discussions and books: 'cultural capital'. Inversely, my partner's parents grew up without the trappings of education but became economically stable, and he describes a lack of 'cultural codes'. It is a common joke between us that as his immigrant family sent him climbing up the economic ladder, I fell tumbling down, and we met somewhere in the middle. We share the experience of being interlopers, sliding up and down the class scale, sometimes wondering who we are, and sometimes pretending to be somebody else. Having lived in France for over half our lives, we have learnt to negotiate another language, class system and culture. Bits of our

Britishness have now disappeared, and we don't belong either here or there. Elsewhere has become our home.

In the psychiatric units where I work, patients are often asked about their antecedents, the perplexing history of their families. Nurses help patients draw their family tree, and biro lines on paper connect the present to the past. Genograms allow us to see hereditary patterns of behaviour, medical and psychological factors. For instance, findings show that children of alcoholics are about four times more likely than the general population to develop addictive behaviour. Affecting about 1 per cent of the population, schizophrenia is approximately 80 per cent inheritable. The past is written in our bones. Yet, while we are creatures of nature, we are also nurtured. Ask most sociologists, genetic scientists, anthropologists, historians and psychologists, how do we become who we are? Despite the ongoing debates about nature and nurture, each of them will agree with my friend the archaeologist in Pompeii that you must brush the earth off the artefact and examine both: our history, and what we've learnt.

In late sixties Britain, my parents fit together like two pieces of unadorned, well-made furniture, good-quality fittings for a durable home. They were both kind, hard-working and well-intentioned. Both grew up on continents separate from their parents. From the age of five, they carried their belongings in trunks onto planes, boats and trains, and slept in different countries to their mums and dads. In dormitories, they were confronted by rows of metal beds.

Twenty to a room. The youngest the furthest away from the toilets. The lights were turned out, but no one could cry. When I think of their childhoods, I often picture very small children alone in the darkness, far from home.

Newlywed, in their early twenties, he passed law exams and then worked for local government. She stayed at home, and they had three breastfed babies. She read books on child-rearing, and I was the youngest when it happened. 'It is Fortuna,' my archaeologist friend would say, referring to the blindfolded Roman goddess spinning the wheel of life, for Ovid tells us luck is blind. One of the reasons we arrived at the community was not nature or nurture. In our case, it began with a wall.

This is how I imagine the scene.

It is mid-July, six years before the commune move, and five years before the meetings with Alfredo. In comfortable suburbia, we are returning from collecting my sister Rachel from school. I am three months old, a tiny just-made scrap of life, lying in an old-fashioned metal Silver Cross pram; the suspension guaranteed to provide a smooth ride. Strapped on top, with belts and buckles, is a wriggling, lively toddler Claire. Our elder sister, Rachel, walks ahead.

A moss-covered wall overshadows our path. It is a winding, ancient stone blockade. Sheer sunlight is fractured by an overhang of trees. A jewelled jade lustre sways in the breeze. The gentle English heat makes sweat in dimpled baby flesh. The wall is close enough to see the balance of matter. The lichen on the surface grows a vivid green. Sounds fuse together: insect hum, the distant chimes of an ice-cream van. Cornish whip. The taste of summer is on Mum's breath. These are the last days of school, and five-year-old Rachel skips just out of reach. She darts jauntily, one foot to another. Her white socks dangling round her ankles. Perhaps the baby cries, the toddler chatters, 'Mummy, I want ice cream. Mummy.' We are an exuberant orchestra, three incessant pink sisters.

Nearby, a man on a tractor ploughs a field. Maybe he thinks of what he'll be eating for his dinner, as he turns the rows of earth. Perhaps he hums Donny Osmond's 'Puppy Love', for it is a summer hit that year. At a certain moment, his rotating plough discs meet a tree root, a wooden anchor that is embedded in the wall. The plough discs spin, the lost tree root is displaced, and the wall running alongside our path is broken into pieces. The wall falls on the three sisters. It is as fast as a toppling house of cards, as simple as daybreak, as the turn of a hand. One side or the other: Luck. Chance. Fortuna. The wall tumbles so quickly you cannot stop it. Rachel dies. The Silver Cross pram is crushed, and Claire and I are flung into the air. We fly across the road, spinning like stars. In clouds of dust, we land in the undergrowth, realigning our constellations. Among thorns and brambles we alight, and we have survived.

They say that losing a child is the worst thing that can happen in your lifetime. The French describe it as *contre l'ordre des choses*, against the order of things. We freeze: Mum, Dad, Claire and me. They stop and we stop in that moment. Trauma stops things. Trauma cuts through temporality, through clocks, through the stream of time, because trauma creates time that is always the same: the events, sensations, sights, jangles and thuds. This is why trauma victims find a smell or sound can trigger deep panic, distress and flashbacks. Rachel is dead.

As I grow up, the falling wall will become my starting line, a compass to my universe. Something inevitable happened, and the community ideology prolongs this murky sentiment of fate, for Marx believed capitalism controls us all, the feminists link all suffering to the patriarchy, and nuclear annihilation will surely destroy the world. Something fatalistic overshadows my childhood, an unescapable sense of being wedged into disaster. The day of the wall is like an exploding magmatic force. It broke the earth's crust and erupted into our lives, flattening and reshaping everything.

Straight after the accident, we leave suburbia. The house is packed, baby clothes placed in boxes, educational toys filling an old school trunk marked with Dad's name. We arrive at No. 5, a house backing onto the park. The move was planned before the tragedy, for Dad's new job at the council. No one knows us here and no one ever knew Rachel. We have turned another page, and the boxes are unpacked. Our *locus* is white. Our past, before the accident, is a vast piece of nothing. We learn silence because trauma doesn't have words. Our bodies sit on high alert, fight or flight; in the amygdala part of our brain, red lights flash. The seeds of not speaking are sown.

The accident is inside us, at the bottom of our oceans, buried so deep we forget it is there and stay away from remembering. A Spanish psychiatrist I collaborate with frequently reassures patients who are wrestling with their avoidance of past events: 'Defence mechanisms are healthy things that we use when trauma is too much.' Even Freud believed that unconscious psychological responses such as denial and repression were understandable and often necessary. Throughout my life, I will find myself unconsciously eluding discussions about what happened with the wall, and I will live with my partner for three years, thinking I have told him about the accident, only to discover at a meal with his parents that he had no idea.

The only relics from this time are faded newspaper clippings about my sister's death. The clothes she wore the day she died. Years later, I will discover these things in the drawer at the back of a filing cabinet: a small, folded dress; a handful of headlines. They are proof that Rachel was here.

Eighteen months after the accident, when I am nearly two, my younger brother is born. Weeks after his birth, Dad leaves No. 5. He walks away and shuts the door, drives out of the street, out of our lives. He runs from tragedy. Dad is rushing away, and he is going, going, gone. There are so many different verbs to describe his actions, and we will never live with him again. Mum is left in No. 5 with a baby and two very small girls.

We will stay in our house for five years. It is a corridor between the accident and the community.

When Dad leaves, Mum works for a Quaker group for homeless people. She witnesses bottle fights and ladles out soup. She paints our new house with her sister, advancing stoically, step by step. Later, she will tell a story about me that becomes family folklore: 'Susie was so bright, she spoke in sentences before she was one. She did jigsaw puzzles with three hundred pieces or more at the age of two! I would put her in the playpen with all her puzzles, and put her brother and sister outside, so she would be able to do her jigsaws calmly. She taught herself to read before going to school.'

Occasionally, Dad visits. Mum tells Claire and I, 'Go to the sweet shop.' Down the road, we buy white paper bags filled with sticky delights. Dad calls us 'poppets' and then disappears. Dad is always arriving and departing; like a bus or a train he is never there.

Our world is unhinged. The hinge is the axis of the universe. We roll, rock and roll.

In the years that follow, Britain has four prime ministers, four general elections, five official states of emergency. There are two oil crises and two property booms. The decade is marked by violence and hippiedom, possibility and entropy, luxury excess and power cuts. The free market vibrates with hedonism as workers take to the streets. There is austerity and decadence, something sleazy and a certain innocence.

Mum attends women's groups and trousers become a two-legged symbol of freedom. At school, as part of our brown and mustard-yellow uniform, we must wear skirts, and are only allowed to wear trousers at breaktime. On her return from a school meeting, Mum says, outraged, 'I was the only woman not wearing a dress.'

Journalist and author Eva Figes, who was abandoned by

her husband and left with two small children, writes extensively about the inequalities of marriage and divorce at this time. She describes the loss of personal ambition and economic independence, and becoming bankrupt, economically and psychologically. It is difficult today to imagine the psychological, legal and social precarity faced by divorced women with children in the late seventies. Figes is another thinker espousing 'communal living . . . where there are young children to be looked after'.

Meanwhile, we go to free festivals in fields, and I attend playgroup and school. Bearded men rent out our spare room, and our cat Johannes is named after a German lodger.

In the only few snapshots taken by my aunt from these first six years of my life, my sister, my brother and I appear blurred next to the wooden fence. There is a sense of things lost. A solitary boat flails in the middle of the ocean. Mum is the only thing preventing us from drifting, and we cling on to her tight. Mum never complains. She lifts her chin up, sings and advances. We dance around the living room. She is vertical, and fights against the odds. We know we must help her, as children know without being told. Sharks swim around our existence and we must keep watch in case they bite. Silence swallows everything. It has more power than a million words, or shouted insults. Part of our history is simply amputated. No one mentions the accident. Our sister is dead. Our dad has left us.

We learn that much of human history is subaqueous, unseen. Instead, our family reverts to the imperative of forgetting, of letting the blood dry. We ignore our history.

Polish poet Wisława Szymborska, who lived through Poland's suffering under German and Russian occupations, writes:

> Reality demands
> we also state the following:
> life goes on.

She is expressing the ethical imperative of forgetting.

Mum needs to rebuild, start again with us, and she goes to meetings and meets Alfredo. They find the mansion. In 1978, she packs up No. 5. We put the boxes in a car, and go and live in the community.

One early June morning, shortly after moving into our new house in France, our three-month-old baby is staring at our living room wall. A face floats on glimmering onyx. A painted white ruffled collar encircles an archly trimmed beard. Inside the gilded frame is a three-hundred-year-old portrait of Sir Francis Walsingham, Elizabeth I's right-hand man. He was a spymaster, who secured the execution of Mary, Queen of Scots. That morning, I step back from the painting, the baby in my arms. 'What do you think?'

A looks up. 'The picture is unnerving. As though he is watching our every move.'

The picture belonged to my paternal grandparents. My dad has just emptied a storage container and has given me the portrait, along with cardboard boxes containing a selection of his parents' belongings. With my two eldest daughters, we have ripped through gaffer tape and discovered my granddad's dusty bibles, school diaries, a gilded broken Hermès teapot, and tinted ink drawings of a solemn wig-wearing judge. Twenty boxes of books. My older daughters smile. 'Look at all this treasure.' Crunched packing-paper balls pile up into a feather-light snowdrift. Perhaps, I think, I should keep this paper rather than the stuff. It is less of a weight, a confusion.

One evening, A tells me, 'You fit into these things like an old jumper.'

'But I only saw my grandparents a couple of times a year. Our lives couldn't have been more different.'

That summer, friends come over. I pour tea into newly acquired green Paragon cups and put biscuits on mismatched flowery plates. Pointing at the porcelain, the hardback volumes, and a silver spoon with a leaping-deer engraved handle, I explain, 'These things belonged to my grandparents, and then my dad. I've only had them for a few weeks.'

A woman asks about my relatives, and I continue. 'My grandparents came from a very upper-class family. One of my ancestors was Luke Howard, famous for looking up and naming the clouds, inventing the terms – cirrus, cirrostratus, cirrocumulus. He inspired Constable. But I had a very different upbringing, really nothing like them at all . . .'

I trail off coughing, suddenly disoriented; travelling from Constable to the community is a mighty leap. I bounce between the cloud-namer and a guru rebirther in a purple cloak, leading moaning hippies through a dirty sheet; juggle missionaries in dog collars, and hairy nudists' bums; dart between wealth and poverty. Sipping tea, I hope no one will ask about my childhood, as I never seem to get it right.

The language is a masquerade, and masked words provoke unexpected reactions. A utopia is a project of radical personal transformation, and people are excessively curious. Since I left the community, perfect strangers have enquired: 'Did you take drugs as a child?' 'Did you witness orgies?' 'Was it heaven?' 'What about incest?' 'Was your commune a cult?' It feels like each question is inserted gently, like a pin, until I find my past and me splayed open like a butterfly. Wings attached, I have been immobilized, a collected freak. Then people say, 'You don't look like you grew up in a commune,' as though I am not what is to be expected.

I talk to A about this one day, and he says that when people say similar things to him about his childhood, he feels proud not to conform to expectations. Whereas I feel I have betrayed utopian ideals. I look too normal, am a fallen angel from paradise. There is a clash that Milan Kundera evokes in his novel *Ignorance*. A woman returns to the Czech Republic after twenty years in Paris, and when she meets people 'they are trying to stitch her old past onto her present life. As if they were amputating her forearms and attaching the hand directly to the elbow; as if they were amputating calves and joining her feet to her knees.'

For over a decade, as part of my drama-therapy practice, I work as a clown. In child psychiatric units, in special schools, during international conferences, I put on a red nose. My clown goes most frequently to a child psychiatric daycare centre where I work every week. The story of the clown always starts the same way.

Once everyone is seated in a row (four children and a

nurse), my clown begins singing circus music, 'DA da dadadada DA da da . . .' then turns and proclaims, 'Ladies and gentlemen, boys and girls, welcome to the circus. I am pleased to introduce myself, I am the clown.' My clown bows dramatically. The five audience members clap. My clown says, 'As you can see, I have a red nose. All clowns wear red noses.' My clown is proud of this knowledge, of their professional attitude. My clown points to their nose, and the children start giggling. The clown insists, 'Look, here is my red nose.' The children laugh louder, and explain, 'But you haven't got a red nose.'

At this point, my clown touches their nose and realizes it is bare. No nose! My clown is mortified, panicked, and begins searching frantically for the red nose, lifting theatre mats, patting walls, and seeking out hiding places behind doors. All the while, the children are laughing louder. My clown begins to weep theatrically: 'I cannot find my nose. I can't be a real clown. How can I be a clown without a nose?'

My clown wipes imaginary tears from their cheeks. 'Could you help me find my nose? I need my nose, all real clowns wear red noses.'

The children nod; they always help my clown, come to rescue the clown from this moment of loss, this question of identity. The children may have autism, bite their siblings, be non-verbal, rip bed sheets, be victims of sexual abuse, or have foetal alcohol spectrum disorder or learning difficulties, but they always help the clown. A girl (the twelfth child born to an alcoholic mother) comes and strokes the clown's arm. A boy with ADHD, who scratches deep holes in his bedroom wall every night, offers my clown a pill. Another boy tries to convince my clown, '*We* will find your nose.'

My clown and the audience search for the nose together. Finally, miraculously, the clown looks inside a little girl's sock, and by some amazing turn of magic finds the nose. 'It is here. We have found the nose.' Everyone is thrilled. My clown feels utterly stupendous and is eternally grateful to the audience. At last, the clown says, 'Let the show begin . . .'

Clown experts say a clown has no function, no status and no responsibility. A clown comes from nowhere, and can be old and young, sick and healthy, a lady and a tramp. A clown takes everything seriously and couldn't care less. In Western theatre, the history of clowns and jesters spans from the ancient Greek Dorian Mimes, via medieval buffoons and *commedia dell'arte*, to the twentieth-century clown trainer Jacques Lecoq. Clown theory states that everyone can find their clown. This is why I write 'my clown', because the clown's story found me. A clown is a doppelganger, an alter ego. In the TV series *Modern Family*, the character Cam reveals his clown persona Fizbo and his deep attachment to this buffoon. For whereas an actor puts on a mask to bring a character to life, a clown takes off a mask to reveal their inner fool.

A clown cannot be utopian because a clown is always imperfect. But a clown is probably a good example of what Camus meant when he wrote in *The Rebel*: 'Beauty, no doubt, does not make revolutions. But a day will come when revolutions will have need of beauty.' Clowning, they say, requires a dancing of the soul.

I give a lecture on this psychiatric clown work at a conference at Heidelberg University. Facing an audience of strait-laced academics and serious psychiatrists, I put on a red nose, beginning: 'The red nose is the smallest mask in the world. It doesn't hide us. Instead, it reveals.' My clown story was imagined one day, and for years I use it every week. Sometimes, I wonder why I chose this story, about this clown who is so worried about not being a clown, who needs a costume not to feel like a fake, who suffers from imposter syndrome, is an outsider trying to get in. Perhaps it is obvious, but maybe it isn't. It is a riddle.

3. Inside/Outside

'And to the degree that the individual maintains a show before others that he himself does not believe, he can come to experience a special kind of alienation from self and a special kind of wariness of others.'

Erving Goffman, *The Presentation of Self in Everyday Life*

'The outer and inner are in a continual volatile dynamic relationship . . . Such is the creation and growth of the individual, the person who is in innumerable ways special, unique, different from his neighbour. This is the concept for which, in 1989, the people of eastern Europe fought their tyrants.'

Iris Murdoch, *Metaphysics as a Guide to Morals*

By the end of the first summer, Alfredo, Barbara and the Adults have set our new life into motion. Our utopian machine is turning. Cogs rotate and spin, yet the blueprint of our home and life is sketchy. The list of fors and againsts is always changing, and it is difficult to remember everything. It depends on who you meet in the Kitchen or the Garden. We live inside a workshop where life is improvised.

We must love nature, but an American man gets cross when I give him a bunch of cow parsley, for flowers must be left to grow wild. Barbara screams at a meeting, 'Everyone must cook,' because no one must be freer than anyone else. Yet Eagle sits for hours in the Yoga Room, as she just read *Zen and the Art of Motorcycle Maintenance* and is learning to 'be'.

As well as understanding the new rules inside our home, we are soon confronted by going outside, and what happens when the people from the outside come in. We are about to start school and our friends might come to play, and they will walk through our doors into utopia.

We can distinguish individual houses by their management of privacy, how they let people in and out, for all homes invent rules for disclosure and discretion. What is shown or hidden is translated in the use of shutters, curtains, locks and doors. When I look back, this intrigues me about the community. Who was allowed to enter, and how did they get in?

During the fifteen years my family lives in the community, journalists from the radio, newspapers and TV regularly come to investigate our home. They are some of our first visitors. In late August, we are informed by Alfredo, 'The crew will be filming you fly-on-the-wall style.' The Adults say, 'Act normal. They start tomorrow at breakfast.' Like most children, I want to be on TV, and Barbara adds, 'It is *cinéma vérité*,' which means it is the truth. That night, in my bed, I wonder what the film crew might want to see, and who they might want me to be.

The following morning, I put on a blue plastic waterproof cagoule – the smartest thing I own. In the giant communal Kitchen, by a bookshelf piled with greasy copies of the *Moosewood Cookbook* and the *Mennonite Community Cookbook*, a cameraman is filming. Another man holds a microphone. The Kitchen is a cave to shelter all community members. At the central stove, I light one of the twelve gas rings, heat a cast-iron pan, add oil, and crack an egg. The camera swivels towards me; I manage not to break the yolk. It is a triumph against all odds, for a yellow globe sings in an oval of white. With a metal spatula, I slide the egg onto a buttered doorstep of home-made bread. By the stove, in my raincoat, I stand proudly with my breakfast. This becomes the opening sequence of the documentary.

Donald Winnicott, the celebrated child psychiatrist, developed the concept of the 'false self', explaining that when children do not feel secure, they create a double. What they show to the outside is what they think the outside wants to see. It is a defensible façade. 'Yes' people, they become adaptable, always trying to fit in. These children repress inner, authentic, spontaneous experiences, and other people's expectations become their goal. Over the years, I became practised at this play-acting for journalists, but also inside and outside the community. For if a house is a shelter for dreaming, it feels urgent, as I write now, to finally ask who wrote my dream script, imagined my dream childhood and chose what role I played?

*

On a Monday morning in September, the Kids get in our van. Our messy gang leaves the house for our new school. The twins do not come because their parents forgot to wake them. Sunshine and Troy stay at home because they are homeschooled. Walker is our driver today and takes us four miles – another number to remember – and drops us at the pretty village green.

When we get out of the van, Jason smacks me on the head. 'Crybaby.' It's because of what happened yesterday, when we did something scary at the community. We climbed down a ladder, like a hole into nowhere, into an air-raid shelter. 'There could be bombs,' Saskia said. I thought I'd wet my pants, because Barbara recently showed me a nuclear bomb documentary. Little girls annihilated, turned to lines of dust. In the dark shelter, Jason shone a torch in my eyes, and saw my tears. 'Crybaby. Crybaby.'

At the village green, he whacks me again. 'Crybaby.' It hurts, and I would like to hit him back, but know it's better to laugh like I don't care. Instead, we run towards the churchyard which leads to our school. Through the gate, I look for children's graves. Secretly, I'm always doing this, trying to find proof of a family story like mine, where a child died like Rachel, because I don't understand. Among the headstones, I search for closely marked dates of birth and death; 'Two years old', 'Five years old', 'A beloved child'. Then, I exit the churchyard, and when I enter the stage of the school, the costumes, script and characters have changed.

*

Sociologist Erving Goffman wrote extensively on role-playing and used the metaphor of the theatre to describe everyday interactions and social norms. He used dramaturgy to explore what we expect from each other in terms of clothes, language, and formal or informal behaviour. What do we consider to be 'normal behaviour' in a street, at work, at home for a parent or a child? When I teach this to medical teams in university hospitals, I often explain his theory using our expectations of the role of the doctor as a knowledgeable decision-maker – leading a team, using formal language – and how we are shocked when these things are not immutable facts. When I was a child in the community, instead of being spontaneous, conscious role-playing became part of my everyday.

At the wooden school gates, women gather in pastel jumpers and skirts; they wear pink lipstick, kiss their children and wave goodbye. Softness wafts from them, hairspray and fluff. Little boys and girls say, 'Bye bye, Mummy.' Inside the school, we call the teachers 'Mr' and 'Mrs'. There are no first names, scarlet nipples or hand-milked cows. No one says 'shit', or mentions nukes or the golden age of preindustrial rural life, or asks our opinion, then tells us to shut up, be free and 'What about Marxist weekend schools and the fucking revolution?' At assembly, our headmaster, a besuited long-legged man, instructs us solemnly, 'Put your hands together and pray.' Outside of the community, everything is different.

That first week, in a classroom, an enormous old teacher with a hairy chin tests what she calls my 'reading levels'.

Peering over dirty glasses balanced on a blotchy nose, she hands me books: 'Can you read this, dear?' Book after book, I answer, 'Yes.' The books pile up, until I am no longer interested and between us stands an alphabetic wall.

At breaktime, I wander around. Brandy is in my class, but she has gone somewhere. In a corner, a boy and girl sit quietly together on a bench. She has pink round glasses, and her black bob swings in a perfect line. He is plump and pale and wears crumpled trousers. A weeping willow tree hangs behind them, and the branches flow to the ground. Smiling shyly, I walk towards them. 'Hello.' He blows his nose, and the girl says precisely, 'I am Mary, and I am half-Australian, and Paul is half-Irish.'

He says, 'I like trains, especially the bright yellow and blue new Intercity 125.'

I say, 'I have been on tube trains, but you must be sensible and careful of the tracks.'

Mary and Paul nod, and I sit beside them in their green cave, beneath the rush of willow. Mary and Paul become my friends, and we are friends off and on. On and off.

One Tuesday, I ask Alison, 'Can Mary come to play?' She agrees, and the following weekend Mary's mum drops her off in the courtyard. She has a dark green padded jacket, and a silky flowery scarf. Alison is in a mud-stained boiler-suit. When Alison offers tea, Mary's mum refuses – 'I have to walk the dogs' – and suddenly, she jumps into her car. Mary's eyes scan over the community, taking in the thousand bricks, the air-raid shelter, the outbuildings crammed with broken furniture and bikes.

Face to face, we stand trembling. Excitement flares

between us in a blaze. I grab her hand and our small fingers interlace, and I pull her through into the Kitchen. Thomas is doing the washing-up, tackling a mountain of week-old food-encrusted pans. He ignores us, but at the central stove, Alfredo says, 'Hello, girls.' He is frying onions, the scent of spices perfumes the air, and he scoops spoonfuls of brightly coloured powder from giant jars labelled 'Cumin' and 'Turmeric'. Alfredo explains he is teaching Barbara how to make Keralan curry – he was taught the recipe when he lived in Cochin. They elbow each other. 'You see, I am not a bloody MCP.'

Mary whispers in my ear, 'What's an MCP?' She stands close to the wall, near the door, and I tell her, 'An MCP is a male chauvinist pig.' Mary looks at me, wide-eyed. In the corner, Tripti sips tea, heavily pregnant. A woman comes in, a baby attached to one naked breast. She says, 'Hello, girls,' and plucks the baby from her body, and hands it to Alfredo. 'I need to piss.' Alison arrives, and Tripti begins talking about the strikes in car plants across the UK, and a new member, David. 'He's working-class. They say he was in prison.'

I say, 'Hello, Tripti.' Mary says nothing. Her silence is too long, and she leans down and pulls her socks straight. Sunshine and Brandy run into the Kitchen, yelling 'Ban the Bomb', and Brandy shouts, 'We're off to play British Bulldog,' and I grab Mary's hand. 'Let's go and play in my Unit.' We charge up the dark wooden stairs.

By our Unit, we bump into Bill. Bill is Alison's boyfriend now. Bill knows the name of every flower, even in a language called 'Latin'. He has a dark beard, long hair, wears a velvet jacket, jeans and high-heeled leather boots. When he goes through airport customs, he tells us, 'They X-ray my heels for drugs.' Bill works in German forests, and on his return gives us dark, spicy, gingerbread hearts decorated with hard swirls of pink iced flowers. Bill is not our dad, Alison insists. 'He is free, and has his own room in the community.' This is important, and we are told to never forget that Bill is free. But when we wake up in the morning, he is beneath Alison's green and white duvet. It rises and falls to the sound of his breath. Bill whistles through his teeth, 'Have fun, girls,' and we giggle.

Mary is wearing a pretty dress, and I wish that I had one. Alison often tells us, 'We have no money.' Claire, our brother and I are not allowed and must not want sliced white bread, Mr Kipling's pastel French Fancies fondant cakes, a beaker of fruit squash, a purple ruffled rah-rah skirt, or a family day trip to the seaside. Inside the community, our poorness is seen as good. We're told the working class are good and they are poor. But our poorness bites with sharp teeth when we want things like people outside. We have no money for school trips, and Alison says, 'Don't eat the food in the fridge.' Child Maintenance from Dad is not enough. It is better to choose the cheapest thing, or simply not to want. Outside the community, at school they soon laugh at us for the way we are dressed. Our clothes are from jumble sales and shared with the other Kids. Claire and I learn to sift through piles of clothes and find the thing that fits, a treasured leopard-skin coat or a duchess's hat.

'People bullied me every day at school,' my sister will tell me years later. 'They said I didn't wash, which was true, that I smelt, which was also true, and that we were poor. It was true as well.'

In my bedroom, I say to Mary, 'Let's play babies.' She nods her head and I am pleased. Normally, I only play with Dolly on my own, and I dream of having a real baby. But you can't play with dollies with the Kids. We play boy games because that is equality. I get my Dolly and Mary says, 'Let's change her nappy,' and I try to unplug a floor lamp so we can lay her down. The lamp is in our way, but the plug is stuck. All the plugs in the community are old, the wiring is bad; I yank and push, but nothing moves. Seeing a thin crack between the socket and the plug, I decide the best solution is a knife and fetch one from our kitchenette.

I say to Mary, 'This will work,' and stick the metal blade into the socket. There is a thud. A bang. Mary and Dolly watch. Their blue eyes open and close, while the electricity travels from the socket, through the knife, to me. It is like being shaken by a giant hand. When it stops, Mary is crying, and I cry too. Dolly watches us, motionless. Mary takes off her glasses and wants to wipe her nose. There are no tissues, so I get a roll of loo paper. It is recycled and grey. I rip off sheets and we leave them in piles on the floor.

We go to find Alison in the Kitchen. In the industrial mixer, wholemeal dough turns. Mum is making bread, and her face creases into worry when I tell her what has happened. 'Poor thing. You electrocuted yourself. The electricity must have been stopped by your new shoes.' I smile and say, 'My new boys' shoes,' because I am proud they came from the boys' section of the shoe shop. But Mary is quiet, and I want to tell her I am fine. Then Barbara arrives, talking about the Friday Meeting Agenda, and Alison grabs a notebook and writes things down. Soon they are discussing Tripti's pregnancy, and it is often like this in the community. Other things are more important than us. I look at my crêpe soles and think: *they saved my life.*

I am relieved, but Mary still seems worried. I take her back to my Unit and as we walk up the stairs, we hear wails and screams. 'It's Tripti's baby being born,' I explain, because Barbara said it would be today. Mary says nothing. That night, I am sick in my sink – 'from the electric shock', according to Alison. Eventually, when it is time to go to sleep, Mary and I whisper, 'Goodnight.'

The next time I see Mary at school, she says clearly, 'I am not allowed to come and stay or play at your house, ever again.' My stomach lurches. I nod and ignore this fact. Mary ignores this fact. After this, the mummies in the pastel jumpers at the gate seem to look at me. Something is wrong, out of kilter, and I try to make it better, and be polite. None of my school friends are allowed to come to my house. But I go to Mary's, and in a large farm kitchen, surrounded by small barking dogs, her mum hands us lemon squash in plastic beakers. On a plate are fairy cakes in frilly papers sprinkled with icing sugar, white powder from the firmament. The cakes are irresistible, and I take six or more, because I am always hungry. But her mummy looks at me, even though I say 'Please' and 'Thank you' and try to make her like me because Alison always tells me to thank people for having me. I devour cake after cake.

*

In his book on stigma, Erving Goffman explains that: 'The stigmatized individual is asked to act so as to imply neither that his burden is heavy nor that bearing it has made him different from us; at the same time he must keep himself at that remove from us which assures our painlessly being able to confirm this belief about him.' This means the stigmatized individual must feign acceptance of the situation, pretending everything is fine, providing a base for a phantom normalcy. The etymology of the word 'stigma' implies a mark on the outside of the body, the skin. Stigma, for Goffman, is spoiled identity.

One day, I talk to a therapist about this, explaining that during my childhood I felt branded. It is a complex explanation, as I am speaking in French, a foreign language, trying to explain an alienated childhood. I don't know the French word for 'branded', and so I talk about cattle being burnt with hot irons so they can be identified. Surprisingly, doing therapy work in French is liberating. This second language and culture forces me to use new words for my utopian upbringing. Through unfamiliar linguistics, I understand my childhood home another way.

Before anyone is allowed to come to the house, their names are written on the dusty Kitchen board. Then, wiped off when they go. Nobody enters or leaves without their names appearing in chalk. When visitors arrive, everything feels a little wonky because our home is reflected in their eyes. Regularly, Alfredo takes visitors round the Estate. Often, Sunshine and I follow them. Many are 'potential members', and the goal is to show them our way of life and explain this is a community, not a commune – 'We are not hippies.' This distinction is vital, and as Tripti insists, 'We are more serious.' We learn to become efficient guides, wound up like radical clockwork dolls.

Often, Alfredo begins, 'Initially this house and land were a private estate.' He talks a little about what came before. But when she's there, Barbara interrupts him. 'Alfredo, we're not interested in history or the past.' She wants to explain about Carol Hanisch and 'the personal is political'. Born from a New York women's consciousness-raising group, this phrase distinguishes between suffering that requires therapy (which indicates individual difficulties) and political repression (which requires collective political action). These four words will impact generations of feminism, infusing them with the radical idea (also found during the French Revolution) that what happens in the intimate realms of our lives is due to society's oppressive structures.

But Alfredo ignores her. 'In the nineteenth and early twentieth centuries, the house was passed, like a jewel, between the hands of high society. Later it was converted into an old people's home.' Potential members chase after Alfredo's words like diamonds. His gestures are shooting stars. Alfredo is a leader like Che Guevara, and we understand that means he does not have inherited privileges, is not here because of traditional rules. Instead, he is a white, male, charismatic hero channelling a revolutionary otherworldly force.

Barbara stands in front of Alfredo. She knows about utopias and politics. 'What's important is now.' She begins quoting French – Barbara likes to do this. 'They say in

French *maintenant*. It means the holding hand. Now, we can change things. Now, we can liberate our children.' She points at Sunshine and me. 'Their *personal* life is *political* in this house. They can eat, sleep, work and play radically. They are *libre*!' We grin awkwardly. The visitors watch. Eyes on fire.

Other visitors are the divorced dads, and these visits from the outside are different. One morning, Alison writes on the communal noticeboard: 'Saturday afternoon: Jack'. Dad parks his car, I am practising handstands with the Kids on the lawn, and Alison calls, 'Come on a tour with us.' Dad hugs me, and his shirt buttons press into my face. I see he is wearing polished shoes. On the ground floor, Alison says, 'Here are the Lounge, the Dining Room, the Kids' Room, the Yoga Room and the Mattress Room.' The Mattress Room is a dark, windowless cupboard where old bedding and stained mattresses are stored.

Alison's voice floats like a balloon, full of air and promises. Dad looks worried, and I grab his hand. Alison opens another door. 'And here's the Laundry Room.' From top to bottom, the walls are covered with racks. Crumpled jeans, holey T-shirts, pink towels and purple ragged knickers dangle from wooden bars. Dripping water forms puddles on the floor. Strung on the ceiling with pulleys and ropes are more racks. It smells. Alison points to me. 'Susie is learning how to operate the machine. It's important for her independence.'

Nodding, I add, 'And for women's rights,' and I smile because I am learning about machines and feminism. But Dad frowns again. Sometimes, visitors are like this. Their faces shut, and I feel it in my stomach. But I want to reassure Dad everything is fine; it doesn't matter if I regularly walk in on seas of moving sheets, naked limbs and couples having sex. It doesn't matter if I often feel abandoned and scared. I am learning to adapt. 'It's just normal, how we live,' I tell visitors proudly, when I am asked if I like living in the community. One day, a therapist will tell me this pride is a defence mechanism, like the pleasure felt by a child soldier given a gun.

Alison opens the door to the Egg Room, and then the Post Room, where letters are sorted into pigeonholes. By the Dark Room, she says, 'There are many talented photographers.' Her voice is stronger now. 'In the community, we have diggers and dreamers.' Beyond the Dark Room are two Visitors' Rooms. A French visitor lies in his underpants. 'Hi. I am reading *The Anarchist Cookbook*,' he giggles. 'It even shows you how to make a bomb.' The man strokes a black beard, pushes thick glasses up his nose. Dad is looking more worried, and I don't know why.

'Dad!' says a voice from behind us. Claire rushes in barefoot, wearing a shirt with no buttons and Michael's jeans. She throws herself into Dad's arms. He holds her so tight that Claire says, 'Let go, you're hurting me.' Looking away from the half-naked man, Dad coughs. The man turns back to his book and his underpants slip down. I stare; it is difficult not to look, through the open door, at the two soft, white hairy moons.

Dad leaves, and I want him to come back because he is not often there. He says he'll do things but he forgets. His name appears most months in chalk on the board, and he walks through the doors. One day, I try calling him by his first name, Jack. But he frowns, and asks me, almost whispering, 'Please don't call me that.' I stop instantly and I will never call him by his first name again. I cannot risk losing him, because he is already so far away. He circles our world like a satellite. Each letter of him flashes in the darkness: D-A-D.

One day, my grandma visits. Mutti, Alison and I are in the bathroom and I am getting undressed. It is a special treat to be alone with Mum and Mutti. In the community we're rarely alone with our family. In our Unit we have a private bathroom but there is no hot water, so the three of us have gone to the communal bathroom. Dirt draws squiggly black lines here and there, clings to windows in grimy swirls. In the sink, yellow and brown marks are like the lines on rocks. But, Alfredo says, 'Dirt is good.' As the bath runs, Alison hums 'Little Wheel Spin and Spin' by Buffy Sainte-Marie. This is a protest song, and tells you how small things lead to hate. Alison also has a tape of the UK hit 'The Floral Dance'. In our Unit we dance together, pretending to play trumpets and bang on drums, spinning in happy circles.

In the communal bathroom, Alison informs Mutti, 'Look, Susie takes her baths on her own.'

I smile because this year I have learnt to wash my hair, and in the community it is as if you get a prize when you are a Kid being an Adult and going it alone. Each act of independence is a notch on a stick. I don't know Mutti well, but I want her to like me.

At the foot of the bath, she is polished and clean,

textured differently from the community women. This morning, I saw her put on face powder, lipstick and perfume, covering her skin in these things. Mutti wears a fawn twinset, and ironed trousers she calls 'slacks'. On her feet are tan-coloured socks called 'nylons', and slip-on shoes. She is dressed like the school-gate mums.

Alison turns the taps off, strides away. I am alone with Mutti, and I check she is watching, then put shampoo on my head and make a bubbly mountain. 'Look, Mutti.' Carefully, I tip my head under the water, wriggle my limbs and close my eyes. I am a mermaid, swimming in hot water, rinsing the shampoo from my head. Opening my eyes, I am ready to see my grandma, and think she will tell me I am grown-up because I wash my hair. To be grown-up is to do all the right things. Instead, she stares at me with worried eyes, suspicion in the creases of her powdered skin. Mutti pulls her cardigan close, and gives me a look. I recognize it as the look from the mums at the school gate. It means there is awkwardness; 'awkward', from the Old Norse for 'turned the wrong way'. In the bathroom, we are upside down and inside out. I think perhaps I did not wash the shampoo from my hair. I want my grandma to be proud of me. She never comes to visit again.

According to leading British psychoanalyst Adam Phillips, the child's 'false self' has three functions: it helps look after parenting figures; it shields and hides the true self by conforming with environmental demands; and finally, it is a caretaker for the environment that has failed. It is a basic form of 'self-sufficiency in the absence of nurture'.

Now, at school fetes, in child psychiatric services or at kids' birthday parties, I recognize children developing false selves. They have learnt to hide the reality of their lives. Overfriendly, they are willing to please, and their eyes shine bright. Recalling Winnicott, I see my own childhood false self trying to cover the deepening cracks. It is odd when you grow up desperate to belong, not just within a group but also inside your own skin. The false self is a superhero costume against loneliness. But there is a huge risk, and it is a constant, exhausting struggle to keep the mask straight.

'Our bodies are political. The mainstream is so oppressive, they say it is the Year of the Leg,' Violet tells me. In her hand she's holding a copy of *Spare Rib*, and she reads out: 'Lipstick is rape exploitation.' Over the following months in the community, babies arrive like falling rain. Women grow round stomachs, have homebirths and breastfeed everywhere. Babies shit, and in the Dining Room, Barbara, Walker and Tripti say 'shit'. Occasionally Barbara says '*merde*'. The babies shit and the Adults say 'I need a shit'. This word is applauded because shit is shit. It is like 'fuck' for sex.

These words are pointed like arrows and can be fired into a face. The Adults say them jubilantly, like children farting in a museum and enjoying the stench. In our house, intimate things are talked about everywhere. There is no difference between private and public conversations, between the inside and the outside. No euphemisms. Vaginas are discussed over breakfast alongside domestic violence and nuclear bombs. At the Friday Meetings,

Alfredo says, 'There are no linguistic illusions.' Barbara says, 'Life is not a bourgeois metaphor.'

In the community, language is a vehicle for hard truths, which can be confronted if named factually. I understand it must have been liberating for the Adults, but when I look back, it was often dehumanizing and sometimes cruel for a Kid. The ethics of treading carefully are not considered. Our small bodies and minds must understand rape, the menstrual blues, and women being stretched to breaking point in mental hospitals. Despite the number of discussions in the community on the subject of 'kids', there is little acknowledgement of child development theory or what UNICEF now calls age-appropriateness. It is when I train to work in child psychiatry that I will discover authors such as Jean Piaget, the eminent Swiss developmental psychologist, who established that children's minds work in different ways at different ages. I will learn about how few human societies deny the specificity of childhood as being distinct from adulthood, and how it requires a different language and behaviour due to a child's different perception of the world.

That year, community women learn to drive tractors, cut hay and muck out stalls. They are Second Wave feminists, inspired by Andrea Dworkin and Judith Butler. Barbara dramatically reads Claire and I lines from Annie Leclerc's *Parole de femme* – 'To be this vagina, an open eye in life's nocturnal fermentation' – and later we laugh so much our stomachs hurt. With Brandy and Sunshine, I build camps in the woods, as the women get stuck into mud. During maintenance weeks, they do what they describe as renovating, painting and restoring. Fields are fenced and chickens slaughtered. Women hoe and dig gardens, repair roofs. Alison yells, 'I can lift that bale.' She throws a twenty-pound rectangle of hay to Barbara. Calves are born, and within days, as Barbara points out, 'they are immediately independent'. We invent dance routines and show them to the new member, David. Lying under his duvet, he claps and claps.

From now on, I want to be a boy because being like a boy is being strong, and being like a boy is being sexless. I must ignore my winkle (or call it a vagina); it shouldn't be there. My body is a contraption to be undone. All my parts remodelled a different way. I get my hair cut short, feel the wind on my neck. Often, people think I am a boy, like the community boy-Kids who have bones like pistons, roll in dirt and throw punches. Most of the girls now do the same, and later, when Dad remarries, I rip my bridesmaid dress and throw a boy to the ground, because he says, 'Girls are weak!' Being like a boy is being powerful like the commune women, larger than the heads on Easter Island, holy ova carved in stone.

Alison says, 'We are not mainstream.' Tripti says, 'We will not conform to oppressive ideals.' Eagle reads an article which says clothing has jaws and is designed to make women into sex objects. Barbara tells a friend on the telephone, 'I refuse to paint my lips for a man.' Firefly has read: 'Female magazines only let you be a virgin, a mother, a whore.' These goddesses are stronger than all things, can be anything: builders, shepherds, cowhands or Friday Meeting leaders. Most of them are middle-class and were privately educated; they own varying cultural and economic capital. Some have a comfortable 'outside' income (I only realize this now, as I write this book), and some, like us, barely have enough. They are women dressed as seventies men dressed as hippy peasants dressed as a Marxist feminist democracy.

'Your grandma and those women fought for so many of our freedoms,' I am saying to my eldest daughter. We are discussing whether we shave our legs, and I am explaining I love the feeling of my soft, waxed skin. It's something I need to physically reclaim. Yet I tell her I have great respect for these women who fought against abhorrent sexism: in the US, in the seventies, marital rape was still legal in fifty states.

'Their struggles gave us choices,' agrees my daughter, who is eighteen and studying Gender Politics. 'Because of them, you can choose to work and be a mother, and share domestic work, and you've passed this freedom on to us.' And she begins talking about how women's bodies have historically been tyrannically controlled from the outside, how the commune women must have felt powerful and free. My daughter then asks, 'So what went wrong, Mama?'

Foucault wrote, 'The human body is the principal actor in all utopias.' And I try to explain to my daughter that in the community, patriarchal objectification was replaced by another dogma. As a child, it seeped into my bones. My small body was not a place of pleasure or expression. It became a place for politics, a house that had to be armed.

*

When I am seven, nearly eight, David – the new member – informs me daily that he loves me. In his room, I curl up on his lap like a cat, and he says, 'Of course I love you,' and I say, 'I love you too,' and cuddle him. David's black hair falls in curls on his shoulders, and he is half-French and says he has gypsy blood. The Adults whisper, 'David was beaten as a child, and used to deal cocaine.' On David's bedroom wall is a photo of him in a cowboy hat. He can cook, play guitar and mend cars, and he has a temper. He is one of the many single men at the community.

David is one of my best friends, and insists, 'You are not just attractive. You are beautiful. Your friend' – I think he is talking about Brandy – 'is just attractive. One day, you will be a beautiful woman.' He smiles, and I feel awkward but thrilled. Brandy has thirty-seven freckles – we counted them – and spins in cartwheels on the lawn. She is the daughter of Dole royalty. I am a crybaby and read books. 'You will be a very beautiful woman,' David repeats, and I drink in his words, gobble up the love.

One day, he confides, 'I have decided I will marry you, but don't tell anyone. It is our special secret.' It is a proposal. I sigh and believe him, for I am nearly eight now, we've lived in the community for almost a year, and I spend hours alone with David. In my bedroom, I confide in Brandy, 'David wants to marry me.'

The following day, when I walk into the playground at lunchtime, something is wrong. Boys and girls are shouting, 'She thinks a man wants to marry her.' The tease thunders from mouth to mouth. Brandy has told a girl at school. Everyone joins in, even Mary and Paul: 'She thinks a man will marry her!' Stuck inside the circles painted on the playground floor, I try to hold my ground because I am telling the truth: David loves me. The class forms a knotted chain of arms and legs, and I am trapped inside, bullied for what feels like weeks and months. A teacher says to me, teasing, 'Why are you looking so serious?' I just wish I could disappear, get smaller and smaller until I am not here.

At milking time, I go to see Alison. The small stall is dusky with the scent of hay. On three-legged wooden stools, we sit either side of a cow, separated by soft, brown flanks. It is our only time alone. From here, all I see is Alison's hands and the cow's pink teats. The teats stretch and elongate. Streaks of white milk land in the bucket. Alison is reliable; she never misses a milking shift. Scuffling my feet in straw, I say, 'They're picking on me at school.'

She doesn't seem to hear me and says, 'Oh, just ignore them. You poor thing,' and I start to speak again, tears in my eyes, but Alison has picked up the milk bucket. She is walking across the courtyard. I want to tell her about David and the proposal even though I know that I am not supposed to need my mum. I follow her to the Kitchen, and she puts the milk in the fridge. My mouth opens and closes, and I don't say anything as she fills industrial dishes with layers of apricot crumble, preparing for a visiting family from Sheffield. They are important because they are striking about steel and have been queuing for bread. I realize I need to find my own solution to the bullying.

My plan involves the communal bathroom and a book called *What Katy Did*. The communal bathroom is purple now. Recently, in a fit of anger, Lawrence slopped paint everywhere. The walls are coated in purple stalactites. I turn the cold tap on and lock the door. In the house, this is the only room with a lock. When the bath is full, I undress, and then get into the chilly water.

In the freezing bath, I look at the purple ceiling and pray to my god, Lardy, for the playground game to stop, and for me to get ill, to have a fever, and become so sick someone will take care of me. This is my solution: they will put me in a warm bed, with hot soup, like in *What Katy Did*. In the 1860s she fell from a swing and people sent her boxes filled with fruit and candy, tied with pale blue silk bows. In hospitals, I think, even strangers love you. Surrounded by the purple walls, I count the seconds as I pray. It is unbearable, but I must stay here until the cold touches my core. Brandy betrayed me, and she knew the outside rules better: the difference between what happens inside our home and at school. The cold water moves from skin, through muscle to bone. It reaches me.

For over a decade, I work in child psychiatry, and often in a daycare unit for children on the autistic spectrum. One of my favourite drama-therapy exercises involves creating an imaginary world. With the nurse and the four children in the group, we leave our imaginary home, get into an imaginary car and drive to an imaginary mountain. We always get lost on the way, because I have lost my map, and the children have to tell me to turn left or right. Upon arrival, we get out of the car, put on raincoats because of the rain or sunscreen because of the sun. We venture across muddy fields requiring imagined boots, dip our toes into freezing seas, climb mountains by pulling each other to the summit. At the top, we plant a flag. We always stop for an imaginary picnic, and take a series of imaginary photos as we eat the best sandwiches we've ever tasted and sample the most delicious cake. Then, suddenly, it is time to go, and we have to rush our journey getting back down the mountain, along the coast, across the fields, until we reach our car and can head home.

During an annual clinical day with the multidisciplinary team, I present the drama-therapy project, drawing a map of our world. When I finish, the Head of Child Psychiatry, a tall blond French man with glasses, turns to me. 'I wish I could go there.'

In the children's therapy workshop, we expand body movement – skipping, stretching, pulling and pushing – experiment with emotions of joy and fear, and imagine another place. Yet crucially this world provides *both* risk and safety. It is an ever-expanding yet ever-similar space. Researchers such as Lev Vygotsky, Piaget and Winnicott consistently explain that repetition and stability are fundamental to child development. While the community provided a bewildering openness, in the daycare centre our imagined world balances a child's developmental need for ritual *and* adventure, ordinary safety *and* the dream.

In the community, our instability extended to childcare. Rather than attempt to share childcare between men and women, in a move to free women from domestic labour, we were often abandoned to each other or to ourselves. In this autonomous dream, I took care of younger children while still a child myself, going off for three-hour picnics with a gang of little kids in tow. A few times, from when I was seven, I even took them to a café in the local village, and under the astonished gaze of the waitress ordered myself a pot of tea. In Melford Spiro and Bruno Bettelheim's studies of the Israeli kibbutz, the largest utopian movement in history, they examine the effects of children living separately from parents. Bettelheim quotes a nursery worker who cared for children for more than thirty years, who says, 'Let's face it, the kibbutz wasn't built for children, but to make us [the adults] free.'

As our first year at the community draws to a close, I feel the world dividing. There are two languages, two value systems and ways of being, an inside and an outside. At school, and with my dad, no one uses the same words to describe home, meal, bedtime, adult, parent or child. We live in Units, but a Unit is a number, a Unit is not a home. It is as though while attempting to build an alternative anti-capitalist utopia, an equally repressive institution has been established. What was promised is not what is practised. As Arendt writes in *The Origins of Totalitarianism*, 'the self-compulsion of ideological thinking ruins all relationship with reality.' Institutional power structures are replicated; their impact is ignored.

Later, a member of my extended family, when we talk about my childhood, will say to me dismissively, 'It was just like Hampstead but in the countryside,' and I will be shocked because while our house has remnants of left-wing, wealthy Hampstead, the reality of our life is nothing like it at all. As we run free, people like David, who are vulnerable and damaged, become our closest friends. On some days, I wish it was more normal and simpler, less hard work just to be alive.

One rainy Sunday, on Alison's bookshelf, I find a book: *Survive the Savage Sea*. The cover is a turquoise swirl of waves. In my bedroom, I read as rain splatters on the windowpane, and I will reread this book throughout my childhood. It is the story of how one June morning, in the Pacific Ocean, a forty-three-foot yacht, sailed by a Scottish ex-farmer and his family, is attacked by killer whales, sinking in sixty seconds. Left with an inflatable rubber raft and a nine-foot fibreglass dinghy to tow it, the two parents, eighteen-year-old son, twelve-year-old twin boys and their student friend decide to make for the coast, one thousand miles and an estimated fifty days away. They have enough emergency rations for three days. The author writes about cutting turtle flesh into strips, bodies organized for maximum sleep, the benefits of flotation chambers and careful food planning to survive.

As a child, what I understand from this book is that life is to be survived. To survive is to outlive, endure, persist and remain. The antonyms of survival are 'succumbing' and 'death'. To survive is to keep a calm head, a brave face; to be helpful and not complain. *Survive the Savage Sea* becomes a kind of bible, and from then on, I structure my days. In my bedroom, I print between wobbly lines: 'Monday 5pm: Play, 5.30–6pm: Garden, 6–7pm: Read, 7–8pm: Write, 8–8.30pm: Practise my recorder.' I keep these timetables for decades, ordering my days like the Adults when they organize their meetings. The timetables are a weapon in my battle when I move between outer and inner worlds. I am a little girl, and it will take me forty years to understand that surviving is not living; to survive is an addition to life. It is the *sur* added to *vie*, a survivor is a thing that remains. It is a replacement. To survive is not to be.

Recently, I met a man who grew up in a similar environment, an Australian religious community, where he cooked meals for sixty and gave sermons as a child. We shared stories of what we had gained from our childhoods – feral autonomy, self-reliance, open-mindedness and creativity – and what we had lost. With resignation, he told me, 'I will always be an outsider now, forever. I'll never fit in anywhere. That's just the way it is.'

His fatalism reminded me of Sisyphus, forever pushing a boulder up a hill, only to watch it fall and be obliged to push it up again. Listening, I wanted to insist, to tell him that this was not the case. I wanted to persuade him he could find different ways to come in from the outside and feel at home, that it is nearly always possible to make things different.

As a therapist and when I work lecturing and supervising, I often talk about hope, and my refusal to give up or be cynical. When I was running a seminar in Paris on stress management for an international MBA, I asked the group to identify their images of hope. An Egyptian woman said, 'I always picture myself as a young woman, just before my final high school exams. I'd spent years inside the high school, studying. I was the first person in my family heading for university.' She explained how much she'd felt like an outsider at school, but that somehow this had given her a special strength. 'In Alexandria, I was standing overlooking the sea, and I stretched my arms wide open. I thought, I am at the edge of the continent, about to step outside into the beginning of the world.'

4. Dads' Worlds

'"To understand history," Chacko said, "we have to go inside and listen to what they're saying. And look at the books and the pictures on the wall. And smell the smells."'

Arundhati Roy, *The God of Small Things*

'Gender is a key marker of power and powerlessness.'

Mary Beard, interviewed in the *Sunday Edition*

From beside Claire, I look out of the train window. Trees, houses and fields. Black train cables strung across the sky. We're going to see Dad. The train journey takes an hour, and we're on our own. My big sister is nine, I am seven and our brother is five. On the rack overhead is our luggage. Somebody left their copy of the *Sunday People* newspaper on the seat, and I am reading about 'The Face of the Ripper: British women being raped and murdered' and 'The price of petrol soars'. Claire prods me and I prod her, and then I turn back to a photo of a granny on a motorbike. Policemen pursue her to chat her up because she rides her bike in a bikini. On another page is Diana, yet to be married, aged nineteen, blushing in a see-through skirt.

In the newspaper, women are wide-eyed and innocent, sexy, or raped and dead. 'Time to change trains,' Claire says.

For a while, Dad drove to the community. When any dad visits, all the Kids ask questions, and we want our dads to be the biggest and best. 'My dad can do karate and threw a man across a room,' I tell Jason, even though it is a lie. I don't think my dad can even kick a football. Dad brings chicken casserole in a brown Le Creuset dish. He has been on a course called 'Cookery for Men' and learnt to make five dishes that he can rotate through. Dad likes things to be the same. He eats an orange every night before going to bed and keeps his wellington boots for twenty years. At the community, we eat with him around a borrowed table, in Alison's room, in our Unit.

Now, it's been decided we can journey alone, and we will travel across the country regularly for fifteen years, carrying our weekend bags. Sometimes, Dad gives us money for food on the return journey, but as we have little money, we save it to spend on sweets, showing off in front of the Kids. Slowly, I develop a taste for other worlds.

Later, as an adult, I will end up working on three continents and I will never lose the itch to travel. Each time I get on a train, or settle into a bus or plane seat, my heart skips. Packing a suitcase is one of my favourite activities. Travelling becomes an escape pod, a corridor, or perhaps it is a bridge?

When we're at Dad's house, getting dressed in our mismatched clothes, we meet his girlfriend. She snaps, 'What are you wearing?' None of us answer. We dislike her for this. She calls me Kate Bush because I never brush my hair. Dad's girlfriend speaks her mind and decides things at the last minute: to bet on a racehorse, make us bacon butties or bake a Sachertorte. Neither Alison nor Dad is like this. Like Bill, Dad's girlfriend is a stuck-on part of our lives. Our Single Parent Family is attached to other people with Sellotape and Velcro; we are tied together with lengths of worn-out string. In social gatherings outside the community, we are the exception.

Nowadays, family structures have become more fluid. Statistics show almost one in two marriages ends in divorce, and stepfamilies are the norm. The waters are shifting to include non-married families, same-sex families, blended families, polyamorous families, and families with no children built from groups of friends. Our own family and home, extending out from the Breton house, includes many versions of these. When I look around at my daughters, friends and family, I relish the idea that families can evolve, that we can accept different structures and ways of being. In her compassionate book *Every Family Has a Story*, renowned family therapist Julia Samuel writes that 'the underpinning predictable resource' for every family is love.

At first, we visit Dad for one weekend every fortnight and two weeks during the summer holidays. At Dad's flat, two of us sleep in a bunk bed stacked in a spare room. The third child is on the sofa. Dad says, 'Night-night, flopsy bunnies.' He says words like this: 'poppets', 'bunnies', 'dear'. At Dad's, we always sleep in a spare room, even later when he marries his girlfriend and they buy a three-floored, elegant townhouse with mauve hydrangea bushes and an extension. Car wheels crunch on a gravel drive and they make extravagant promises of bedrooms for the three of us. There are always interior decorations involved and we're told it could be done Laura Ashley style. For years, I imagine this room in this home: a crisp turned sheet, floral walls and a dressing table. But instead, there are mattresses on floors and makeshift attic beds. Sometimes I wake up in the night, startled, not knowing where the door is, or how to turn on the light. The bedrooms never appear. This other house that is not a home is an absence that weighs heavily. But when we get back to the community, and Mum asks if we have had a good weekend, we just answer 'Fine'.

When we are little, before Dad has more children, he says, 'Let's go swimming,' and takes us to the pool. Afterwards, he buys us Wagon Wheels. A biscuit, big as your hand, topped with marshmallow fluff and coated in thick milk chocolate. Dad does things like this: swimming lessons, puppet theatre and ice-skating sessions. He takes us to Saturday cinema to see *Raiders of the Lost Ark*, falls asleep, snores, and wakes up to clap loudly at Indiana Jones. Dad embarrasses us, perfectly.

Occasionally, Dad has friends over for dinner parties, and at one, a woman in a scarlet silky jacket with padded shoulders flicks her perm and asks us prying questions about the community and we say it is 'Fine'. She enquires about where Bill and Alison go out, and Claire and I frown. We don't know what she is talking about because no one at the community 'goes out' in couples or as families. Instead, collectively we attend Marxist conferences, and go on marches. Very occasionally, the whole community goes punting in Oxford and we advance along the dark river in boats.

Bill now sleeps in our Unit most nights. He also has a small, dark room in the community. There is a single bed, dusty shelves stacked with botanical books, and he tacks the pictures that I draw for him on his walls. In our Unit, he and Alison share a double bed, but Alison says, 'Bill does not live with us, and he is not your stepdad.' Sometimes, Bill puts on music so loud, we run around Alison's room to a song called 'Harry Irene'. Bill has a glass eye, and if we ask specially, he taps it with a spoon. We chant, 'Tap your eye. Please, Bill, please.' My sister and I vie for his attention. Bill taps his eye. Clunk. Metal against glass. We shriek and Alison cringes. Sometimes, Bill sticks needles in his cheeks to make us laugh. He is a magician.

But our family arrangement is hazy, a shape without contours, and this is perhaps one of the problems. No one talks about anything. Dad never talks or asks us about the community, and Alison never asks about life at his house. Their silence is respectful and dignified. Yet, there is constant collapse when we travel between their worlds. Their silence stops connections, and it builds a wall so high communication becomes impossible. There is a room with a light turned on, but no one is there. Instead, we journey between three spaces, cross gateways between the community, school and Dad's world. Three cultures. Three languages. Inside each cosmos is a separate way to move and speak. I am six, seven, nearly eight, and I create my own escape pod for passing through each firewall: I'm fine. Fine. Fine.

In 1987, J. E. Goldthorpe, an eminent sociologist, published *Family Life in Western Societies: A Historical Sociology of Family Relationships in Britain and North America*. The book opens with the words 'Everybody is somebody's daughter or son', and Goldthorpe writes that of all the social worlds that sociologists study, the family is one of the hardest to observe. From psychoanalysts to fundamentalist Christians and Soviet theorists, different thinkers, eras, cultures and creeds have tried to regulate and/or understand our basic social group. Having worked in mental health for decades, I am still amazed by the power of families to dominate our lives, whether we are six or sixty. In consequence, all utopian projects have attempted to control domestic life.

But I wonder how and if we can ever tell objective truths about family and homes? Can we think dispassionately about the most intimate part of our lives?

In an early chapter, Goldthorpe explores post-World War II criticisms of the family, citing the example of sociologist Barrington Moore Jr, who believed 'one of the most obviously obsolete features of the family is the obligation to give affection'. Moore's approach is astonishing, as though love and care are out of fashion, dead and gone. Yet, in our communal upbringing, this outlook influenced the Adults, who believed that parental affection was a trap, and indifference guaranteed freedom.

Goldthorpe also challenges the notion that the smaller nuclear family is a recent invention. He gives extensive historical examples from Northern Europe such as the diaries of the Reverend Ralph Josselin, who was a vicar in Essex in the seventeenth century, detailing a pattern of intense, intimate relationships with an inner circle of near-kin, but non-existent relationships with first cousins. When I read Goldthorpe's book in the British Library, I remembered how in the community, the nuclear family – and the family in general – was considered to be a suffocating social structure invented by patriarchal capitalists.

When my great-aunt (on our dad's side) dies, there is a funeral. Alison sighs and says to me, 'You have nothing to wear.' Before the funeral, I borrow a grey sweatshirt and a matching skirt from Sunshine. The clothes feel awkward, and over a dinner of nut roast, David smiles and kisses my cheek, 'You look pretty.' Lawrence says, 'You are so cute.' Saskia asks me, 'Why are you wearing a skirt?'

Dad drives us to the funeral. His girlfriend is in the car, and Alison comes too because she was very close to my great-aunt. In the back, I wriggle in my skirt. The waistband digs into my skin. After the church service, we go to a house with shiny antique furniture and pictures on the wall. When we walk in, a woman, dressed in a tweed suit, whispers loudly, 'Look, there's Jack with his harem.' People's eyes glance sideways at us, and I brush down my skirt. I am wearing Claire's too-big old shoes, and socks with a hole. They give us milky tea, and fruitcake. A dry sponge spiked with glacé cherries and sweet black dates. But things are not quite right. Dad tells us this is our family. It is in front of our eyes, and we reach out with our hands, but the door stays shut. They are things called: shareholders, lawyers, doctors, solicitors, professors, and chuckling landed gentry. We do not belong here. We have bad clothes and home-cut hair. We stink of communities, of abandonment, of dead sisters. We smell of harems, whatever that means.

A, the girls and I are near Bordeaux. On holiday. We're staying overnight in a *chambre d'hôte*, a squat chateau with a dusty vineyard. It is a special treat. Summer heat caresses the flowers, and the pool is surrounded by plump cushions. 'Let's go swimming, Dad,' the girls say. The youngest naps and the three of them play in the water.

The next morning, after a breakfast of freshly picked strawberries and homemade sweet flan served on Gien porcelain plates, the owner bustles over to me as I write, scolding, '*Il ne faut pas travailler*. Don't work.' I raise my eyebrows. Sometimes, I feel like a carthorse with blinkers, always pulling the plough. My body craves labour: I have a Marxist and Protestant (and possibly a survivor's) devotion to work. A laughs when I tell him about the owner; he says, 'You'll never learn to chill out.' A is much better at relaxing than I am. Our children know who to ask for what. Dad is good for cuddles, plasters, jokes and cash. Mum is good for listening, intense discussions, fashion, crazy dancing, and eating something that has just been dropped on the floor. Both of us are very close to our three daughters. Sometimes, I look at them, gazing at their dad with love and admiration, and I wonder what it must be like to grow up in a family like this. In many ways, A and I are like chalk and cheese, but we share core values, particularly in relation to our three children. When we finish our day exhausted and grouchy, we often say, 'They didn't choose to be born, they are our responsibility,' and we love them so much it hurts.

Childcare and domestic work are divided between us, in a hopeful, beautiful mess. We have no family living in the same country as us, so over the years we have developed self-reliance. He cleans and cooks, and so do I, though his hygiene standards are higher, and I have a feral tendency – a result, he teases, of my 'commune upbringing, and the dirty upper class used to servants'. In our couple, he prefers being at home while I am off climbing metaphorical mountains. He prefers safety, while I thrive on risk, and we've both come to accept what makes the other tick.

Often, I realize how A's involvement in domestic labour or paid work is considered differently to mine. It's as if his involvement is a choice whereas mine is a requirement. Centuries of gender inequality are hard to undo. In the seventies, journalist Eva Figes wrote in *Man and Woman* magazine of how, during the French Revolution, Rousseau thought women should be slaves to men. She also detailed the impact of capitalism on domestic work. From the late eighteenth century, economic development and industrialization divided labour, with new employment located in factories and buildings, and household work left at home. The former became valued as paid labour, the latter was seen as voluntary, natural, unpaid female toil. Work was separated from home – spatially, hierarchically, economically and in terms of gender.

In her fascinating book *(M)otherhood*, behaviour and data scientist Pragya Agarwal unpacks gender expectations and roles, and explores how many workplaces are still patriarchal structures, where women – especially women of colour – are discriminated against. Research shows that it is still assumed that women will choose motherhood and not be as serious about their careers. In the 2020s, being a working mum is still not the same as being a working dad.

When I travel for work, I am told by colleagues and mums at the gate, 'You are so lucky to have a partner who supports you!' and when he picks up the kids, 'What a wonderful dad!' Artist Mary Catherine Starr, in her comic 'An Illustrated Guide to the Double Standards of Parenting', highlights some of the major differences in how society views mums versus dads. The artist told HuffPost, 'I'm tired of our society applauding dads for handling the most basic of parenting duties and expecting perfection from mothers.'

Dad takes us on yearly camping holidays to North Norfolk. We venture out on the flatlands where earth, sky and water make one soft grey-green horizon. He erects an orange and brown family tent by the salt marshes. Mornings spent crabbing stretch into afternoons. When dusk falls, we eat fish and chips at the port, and play on the penny slot machines. Evening lemonade is drunk in pub gardens. Moths circle lights.

In the daytime, at the beach, we swim in the waves. For hours, I play at water babies, like in the Victorian story where chimney sweeps are transformed into nymphs. When we are too blue and too cold, Dad chases us up the long, flat beach. 'Run, children, run!' When I stop, shivering, he wraps me in a big towel and rubs my skin. The feeling of this huge, enveloping rough towel around me and his hands holding me tight is the best thing.

On holiday, his menus are always the same. At the campsite we eat packet mash, packet mince, packet macaroni cheese and packet soup. He cooks on a two-ring camping stove. For lunch, he makes us sandwiches, called rounds: cheese and pickle, tuna and cucumber with vinegar, and cheese and tomato. The sandwiches are stacked inside an empty bread packet. Whichever rounds are not eaten at lunchtime are recycled, fizzy and soggy the following day. Dad always eats the leftovers. 'It is a family tradition from the Quakers. Even my great-grandfather – the High Court judge – insisted on eating the dry bread crusts.'

'*Vos huîtres.* Your oysters, Madame.' We're at a restaurant for the seventh birthday of one of my daughters. Their granddad is here, my dad. In front of me, a waiter places a dish of oysters, weather-worn and barnacled; inside they are glistening white. With a small fork, I cut through the nerve connecting the oyster to its shell, add a spoonful of cider vinegar and diced shallots. The girls are chattering, not listening, and suddenly I ask, 'Dad, do you remember that time when we found a sex doll?' The story has just entered my mind. It seems funny, light-hearted, suitable lunchtime conversation.

Dad shifts uneasily on his chair. A looks at me. I continue, oblivious. 'Yes, you took us out for the day with some of the Kids from the community. We went for a picnic and visited a model village.' I remember the model village well because I loved the tiny, thatched cottages, little red-brick houses and school, and the miniature white-painted hospital. Pint-sized model people worked, waved and pushed prams, and a small train circled the village, stopping at a station for passengers. It felt cosy, filled with dream homes.

In the restaurant, I take another oyster. 'After visiting the model village, we stopped for a picnic in some woods. And one of the Kids found a black bin bag filled with pornography and an inflatable sex toy. A full-size woman.'

'Yes.' My dad shifts again in his chair.

Looking down at my oyster, I cut and scoop. As I tell the story, I am starting to realize how odd it sounds. I talk more quietly. 'We took the doll back to the house. Then, a Kid blew the doll up and we ran round our woods with her on our shoulders. For hours and hours, we just ran and ran.'

A is still looking at me. The girls are chattering. Suddenly, I realize this is not a funny story. We found the doll, took her home, and in our woods, we carried her. Pink plastic skin. Red nipples. Blond plastic hair. All the Kids took her round the fruit trees and the redwoods. We pulled at her arms and legs. Nobody stopped us – not my dad, Alison or the other Adults. Yet this sex doll must have been used, penetrated by a man.

I butter a piece of rye bread and gulp some white wine. Vouvray bubbles fizzle on my tongue. My dad is saying, 'I could never be authoritarian at the community, even with the Kids. I was an outsider. But I was irresponsible.'

However, I am not listening. In telling the story of the sex doll, the funny side has shattered, and something ugly remains. I grab a bread roll, and I feel ashamed. One of the Proto-Indo-European roots of the word 'shame' is **kem-*, 'to cover', and in the restaurant I feel uncovered, and wish I could wipe myself away.

A few times a year, we visit my paternal grandparents' house. Dad packs the three of us kids into his car. He stops for me to be sick and wipes my face. He stops for us to wee, and hands out tissues. We sing 'The Wheels on the Bus' and Dad joins in: 'All day long.' We spend a lot of time with Dad in cars: sliding on the back seat – in the age of no seatbelts – staring out of windows. In a notebook, I count cars and write down registration numbers. The road unfolds like a thin black ribbon, and I think how it would be if we touched the end.

Sometimes, we play I Spy. Claire says, with superiority, 'I spy a PLP.'

'A pretty lovely person?'

'No, a public leaning post.' Claire pushes me and it hurts.

In the car, I say, 'Get off! Dad, Claire's hurting me,' but she scowls, threatening me with her eyes.

I look up, but Dad does not reply. I see his reflection in the rear-view mirror. His eyes are slowly closing, his crinkled eyelids falling. He is battening down the hatches. From here, I can see the lids tumbling. He jerks his eyes open, but they fall and close again. His head jolts as he tries to stay awake. Leaning over, he rips open a packet of Extra Strong Mints, and places one of the large white discs in his mouth.

'Do you want a mint?' He passes the packet to Claire. Dad is often falling asleep like this, as though he opens his eyes to reality, only to shut them quickly again. Everything pulls him towards sleep. He tries to focus on the road, to keep looking at the world, but I wonder whether he sees what is happening inside and outside our car.

Later, we park in a quiet, suburban street. My grandparents' house is set back from the road. A tiny path is edged with lavender; the thick, dry bushes are as tall as me. On each stem are pale, purple flowers. A thousand million seeded blooms. The bushes are filled with bees, and we walk up the path between these frightening, living walls.

Granddad opens the door, grinning. 'Hello. Come in. Come in.' The smile on his face jangles with bells. My granddad is a vicar, a slim good-natured man, dressed in belted trousers and an ironed shirt. Sleeves rolled neatly up, he is a do-gooder, and his hands are as warm as pebbles in the sun. He never seems to give us The Look. 'Come in,' he says again. He welcomes us into the house in a way that my archaeologist friend says features in Homer's *Odyssey*. In ancient Greek, the word *xenia* means both 'hospitality' and 'friend'. The cognate word *xenos* can mean 'stranger' or 'friend', and is linked to an ancient Greek tradition of welcoming strangers, family and friends, feeding them and listening to their stories. It is the opposite of xenophobia.

Through a narrow corridor, we squeeze into their home. Past a large wooden grandfather clock, a steep turn of stairs leads up to three small bedrooms. Downstairs in the dark kitchen, saucepans dangle from the ceiling. On the living room wall, Sir Francis, the Tudor spymaster, faces a watercolour of a West African landscape. Black-and-white photographs of steam trains decorate the dining room.

The house is crammed with desks, Chinese cabinets, carved chairs, bookshelves, tables, footstools and a campaign chest – which can be divided into two pieces – that, they say, crossed paths with Livingstone in the jungle. Cut-off Persian rugs cover the floors. Granddad says there is a mix of terracotta for luck, peacock blue, which symbolizes power and solitude, and yellow for the sun, the joy of life. Dad tells me later, 'Your Grandma Bella placed the rugs under the furniture so you couldn't see the holes.'

'Come in and see your grandma,' Granddad says.

Grandma Bella almost never moves. In the house, she is fixed in the same place, in the same time, in a fawn easy chair by a window. Her throne overlooks a small, enclosed garden. In front of Grandma Bella is a cup of tea on a tray, a biscuit, a book and a pillbox. A black velvet Alice band holds her white hair back from her face. She wears pure wool cardigans and knee-length skirts. She speaks softly, and occasionally recites poetry.

In my worn jeans and straggly T-shirt, I awkwardly inch towards her between the large pieces of furniture that were ordered and designed for a grander house. When I reach her, she places a kiss on my cheek, and she murmurs 'Hello, dear.' There is an odour of face powder. It alights on my hair.

Throughout her lifetime, Dad tells me, 'Bella never owned a washing machine. She handwashed certain clothes and used a laundry service. Her ground coffee was ordered from London and delivered through the post. She and your grandfather drank their morning coffee like the French, from little brown pottery bowls. Bella rarely cooked and had a reputation for exploding boiled puddings in tins.' He talks about Bella's parents, his grandparents, and tells me how every morning my great-granddad would assemble the household for morning prayers. He would sit at one end of the table and my great-grandmother at the other. All the children were down the sides on special little chairs. After prayers, a gong rang. Maids filed into place. Nurses took the children away. Every evening they dressed formally – gowns, jewels and dinner jackets. Dad says, 'Some of this was usual for the time. But your great-granddad, the judge, was a stickler for tradition.'

Bella has what is called Parkinson's. When we visit, she sits, shaking, in her chair. But in the car, on the way back, Dad tells us the same stories about how Grandma Bella was one of the first women to go to Oxford University, the very clever daughter of the High Court judge and the sister of an infamous British cabinet minister. When she dies, at her funeral, a man will say – much to everyone's surprise – that Grandma Bella worked for MI5 during World War II. We will all imagine that she was a spy. Frequently, I am told about her cleverness, and everybody repeats that I am like her.

As an adult, I will realize I have few memories of speaking or playing with my grandma. Yet, through the stories Dad tells me, she comes alive. It is difficult to trace the lineaments of the young in the faces of the old. But from deep inside the quiet elderly woman in the chair, a young bright Bella infiltrates my existence. Running past the Parkinson's shakes, she reads and writes, lives surrounded by books, has adventures and undercover lives. Bella becomes my role model: a woman who thinks. In the playground, I tell Mary and Paul, 'I want to go to Oxford University like my grandma.' I am fiercely determined to grow up into something and someone, and for a while Bella is my North.

Intergenerational relationships between grandchildren and grandparents are radically different to those between parents and their offspring. In *Every Family Has a Story*, Julia Samuel writes, 'It is through looking at their different stories from generation to generation, and how they influence each other, that we begin to understand ourselves.' Between grandparents and grandchildren, pressure is reduced, our desperate need for love is trimmed. My dad describes being left at prep school by his parents at the age of five. After a year, when he met his own father again, he wouldn't talk to him, as he didn't recognize his face. Yet my own memories of my granddad are of a warm, loving man.

My partner A was very close to his vibrant maternal grandmother, Zelda. When I met her, she wore red lipstick and roller-skated. Zelda's own mother had been hospitalized when she was a child, and Zelda was brought up by a flock of loving aunts that we nicknamed the Golden Girls. Zelda had her children very young, at the end of World War II, and later could be a highly demanding parent. With my partner's mum, Zelda would ring complaining about her aches and pains, demanding love from her daughter nearly every day. But with her grandson, she was doting and generous. When we saw her, she always shoved five-pound notes in his hand alongside out-of-date chocolates, bought from the market 'for my favourite'. She did a

French O-level, and when we moved to France she sent us weekly letters in her broken French, signed '*Je vous aime, baiser, baiser*'. Kiss, kiss. Recently I realized that, despite not being married to A, every day I wear Zelda's wedding ring.

At our grandparents' house, we eat afternoon tea, or a hot meal Dad has brought: chicken and mushroom casserole served with peas and rice, or sausage and kidney bean stew with potatoes, dishes from his 'Cookery for Men' course. Food is served on blue Denby plates, on a tablecloth with linen napkins, eaten with a mismatched collection of initialled silver cutlery. We like these meals because they are better than the communal failed recipes from the cookbook *The Vegetarian Epicure*. But when his girlfriend comes, she giggles and out of earshot of my grandparents says, 'Your dad's undercooked sausage stew looks like he makes it from cut-up willies.'

For my eighth birthday, we go to see our grandparents with Alison. We are meant to be going on a canal trip. It is my special birthday treat. But Claire's face keeps crumpling, she is crying from pain: 'My ear hurts.' The boat trip is cancelled, and I am furious with Claire. Alison says to Granddad, 'Claire has an orange pip stuck inside her ear and we cannot get it out. We're going to have to take her to hospital.' Granddad puts us to bed.

Years later, Claire will explain, 'At the community, one of the Kids and me had found some dope. We tried rolling and smoking joints. Then when we were stoned we decided to stick small things in our ears: seeds, pips and stones. The problem was I couldn't get them out.'

When we stay overnight at our grandparents' house, there is a room for us. We sleep in bunk beds. Granddad comes in and kisses us goodnight. He leaves the door open, just a crack. A yellow light shines in, as just off this room, through a small door, is his windowless study. In his office is Granddad's published diary of his travels on the Gold Coast as a Church of England missionary. Alison typed up his notes and helped edit the book. In the back drawers of his desk are a mess of papers: drafted sermons, Love to Lagos collecting boxes, personal letters from the Bishop of Kontum in Vietnam, and pages of notes on his British parishioners. Next to our bunk beds, the walls are covered floor-to-ceiling with books, many of them belonging to my grandma. Upright letters. Alphabets. Titles and lines. Hardbacks. Paperbacks. Novels. Poetry. Plays. Theology. Politics. History. Latin and Greek. Sleeping in this room, next to his office, is like sleeping in a library. It smells of paper, sweet and dry. It is a nest made from words. 'Night, night,' Granddad says.

In amongst the stacks of books are those written by my great-uncle, Bella's brother. He was a philosopher, a radical Oxford don who became a government minister. Dad says, 'Your great-uncle was left-wing. His family thought he was a black sheep as he was disobedient and spoke his mind. Bella was the only one your great-uncle would listen to, because she was as clever as he was!'

Dad explains that our great-uncle published a book applying Platonic ideas to current society. The book criticized Plato and his support of the 'noble lie', which is any myth knowingly propagated by an elite to maintain social harmony. Our great-uncle thought the noble lie silenced the masses. Later, breaking the noble lie became our great-uncle's goal, and when he was a minister for the Labour government, he kept diaries that, in accordance with his wishes, were published after his death.

Our great-uncle became famous for his published diaries, and they were one of the inspirations for the TV series *Yes Minister*. At the community, people talk about the diaries and call our great-uncle a hero. The diaries caused a national scandal, exposing people in power and revealing the hidden side of the British parliament. My great-uncle broke the respectable pact of silence. He sawed an institution in half and opened it up, exposing the inside.

Sometimes I am told by my granddad, 'Go and play, have a look in the toy drawer.' On the Chinese lacquered cabinet, I grasp the wooden handle and ease open the drawer. Inside are dozens of wooden and cardboard boxes with words stamped on lids. There is Uno and Spillikins, a set of spiked batons that you lift and let fall. There are canasta cards, a chequered board, and Ups and Downs in India, with cut-out cardboard men in safari hats. The instructions explain this is 'a fascinating game for boys and girls depicting the adventures of a missionary from the day he sails from the homeland to the triumphant opening of the new church in India'.

Most of the games are incomplete, and yet none of that matters, for this drawer holds my past. My hands sift through leftovers, eye up the junk like a jackdaw. Inside is what came before the wall, the divorce and the community.

A few years later, both my grandparents pass away. First my granddad and then, a few months later, Grandma Bella. 'She died from a broken heart,' Dad says. We cry at their funerals, these warm-hearted people who made us feel loved. They link us to a white, colonizing, moralizing, well-read, Christian, privileged, public-school-educated, upper-middle-class family. We sleep in the bunk beds a final time. Dad and his sister clear out the house. On a bottom shelf, among some magazines, my cousins and I find our granddad's soft porn magazines: images of *Playboy* blonds and lusty brunettes in lace-trimmed lingerie, exposed curls of pubic hair and pink genitalia. We giggle hysterically, until Dad grabs them, horrified.

It is a hot August day in North-West France. In my office, on the top floor, I am drinking icy water, trying to keep cool. All days dwindle, and as this day ends I work at my granddad's desk. This piece of furniture is now in our house here in Brittany. The family books are stacked on the shelves in my office and have accumulated downstairs in the living room. The volumes line the landing between my daughters' bedrooms and are piled in slapdash heaps by my bed. There are gold-embossed family bibles, annotated first editions of Edward Lear, books by Katherine Mansfield, and volumes of Auden's poetry. Inside, paragraphs are interrupted by my grandma's pencil commentaries.

Recently, I found my granddad's sermons and notes on his parishioners, crammed into the back drawer of his desk. In 1957, he wrote: 'Mrs Harvey. Lost glove. Her mother: suicide. She says, "Can I go into a church? I wouldn't like to take a liberty."' Strangely, his notes resemble mine. My clinical notes, novel and essay ideas, and lecture plans also echo Bella's writings in her notebooks. There is a sense of connection, of continuity, of things passed from hand to hand. My great-uncle, the government minister, tried to find the truth. He wrote, 'The most useful contribution I can make to public life is to expose the cowardice of conformity wherever I detect it, and challenge the organized hypocrisy of the Establishment', and as I write this book I often think of him, and the idea of opening up and exposing institutions.

My two oldest daughters sit on my office floor, squeezed between the stacks of books and dusty journals. We begin an impromptu discussion about this book, home and families. 'Since you were little,' I tell them, 'I've really wanted to talk to you about your family. I mean the generations that came before you' – stories about the living and the dead. It is as though I want to avoid secrets and silence, shine small lights on their knotty heritage. But there's a difference between my intentions and their experience.

'We have tons of family anecdotes,' my oldest daughter says. 'Whenever I'm with friends, I'll tell them about Dad's cousin, the journalist who met Marilyn Monroe, or your connections with Goethe and the man who named the clouds.'

'I'm just obsessed with World War Two films,' my middle daughter sighs, and I know this is a painful part of their past and present. The Holocaust, antisemitic jokes and racism.

'Another thing is,' my elder daughter adds, 'because you

and Dad talked so much about the complexities of both your upbringings, and one was traditional and the other alternative, I grew up knowing both right- and left-wing solutions can be tyrannical.'

Her sister chimes in, 'It's so true. As I've got older, I've realized that any political stance can cause suffering.'

I nod my head and think of a radio programme I listened to recently about political extremes and Milton Rokeach. His 1979 work on open and closed minds was born out of a need to 'resist continuing pressures during my earlier years on my intellectual independence, on the one side from orthodox religion and on the other side from orthodox Marxism-Leninism'. Rokeach stated that open and closed minds exist independently, regardless of the political, religious or scientific content.

Yet, talking with my daughters about the community is a plate-balancing act. I want to tell them something truthful, but don't want to burden them with stories that cast a shadow over their days. I adapt the information, according to age. As we talk, their younger sister skips into my office. It is the summer holidays, and she is bored. 'Maman, did you miss your friends when school was closed?' she asks.

'Well, I always had Kids around to play with,' I explain, and when she asks what it was like, I answer: 'It was complicated. You know when you're in the school playground and having a bad day? All the mean games.' She nods her head because we've talked about playground politics. 'Well, when I was little, it was like living in the playground, day and night, and never going home.'

*

My great-uncle thought that it was his responsibility to tell the truth, and if I think of my own responsibility in telling the truth about the community, I know each person who lived there will have a different story to tell. My own understanding of my upbringing has transformed over the years. For memory, as philosopher Paul Ricoeur writes, is an ever-changing thing. Often, I think of François Cheng, a Chinese French philosopher. The important thing, he believes, is not to tell 'the truth', as though only one truth can be told, but *being* truthful. He draws upon Taoism and its central idea of living truthfully in harmony with the world. As Grandma Bella used to quote from Keats: 'Beauty is truth, truth is beauty, that is all ye know on earth, and all ye need to know.' Authenticity is a felt, lived experience. When it comes to my childhood, certain memories have always been there, like a horde of living ghosts, pestering my present days.

5. The Elephants

'All the sacred rights of humanity are violated by insisting on blind obedience.'
Mary Wollstonecraft,
A Vindication of the Rights of Woman

'When does something start to become a relic? When we tremble before the most insignificant object for the mere reason that a loved one held it in their hands?'
Elias Canetti, *The Book Against Death*

Alison packs Claire's bag, folding clothes, selecting small garments for a hot climate: shorts, T-shirts and sandals. My big, nearly ten-year-old sister is going to the other side of the earth, to what they call 'another continent'. This is like the word 'content', which means what is inside a book, and can be ideological, sexist and racist. Tripti is heading to India with Lawrence (who has split up with Barbara and is the dad of Tripti's baby). They are going to India to write and study Marxism. Lawrence has a niece who will be in India and she's the same age as Claire. So, Claire is going with them to play with the niece. When he hears the news, David shakes his head. 'Everyone knows they want to write a book, a bestseller for the revolution, if they get the fucking money.'

When Claire announces her trip, the Adults say to her, 'What an opportunity!' The Adults often say this word to us, and it comes from the Old French *opportunite*, 'a fit, convenient, or seasonable time', and the Latin *ob portum veniens*, 'coming towards a port'. Alison says this word to Claire as well; it is part of the language we speak and the values we hold. An opportunity means the wind blows your boat in the right direction. This is like when Robin Cousins the ice skater wins the Winter Olympics gold medal, twirling and turning on frozen water. Cousins skates at a gala, and Dad takes us, and when he spins past, Cousins reaches out and touches my hand, a fleeting brush with glory. Claire is now heading toward India, and at the ice rink Dad says, 'I don't want you to go.' On the community roof, the Fates and the Furies discuss the dangers, and they whisper 'Beware'. But Claire is very excited and I am jealous because I want to go to India, travel ten hours on an airplane, sniff spicy pepper plants, dance amongst the lions and walk in a forest with elephants.

Before Claire leaves, I stand outside a Unit. Inside are Tripti and Lawrence. On the door, four pieces of Sellotape hold the curling corners of a poster showing a woman and a cello. I read Tripti's name in capitals, the concert and location announced: Bach, Six Cello Suites, Paris. In the picture, one of Tripti's arms rises. Her long fingers hold the instrument's neck. She angles the bow. Black hair tumbles around bare shoulders. Tripti once defied gravity. By the door, I try to decide if I should open it or leave it shut. You never know what you will find.

In the community, there are no rituals for opening doors, no gates or knocks, no bells, neither visiting cards nor telephone calls to say 'I am coming round', 'Is it a good time?' or 'Can I come in?' Later, I will understand that there are no spaces humans have slept in that we have not barricaded, nor fields we have not fenced. Human beings open and close doors six hundred times a day, and ethnologist Pascal Dibie wrote a book exploring how cultures imagine gateways, and our relationship with doors from the *mundus* of Rome via medieval drawbridges to the revolving door. Doors protect, shut out and allow transitions. One day, my colleague the archaeologist sends me a photograph of Rome's *mundus*, a snapshot of a crumbling hut overgrown with grass. He writes: 'Inside is a hole dating from Rome's beginning. It marked the exact spot of the city centre, was a gateway to the underworld, between the living and the dead. It was so dangerous it was only opened three times a year.'

At the community, I decide to be brave and push open the door, and inside, on the floor, Lawrence and Tripti lie naked on a mattress. Around them everything is undone, half-done: opened books, half-drunk cups of tea, stranded trousers, dirty plates, piles of articles almost read. A lot of things are like this in the community – left unfinished.

'Hello.' Tripti sits up to greet me, revealing breasts, two soft brown globes. She looks up at me, unperturbed. Even when dressed in dreary commune clothes – the shapeless, dirty things she picks up from the floor – Tripti is a living drawing, a delicate study of grace. Now, Lawrence lurches up, leaving the baby by his feet. He has a white hairy body and a dangling willy. The Adults call it a 'penis'. Lawrence is tight muscle covered in dark fur.

He says, 'Fuck,' and wraps a lungi – bought on a recent trip to India – around his naked form, then yells, 'What a fucking awful day. We need to book the flights to India, contact the publishers!'

The baby cries. Tripti giggles and pulls trousers over her long legs. I stand watching them and smile shyly. I think Tripti is kind. She often takes me aside and tells me I am clever and gives me books to read with drawings by Chinese children of everyday communist life, where lines of tiny identical figures play, live and share in delicate brushstrokes. She tells me, 'I no longer play the cello because I have become a Marxist.' Lawrence is her strident Israeli prince. His nose is arched, his eyebrows drawn. Precise words crash from his lips, sentences between a giggle and a snarl: 'Fuck. Marxism. Babies. Books.'

Standing by the door, I tell Lawrence, proudly, 'I am going to perform *Alice in Wonderland* for a drama festival. I've learnt it off by heart.'

I have just started drama lessons with an unemployed actress who lives on the other side of our woods. In a damp room crammed with furniture swathed in dust sheets, yellow curtains tightly closed, Mrs Neel instructs me in the 'art of theatre' and 'elocution'. Mrs Neel thinks I may 'have potential', and I wonder whether, if I became a Marxist, Lawrence might write about me in his book, because he has a paperback by a man called Bettelheim about kibbutz children in

Israel who are 'the children of the dream'. It is strange to belong to a dream, and it makes me feel like I am made of air, like I am a kite that is not attached, not held by someone's hands, and if a kite is not held, then is it still a kite, or just a scrap, a rag carried in the wind. Standing in front of him, almost stepping on the baby, I position myself, and pronounce Alice's first lines on entering Wonderland: 'Curiouser and curiouser . . .'

But Lawrence interrupts me, holds a hand to my face. 'The Irrational Forces in Wonderland may resemble Market Forces. And the Rules of the Croquet Game can be compared to the Arbitrary Rules of the Justice System. But the book also naturalizes the Class System.' His words fire at machine-gun speed, and I dodge and run for cover. He glares. 'Read something else! I'm going to make some bloody tea.'

Sweeping out of the room, he strides along the corridor and down the staircase to the Kitchen. I follow his flapping lungi, lost in his words. Like many of the Adults, Lawrence is like a fairground ride: exciting and very scary. Sometimes when I am with him, I want to run away because all his words spin in my head. In the Kitchen, I watch him make tea, and then pickle turnips in murky juice. 'There.' He puts the jar on a top shelf, by the strips of caramel-coloured sticky flypaper. The papers dangle all over the Kitchen ceiling, coated with the black corpses of dead flies.

Tripti and Lawrence plan to write a political novel, a revolutionary bible. He says, 'We need to change the world.' His words echo the canticle of the community, and all aspects of our lives are forced through this song. This couple begin to drift between Manchester, India, Israel and our house. In black-and-white photos, they are divine. Over the years, they will produce a flurry of beautiful children, all of them breastfed naked in bed.

Lawrence's sister is an art teacher. A few times, I go to stay with her. She lives next to the squirrels in a Northern city park. Spanish chestnut and aspen trees grow amongst alders and elms. Her flat is comfortable, the sheets are clean, and everything is as ordered and calm as the pots of pencils and charcoal on her table. She has a friend called Wolf, a Russian artist, who has renamed himself Flow. He draws me, because Lawrence's sister says, 'She's the kind of child who will sit still.'

Nearby, Tripti and Lawrence have a large studio flat. The façade is lime white, held together with a criss-cross of black beams. In the cobbled courtyard, the rich neighbours park sports cars by wandering wisteria and complain about Lawrence and Tripti's cumbersome old van. Inside, the studio flat has a bath, which is transformed with a folding plank into a kitchen table. At the other end of the open-plan space is a chipboard platform made from geometric shapes. Beneath the hexagons is storage space for sleeping bags, book manuscripts and old clothes.

For years, all the Kids stay there for weekends. We don't go to the seaside, or amusement parks, but travel alone on trains to attend political conferences. The big Kids look after the little Kids. We help them, feed them, and when we're crossing cities we hold their hands. During the day, at the conferences, we are instructed in Marxist analysis of Nicaragua, learn about hegemony – which describes how one culture is the boss of another – and watch radical cartoons on Third World trade policy. We are told about exploitation, the proletariat and the CIA. We learn how the world is constructed behind the scenes, how empires are made and fall. Thatcher is coming to get us. We must beware of the capitalist lure. At night, we flee the naked dialectics, and curl into each other on the hard platform, swaddled in old sleeping bags.

We have been living in the community for a couple of years when Tripti and Lawrence take Claire to Kerala. Before they leave, they tell us that Kerala is a radical Marxist state and a mystical land of tropical forests. Lying between the Western Ghats and the Arabian Sea, this idyll is populated by wild peacocks, backwaters, an abundance of flowers, and elephants. Images of these noble pachyderms adorn the temple walls. The elephants are used for religious ceremonies, and they advance, flower-garlanded, to fight battles.

Claire stays in India for a long time. From Kerala, she sends us letters, printed notes. She writes, 'When can I come home?' And again, 'When can I come home?' Her visit is prolonged, her return flights left unbooked. Lawrence and Tripti form a couple that does not organize, cannot get it together. Everyone knows they are unreliable. Walker says, 'They have probably run out of money.'

Claire travels back about four months later. 'Disaster' is such an easy word; it comes from *aster*, a calamity blamed on the unfavourable position of a planet. When my sister returns, she is a fabric ripped apart, a child that has been broken. Slowly, I learn that while my sister was in India she was badly bitten by mosquitoes and had allergic reactions. Giant red welts rose on her legs. The red bumps were hard as rocks, and she itched and scratched. Apparently, Lawrence and Tripti gave her homeopathic cat medicine, little brown pills, and she itched some more. She was bitten again and then her legs were so swollen they put her in a wheelchair. She could not walk.

On her return, Claire hobbles into my bedroom, and gives me a long tube-shaped parcel of newspaper. 'Here you are.' Slowly, I unfold the crumpled newspaper. Inside is a family of elephants, hand-painted in turquoise, black and white. Each elephant is spotted with yellow flowers. 'Thanks,' I say, and Claire says, 'Elephants bring good luck.' I put the elephants on my mantelpiece, lining them up in order of size: big, medium, small and very small. The biggest elephant is the size of my whole hand, and the smallest elephant fits into my palm. The trinkets enter my landscape.

While she was in India, the gardener raped my nine-year-old sister. I only find this out weeks after her return.

It is a moment that goes beyond a word's rim about an act that marks a life, a body, a girl, a teenager, a way of eating, a woman, a sister, a daughter, her children, a belief, a way of thinking, a passion, a love, a century, an epoch, a generation, a family, a house, a home, an architecture, an anatomy, and her destiny.

No one is held responsible.

What happened in India becomes one of those family

secrets that feel like they have always been known, for I do not remember being told. Writing Claire's story in this book feels like being a ventriloquist, an imitated voice emerges from an articulated jaw. Yet ventriloquism was first an ancient Greek practice used to interpret the voices of the dead. I only include these events about her life because they become so linked to my own, but the specific details are not mine to share. And I talk to Claire as I write, like we did when we were young and our life became chaotic and secrets spread. I whisper to her: 'What do you think?'

In order to write these words, I try to picture the Keralan garden, to imagine the impossible: its botanical design, the shades and depths of green, how it looked when the sun rose, or when Claire was there and light left paradise. I discover the *Hortus Malabaricus*, a seventeenth-century, twelve-volume book detailing the floristic botany of Kerala and ancient India. On its pages, I see majestic palms, graceful foliage, climbers and pepper trees; a taxonomy of named plants. Purple orchids and arum lilies. Lilies symbolize the sacred. Rape is a violation of body and soul.

It is something that I wish, wish, wish had never happened. If I could, I would wind back time, and unpack her case, never let her go. I would run on the tarmac and stop the aeroplane. Even now, after her death, it makes me furious. As we grew up, the secret became one of many that held us together in a play that was difficult for the audience to understand, because major events happened off-stage. 'I never knew what was going on with your family,' my partner A often says. While his family shouted at each other over Friday-night Shabbat dinner, lit candles, roast chicken and challah, our dramas were played out elsewhere.

Afterwards, the elephants will accompany me. In the community, we change Units five times, and the elephants are always in my bedroom, staring at my drama books and toys. They walk along my teenage dressing-room table, between lipsticks, a fifties china poodle, and a mannequin's head. Later, when I leave the community, travelling from flats to houses and crossing borders, the elephants will be the first things I unwrap and display. In the crumbling French monastery where we rent rooms, in a seaside town, along cobbled streets, they glimpse Japanese tourists photographing emerald waves. Today, they are inside a glass cabinet in the old stone Breton house.

It takes me years to confront the elephants' biography, and to understand that the objects around us are extensions of our body, that they tell a story. As William Carlos Williams wrote, there are 'no ideas but in things'. If we peer into a home, a house, the community, familiar objects drive our routines; trinkets and prosaic stuff hold our affection and open our world in unexpected ways. Anthropologist Claude Lévi-Strauss said material things were 'good to think with'. Sometimes I think these elephants are like my house gods, like the Lares and Penates statues that Romans kept by the hearth to protect the foyer. Roman families travelled with these statues in their bags, portable spirits of home. Roman scholar Varro said they were 'those through whom we breathe in our inner core'. The Indian deity Ganesh symbolizes power, wisdom, strength, protection of the home, fertility, and good luck. The elephants have become speaking objects, things to think through. There is something deeply innocent about them, and they never stop walking.

Claire is gone now. Months before her death, one of our last conversations is on a northern French beach. The sun shines. A man flies a rainbow kite. A dog barks in the distance. It is low tide. Sheltered by granite rocks, we talk quietly, hoping our children cannot hear. She says, 'Alison has been extraordinary looking after my kids and house while I have chemotherapy. I just need to carry on working and keep life as ordinary as possible.'

We are both silent. We know she's going to die. Behind us, our children build castles in the sand. We talk about our past, as we always do, magnetically drawn back. As Milan Kundera writes, 'The more vast the amount of time we've left behind us, the more irresistible is the voice calling us to return to it.' When we talk about the community, we are perpetually uncomfortable and internally outraged. Our words are hands flung between shipwreck survivors, floating in an unnamed sea. Claire says, 'I always feel sick on the rare occasions when Alison and Bill mention our childhood.' I say, 'I know, I understand. So do I.' Then Claire talks about India, the rape, and she looks at me, bewildered. Neither of us speaks.

Waves tumble on a distant shore, and we spin like tops, overwhelmed by the contradictions between our present and our past, torn by our love and loyalty towards our mum striding through our days. She is the cargo boat that once carried us, and was determined, despite losing a child and a husband, to keep moving through the waves. Now we are adults, she visits, gifts in her suitcase, bakes cakes, reads our children bedtime stories, makes them indoor picnics and sings them songs. But for years we have grappled with paradox and silence. It is as though when we left the community everything that actually happened there became unmentionable. Above the beach, a seagull flies in the wind, carried by gusts of air. A question haunts me: How to look backwards and go forwards?

The facts of the situation are undeniable. Sexual abuse is a severe trauma. It affects mental and physical health, disrupts cognitive processes, increases the risk of addiction, depression and serious health issues. Psychiatrist Leonard Shengold, renowned for his studies on childhood victims of sexual abuse, described it as 'soul murder'.

My sister changes afterwards, and Claire begins to dislike, and then to hate, the community. Weeks after her return, Tripti and Lawrence come back with their baby, and outside, that spring, riots spread across the UK. They begin in Brixton, where over three hundred people are hurt, spread across London to Finsbury Park, Forest Green and Ealing. Windows are smashed, cars burnt. People run in the chaos of hurling crowds. In June, more than eighty arrests are made during clashes between white-power skinheads and black people in Coventry. The National Front is planning a march there later that month, on the same day as an anti-racist concert by The Specials. In July, hundreds of Asians and skinheads riot in Southall, London, Liverpool, Birmingham, Wolverhampton, parts of Coventry, Leicester and Manchester. Margaret Thatcher announces that police will be able to use rubber bullets, water cannons and armoured vehicles against the rioters. Labour leader Michael Foot blames the turbulence on the Conservative government's economic policies, which have seen unemployment rise by more than 70 per cent. Violence rises from incomprehension and abuse. As I arrange and rearrange Claire's elephants on my mantelpiece, Lawrence quotes Martin Luther King, saying that a riot is 'the language of the unheard'. King was not condoning violence, but warning that riots occur when there is a deep injustice that a society or group fails to recognize or hear.

One Tuesday morning, in a British outpatient unit, a client and I face a blank page. 'I can't draw,' she says. We're listening to piano music. A piece by Erik Satie. Intimate notes fill the workshop space. The music dawdles around paint pots, darts between paper stacks, scatters over oil paintings. It skips around trash-can sculptures and sanguine sketches. The woman repeats, 'I can't draw.' She bites her nails. Very thin, she wears a fluffy orange jumper and too-big jeans. She says, 'I should never have stopped work.' She shakes her head. Her voice drops to a repeated hush. 'I should never have stopped.'

Her psychiatrist describes this as her 'litany'. It is a supplication, a daily chant. The woman has just been discharged from a closed ward where she was hospitalized following a suicide attempt. During her childhood, she was sexually abused and, as is frequently the case, it has impacted her adult life.

I say, 'I think everyone can draw. An artist, Paul Klee, said that drawing is just a line going for a walk.'

Placing the nib of my pen on the white sheet, I draw a squiggle that flies across the page. The woman draws another line. Suddenly our two lines turn together, aligned like a skein of geese in flight. As the piano music plays, we fill the white rectangle with black furrows and sudden grooves, bisecting, greeting, copying, avoiding, and running parallel on the page. She has stopped talking and there are short slashes with points, and spirals loop. It is a dialogue between pens, ink and hands.

Ten minutes later, we examine our work. She says, 'But it doesn't look like anything.'

'It could be called a scribble, or a doodle,' I say. 'But when we make art we invent stuff, we don't just copy reality. Imagination is as important as facts. If we wanted art to look exactly like the world, we could take photos. You and I will never draw the same thing, and each time we draw we start from a unique place, a *locus solus*. That's the amazing part.'

'I should never have stopped work,' she whispers again. Her voice is like a petition, a prayer.

'What would you like to draw?'

'A golf course. I used to work on a Scottish golf course.'

'That's a wonderful idea. I know nothing about golf courses, so you'll have to teach me.'

On a new sheet of paper, we map out her golf course:

the Teeing Area, Fairway, Rough and the Greens. She says, smiling for the first time, 'I used to mow the Greens.' For the following forty minutes we draw the blades of grass. Closely trimmed strokes of green, minuscule rows of emerald, a succession of lush grass stems: line after line after line after line of life.

6. An Unbounded Day

'Our imaginations are creatures as
limited as we ourselves are.'
Claudia Rankine and Beth Loffreda,
'On Whiteness and The Racial Imaginary'

'For the clock is not merely a means of
keeping track of the hours, but of synchronizing
the actions of men . . . [it is] a piece of
power-machinery.'
Lewis Mumford, *Technics and Civilization*

Recently, one of my daughters told me about what she called our 'familycore'. 'It's like gothcore or cottagecore,' she explained, meaning there is an aesthetic style to our family, as the current use of the word 'core' distinguishes a taste and way of doing things. Our version of 'familycore' is defined by high/low cultural swing – from Baroque music to Chinese romantic Netflix series, gourmet food to Lidl snacks, dream analysis to eyeliner debates. We are second-hand addicts, bickerers, and often talk about politics, literature and philosophy. Spontaneous eaters of crisps, none of us, except for the youngest, is particularly good at sport.

As my partner and I both once worked as professional

actors, and use drama in our jobs, there are bags of costumes in the garage. Improvised performances happen regularly in our home. Our three daughters devise plays and sing, like a recent musical about the Quest of the Chrismukkah Fairy, combining anarchist, Jewish and Christian themes. We are timekeepers, and forward-planners, though my partner also craves spontaneity. In our house, we also appreciate rituals, like the invention of Sandwich Wednesday. When my eldest daughter was small, we ate a different crazy sandwich every Wednesday, culminating with the epic mashed potato sandwich that was the last, revolting, experiment. Currently we have TV Dinner Wednesday, a moment of midweek indulgence: fried food and inane TV. During lockdown, we had Frozen Pizza Saturday. In this way, while for us 'familycore' contains stable elements, it also changes with time, and is a living thing. It moves.

In the community, long before the sun rises, Alison begins her communal work – milking the cows, putting pounds of kidney beans, chickpeas and white haricot in to soak. They expand as night turns to day. Sometimes, early in the morning, she makes bread dough, because we never buy bread at the community, and enough loaves must be baked for thirty to fifty people. Alison is an excellent baker. But when we come down this morning, yesterday's bread is in the bread bin. Violet made today's and it didn't rise, and so we hack through the stodgy loaf and smear it with peanut butter, dripping with oil.

We've been living in the community for a couple of years now and move through our days at a regular beat.

Our time is rhythmed to a collective pulse, like during the French Revolution, when they invented a decimal clock, hoping to purge time of religious associations and make Chronos egalitarian. Gilles Deleuze and Félix Guattari, two French philosophers, wrote about how we occupy our territories as lived rhythms and refrains. There are beats to each house and home. The music, at this moment in the community, is buoyant and rousing. We are a marching band. Together, we move as one.

On weekdays, we head off to school in the van. A few Kids are homeschooled, because their parents believe that Kids learn better when education is unstructured. Sometimes Walker teaches the homeschooled Kids A-level Maths and Logic, but Sunshine moans, 'I'm only eight. I don't understand.' The rest of us go to school because then we'll know about society. But even though I attend, sometimes I miss classes for days, because I have a tummy ache, or when our teacher gets ill and her replacement is boring. Alison says, 'I think you know more than the teacher.' Regularity is not seen as important. So I read all day or practise my drama performances for Mrs Neel. She is teaching me to act, to speak with received pronunciation, and I love to disappear into these imaginary worlds, reciting Shakespeare: 'Thou art more lovely and more temperate . . .'

Throughout the day, the Adults do communal work. Some are on the Dole, and others have part-time jobs, but everyone must weed, dig, plant and harvest the garden, collect eggs and clean the Chicken Yard, fence the fields, cook in the Kitchen and maintain the house. Our community ideology venerates physical work, and manual skills are learnt by Alison, Violet, Eagle, Barbara, Thomas and all the other Adults. We echo many utopian experiments, like the Shakers, or Brook Farm, a nineteenth-century Transcendental utopian community in Massachusetts who believed in 'a natural union between intellectual and manual labour'. Books are discarded for the fields, and physical work is seen as a transformative collective act, like during the Cultural Revolution in China, when Mao sent privileged urban youth to rural villages in a project called 'Down to the Countryside'. Barbara tells a visitor that luxuries must be rejected for what she calls '*la vie simple*'. The visitor, who worked on an Israeli kibbutz, nods with joy, saying: 'We must live like Spartans. There are more important things than comfort.'

As I write this, I think of Mark Fisher, the punk socialist theorist, who questioned the idealization of pre-capitalist agricultural life and the belief that there is something inherently utopian and pure about muck and graft. During a symposium at Goldsmiths University, he said, 'Hands up who wants to give up their anonymous suburbs and pubs and return to the organic mud of the peasantry.'

In the community, work is scheduled at the Friday Meeting, to ensure enough potatoes are grown to get us through the winter and to stop the roof tiles from falling on our heads. The management of time, I will later read, is not objective but designed, and changes the shape of people's days. During World War II, Spain's fascist leader, Franco, changed the Spanish time zone to Central European Time so that the country could be in line with Nazi Germany.

Earlier, in Renaissance Europe, there was a shift in time management from church bells maintained by the clergy to city clock towers, which were regulated by guilds, traders and merchants. It marked the beginning of a form of capitalist, commercial time.

During community days, the Adults' time is marked by work, but includes breaks for tea, instant coffee and talk. Hours and minutes lull inside the sixty rooms and across the Estate, because, as Eagle says while she lies on the lawn and watches the blades of grass grow: 'It is more about being than doing.' Time is not a thing to be kept but experienced. Things drift.

In comparison, the Kids' time is structured by school, because unlike the Adults we go outside and must be on time with all the people in society. While the Adults are cut off from the outside world, we are in a unique limbo, moving daily between alternative and mainstream time zones. We must adapt to each time. Sometimes, it gives me jet lag.

Mrs Cooper is our teacher for a second year. She has a mop of white hair and wears woollen skirts. In the classroom, I am a good, obedient girl, raising my hand enthusiastically at her stern questions: 'What is twelve times six?' 'Who fought in the Wars of the Roses?' 'How do you spell "dictionary"?' Sat at the front with Mary and Paul, I answer: 'Seventy-two.' 'The Tudors.' 'D-I-C—' Learning is being alive. It is an unwinding ribbon that takes me further, and it never ends.

We used to have milk at school, drunk before prayer time from tiny glass bottles with a plastic straw. But it was stopped by Margaret Thatcher. They call her the 'milk snatcher' for banning free milk in schools. She is everything we are against. She is for the nuclear family, for business and bombs. During prayer time, Mrs Cooper instructs, 'Close eyes, bow heads, hands together, recite the Lord's Prayer.' This year, while everyone prays, I sometimes pull down my knickers to show another little boy my winkle. He looks and I smile, and afterwards, I say, 'Amen.'

A few times, Mrs Cooper invites me to her red-brick bungalow, twenty minutes' walk from the community. I don't know other children who go to their teachers' houses, but I am a gregarious child, who cannot play sports but will talk to anyone and accept any invitation. Mrs Cooper says I am a 'clever girl'. A bookworm, I have read that teachers are to be befriended. In her beige living room, filled with polished brown furniture, she offers me weak tea and custard creams. The room smells empty, and Mrs Cooper looks smaller than in the classroom.

'I've been rehearsing a *Peter Pan* monologue for the drama festival.' I reach for a third biscuit. She pushes her fawn sofa back. 'Show me, dear.' Cocking my head to one side, as Mrs Neel has taught me, I imagine Tinker Bell sulking, and prance round the bungalow. When I act, I love the feeling of being somewhere else, and the magic of this world. When I finish, I hold myself in position, then bow. Mrs Cooper applauds.

At lunchtime we eat school dinners: roast meat and potatoes, steamed raspberry jam puddings and custard, cheese quiche and baked beans, sausages, boiled cabbage and mash. I am always hungry. 'You eat like a horse,' the dinner ladies tell me when I go up for seconds and thirds.

In the afternoons, we undress; change into gym clothes for Music and Movement. In the large, empty hall where we have morning assemblies, the teacher puts a needle tip on vinyl. An ebony disk turns in revolutions. Sound crackles as twenty children move in an English village school while 30,000 march in an unemployment protest in Glasgow. 'Stretch like trees,' instructs a recorded lady's voice over a background of piano music. 'Your branches reaching up to the clouds.' We stretch, and then there is a cymbal crash, a sweep on a xylophone. A whisper: 'Now children, you are a machine. Listen to the music. Your pistons move up and down.' Her voice gets louder, the rhythm quicker. Outside the school, the ZX81, a pioneering British home computer, is launched by Sinclair Research, and the National Coal Board announces widespread pit closures. The voice says, 'Make your machine speed up. The cogs are turning, the lights are flashing. Children, make it work faster.' My pistons churn while Bobby Sands, a twenty-seven-year-old Republican, dies in Northern Ireland's Maze prison after a sixty-six-day hunger strike. With mechanical power, I move head to knee, knee to head. I am speed, composed from separate parts; not the first tool, the axe, an extension of the hand. Born from the Industrial Age, my machine has turbines, and it does not need a body. It goes faster, and more than 100,000 British people gather in London for the TUC-organized People's March For Jobs, and 250,000 protestors attend a CND anti-nuclear march because the bombs may fall. 'Slow down now,' the woman orders, her voice softer. 'Your machine stops.' We no longer move in the village-school hall, because nuclear war may break out. At the community, we've watched the 'Protect and Survive' government films, explaining how to build shelters, avoid fallout, and wrap our dead in polythene. We have seen the maps showing where the bombs will land. We'll have three minutes to hide beneath tables, placing paper bags over our heads. We are Generation X, we face daily annihilation.

Afterwards, we get changed in the classroom. Suddenly, we have naked torsos, freckles and fat. We are packages unwrapped, gifts without paper. We gaze at each other's bodies and underwear. The boys laugh.

'It's only natural,' I say with indignation. 'And why should the boys laugh at us? We're not laughing at them.' The teaching assistant gives me The Look. 'You are very mature for your age.' She frowns but I am pleased. Those six letters describe speaking calmly to adults, being trusted alone to look after little Kids, not to panic or break a bone, and being politically aware. I am M-A-T-U-R-E for my age.

'You stink,' another girl tells me while I am getting dressed, and I don't know why she says this. There is dirt beneath my nails and we are not often clean. Our clothes are shared and torn. Until I am eleven, I don't have my own swimming costume. Our dirt is a rejection of bourgeois norms. In the community, there are no regular bathtimes. Lawrence says, 'The Kids don't need to be washed.' For years after we leave, I don't understand daily bathing and it is with a certain feeling of horror that I will come to realize how dirty I was as a child.

*

That afternoon it is Knitting class. Alison has given me thick, wooden needles, and grey wool she made with her own hands. She has begun breeding sheep, collects their wool, and spins it into yarn. During Friday Meetings she knits, and her clicking needles also produce handmade baggy mohair jumpers that she sells to a woman with an Afro, on a market stall, because we need the money. In the classroom, all the girls have brought thin metal needles, buttercup-yellow and baby-blue balls of wool. The knitting teacher waves my grey wool in the air.

'This is not what I asked you to bring.' Suddenly, from being a homemade triumph, the wool looks like straggles of witch's hair, strands ripped from a sorceress's head. I say calmly, 'But my mum told me to bring this.' I do not call her Alison. That would be a bad idea.

'I don't care what your mummy thinks. I asked for pastel-coloured wool.' The teacher seals her lips. 'And where are your needles?' I hand them over, thick and wooden. 'This is not what I asked for either. You silly girl!'

The teacher is bent over my needles and wool, and I imagine reaching out and grabbing her hair. Yanking her head, I would pull hard and shock her bones. The shock would brighten her eyes. I picture my fingers, her head, a strained neck. Afterwards, I will imagine this scene repeatedly. Inside me, a seed of poison ivy grows. It sprouts and the strands lengthen and uncurl, but when the teacher looks up, I look at the floor and say nothing. I won't say anything to Alison about this either. The world requires adapting, demands sacrifice.

*

At the end of the school day, the Kids meet again on the village green. We are always together, day and night. Ten of us are by the bench. Standing and dangling, we wait for the van. It is hardly ever waiting for us. At the village green, sometimes people throw stones at our vehicle. A boy walks up to us. 'Smelly hippies. You live in a commune. You stink.'

'It's not a commune. It's a community,' I say. Brandy stands up, 'Yeah. It's a community.' Saskia joins us, 'You're a div. It's a community.' Claire gets to her feet, 'It is a community, and you should go now, because our van is arriving and the man driving it was a soldier in Israel and he'll give you a knuckle sandwich.' The boy shouts, 'Him and whose army?' Saskia screams, 'The People's Army.' She lunges towards him as the van chugs its arrival, and the boy disappears.

We jump in through the sliding door like the gang in the TV show *The A-Team*, celebrating our victory. We know who we are, and where we live. The Adults insist on this word, we must say 'community', it is repeated year after year.

Occasionally, we share sweets in the van, bought from a shop on the village green. The oldest Kids have cash. It comes from nowhere. Later, I learn their money is stolen from the drawer of the communal washing machine, or from the jar of coppers in Derek's punk room. We are all constantly poor, but in the community, poverty is a medal pinned on jumble-sale clothes. It makes us equal to 'the working class'. It is almost a version of 'double-tracking', a term coined by writer Tom Wolfe and later explored in a book by the critic Rosanna McLaughlin, who describes it as being 'a bum with the keys to a country retreat'. Double-tracking is to be establishment dressed as counterculture.

It is often like this for the communal Adults. The house is an adventure they will live through, a freeing-up, a chosen experiment, whereas for the Kids it is our life.

In the van, all sweets must be shared. 'It is the rule,' Thomas or Barbara shout as we drive home. '*Égalité!*' The flying saucers, edible rice paper, red-swirled cough candy twists and pink Hubba Bubba bubblegum are passed between our hands. Having read a story about a boy who keeps gum stuck to his desk, I keep a flavourless boulder of bubblegum glued under my bed. For weeks, I mash on a grey, sticky ball coated in fluff. But I do not care. The gum is mine.

On the way back from school, we jostle in the van, a dozen tiny peas waiting to be shelled. When we get home, when we're small there is Kids' Tea, once we're older we eat with the Adults. But first, we play or go to the TV Room. Inside is a VHS machine, belonging to a guy studying at film school, a stack of clunky tapes, and a TV on wheels. It is the only screen in the house. We watch three or four films for days on end, a tangle of kids aged between four and ten. Saskia orders Claire, 'Put *Harold and Maude* on!'

After a small crackle, an image appears. Harold is a rich American kid and drives a black hearse. To get his mother's attention, he fakes suicide: pretending to slash his wrists and perform the hara-kiri knife ritual. He also pretends to drown himself in the pool, and hangs himself from a rope, dangling by a grand piano. Harold likes watching funerals. In a cemetery, he meets and falls in love with seventy-nine-year-old Maude. They blow bubbles, run in flower fields and make love. The film ends as Maude kills herself.

Heartbroken Harold is faced with choosing between life and death. In the final scene, he drives his hearse towards the cliff-edge, as Cat Stevens sings the song 'Trouble'.

We watch this film so often I learn it off by heart. Maude is my heroine. She lives alone but misses the kings of her past. Two fat braids crown the top of her head. Inside her home, a converted railroad car, are a hookah, sculptures, and an umbrella she used to fight for liberty. Maude is a universe, turned into one, running free in intergalactic space. She is alone, and I think she instils in me a certain joyful idea of solitude.

Another film we watch often is *Bloody Kids*. Directed by Stephen Frears, it is a grim and hallucinatory story, taking place over a few days within the British 1970s youth culture at the end of punk. Two eleven-year-olds, manipulative Leo and impressionable Mike, lead us through a landscape of motorways and shopping malls. Rebelling against the police force, Leo gets Mike to help him stage a dark practical joke, and everything goes terribly wrong. There are bags of blood, football matches, knives, men in fur coats, and no parents around. Punks trawl the streets with mohicans and make-up. The boys smoke and drink, then dine and dash at a Chinese restaurant. Leo draws his friend into the darkness of a turbulent night, exclaiming jubilantly, 'We're so young we can do anything.'

Years later, my sister Claire buys me a copy of *Bloody Kids*. She rings me up one afternoon. 'I must tell you. I just rewatched that film we watched every day when we were little, *Bloody Kids*. I can't believe we watched it. I mean, it's not exactly *Teletubbies*!'

She sends it through the post. A fortnight later, I sit through the film feeling undone. The next day, I ring her. 'I can't imagine showing this to my kids. Not because of the themes, but it is so rough, and disturbing.' And there is a silence because we cannot undo what has been done, cannot unsee what we saw.

One day the VHS machine and screen disappear, and someone hangs a dartboard on the wall. When it rains, I learn to close one eye and throw a dart. And we play Round the Clock, and Twenty-One. At Christmas, Eagle buys Sunshine a snooker table, because it is a non-sexist toy. We share these toys collectively. That is another community rule. 'Collect' comes from a Latin word meaning 'gathered together'. Between the fifteen or more Kids, we organize competitions, and learn to balance cues, pot balls, and aim for the bullseye. My skills are average, but they stay with me. As an adult, when I work in southern Africa, I end up dominating a pool table all night at a winner-stays-on club. When I accompany patients to a social centre, I win game after game of darts. The playing is etched into my muscle memory.

Inside my bedroom at the community, Sunshine and I also teach ourselves canasta. We sit on the floor with my paternal grandparents' old deck, clutching thirteen-card hands and making melds. Our heads bow in concentration; my short mop, and Sunshine's long dark hair. She has green fairy eyes and is ethereal. Our games last at least four hours. We miss meals and she counts: one thousand, three hundred and seventy-two points. Simultaneously, we learn mah-jong, forming Pongs, Kongs and Chows, building winds and ivory walls. The black ebony set comes from Sunshine's grandma, who sends her presents by post, things none of us own. One Christmas, she sends Sunshine a dress – layers of soft, twirling fabric with tiny blue cornflowers, smocking and embroidery.

My handwritten timetables still structure my days, like a line I draw through time. Drama practice is planned, along with meals, reading and playtime. Mrs Neel enters me for classes at the annual drama festival. Alison takes me, and I sit in a room where all the girls wear neat black tunics and footless tights. Whispering together, they are a starling murmuration, a harmony of swooping winds. They are pupils at Mrs Sylvia Verona's Private Theatre and Dance School. In Sunshine's new flowery dress and Brandy's shoes – which are too small – I long to be a member of their flock. At home, I practise tirelessly. Slowly, I start to win the Drama Solo, Prose Reading and Mime classes. The judges write: 'Strong opening. A charming voice with musical notes.'

When playtime is scheduled, I grab my bike from the Bike Shed. In the courtyard, Troy says, 'Look at me.' He glides over the black tarmac, arms folded, high-top trainers gracefully balanced on his orange BMX frame. His jaw cuts the perfect angle; he is everyone's boy. But Sunshine doesn't like her brother because he is mean to her, and so I don't like him either.

Saskia says, 'Watch.' She pulls her front wheel up, balances her bicycle in a diagonal pose. She understands the rules of weight, and Saskia could be a boy because she can do anything: wheelies, no hands, and no feet. But if Troy is a prince Saskia is not a princess, she is a girl being a boy, being a punk woman.

Claire calls me. 'Hurry up and come and play.' In our latest bike game, Troy holds a skipping rope across the width of the drive with Claire. 'High or Low?' they taunt us. 'High or Low?'

If it goes High, we must ride and duck our heads to miss the rope, or get knocked from our bikes. If we say Low, the rope could tangle in our wheels. I might skid and fall like Sunshine did last week. A flap of skin split from her knee, and Bill had to pick out each bit of gravel with tweezers. I say 'Low' and I speed forward. But Claire and Troy do not do what I asked. Part of the game is surprise. The rope catches around my neck. I crash onto the drive. Afterwards, I have rope burns and scars around my neck. I joke that it looks like I tried to hang myself, like Harold in the film attempting suicide. When I repeat my suicide joke to Dad when I am at his house, he looks mortified.

Sometimes, Sunshine and I leave the Kids behind. We ride our bikes to the end of the drive, cycle for fifteen minutes and then stop by a gate, where donkeys huddle in a muddy field. Their grey heads are too big and heavy for their scrawny legs. Thin coats show pink patches of skin and bloody sores. Their protruding ribs are like those in the pictures the Adults show us of starving children from the East African Emergency Campaign, eating their last meal. Later, these images will be seen as exploitative – poverty porn.

By the field, Sunshine claims, softly, 'It's wrong to leave the donkeys without food.'

'Yeah, they shouldn't treat animals like that,' I say. We stare into the dark pools of the animals' eyes because we know about society and abusive systems. We are here to help, change the world, and we try to feed them grass but the donkeys ignore us.

Back at the community, it is dinnertime. Alison is not aways there, as a few evenings a week she works at the local youth club. She tells us she must earn more money as the jumpers and Child Maintenance don't bring in enough for shoes, clothes and food. For a while, she and Violet sell Cornish pasties from a food truck at festivals, and we eat them for free, pastry and peppery meat. But again 'it is not enough', and now Alison often gets home late. She cycles five miles to work and back, and I lie awake worrying until I hear our Unit door creak.

At dinnertime, the Gong must be rung; the ringing of the Gong marks our mealtimes, our days. It is kept hung on a string, under the stairs. The staircase is in the centre of our house; it is the twenty-metre-tall throat of our volcano. This communal throat produces what Barbara calls 'linguistics'. The staircase is magnificent. But the space under the stairs is a utopian, communal no man's land, a dumping ground for unwanted stuff: abandoned toys, boxes of papers, broken furniture and worn-out clothes. The mess is a constant source of unaddressed mutterings: 'Who is going to clear up under-the-stairs?' 'What is all that mess under-the-stairs?' In the Kitchen, on the noticeboard, someone scrawls: 'Clean up fucking under-the-stairs!' Later, I will read about how Soviet communal apartments used information boards displaying hand-drawn notes to shame inhabitants that did not conform with the 'socialist ways of living'.

I take the Gong from its hook, and I struggle to hold the weight. Brass rings form concentric circles. Trying to stand steady, I hit the Gong with a mallet. The sound reverberates through me as I walk around the house, banging and banging. Out through a door, the Gong can be heard in the garden, fields and woods, in the Units on the third floor of the stairwell, in the Bike Shed, the Cowshed, and the Workshops, where a visitor from New Zealand saws planks to make a platform bed. Walker and Eagle lift their heads from gathering apples, and Barbara's hands pause on a cow's udder, talk of Lenin and Russia is interrupted, and Bill's fingers freeze on fag-papers turning around tobacco. David's cup of tea is stilled, and children stop in their games. Rainbow lifts her foot from the woodlouse she is about to squash.

It is time. Everyone obeys the Gong. It is our shared watch. We have Friday Meetings, Sunday Cleaning, Mealtimes, Christmas, Maintenance Weeks, the Food Rota and a Gong. We move together to the Dining Room. Adults and Kids skip, talk and fight. It is time to eat.

We have signed up for meals and opted in at Friday Meetings. That is one of the reasons Alfredo has now left. He didn't sign up enough. They said he wasn't committed. There are different leaders now. Depending who is around, and who shouts the loudest, Tripti, Barbara and Thomas take turns. They are Founding Members and explain to new arrivals that signing out and opting out are not encouraged.

Few Adults have the skill to cook for forty-plus mouths. Yet eating the communal food, and not caring if it is disgusting, is seen as a sign of strength.

Sometimes, we break these rules. When we are starving and the person cooking has a bad reputation, Alison signs us out and makes us boiled eggs. In the Kitchen, people glare when we tap the shells with teaspoons, as cooking non-communal food is against the unwritten rules. They look at us as we dip buttered soldiers into yolks. Tripti walks past when we are eating, and frowns. But these eggs are precious, an exception. For a moment, my family becomes more important than the crowd.

Many of the adults in the community grew up in collective institutions. They came from military backgrounds or – as is the case with my mother – went to boarding school. They were cut off from their own parents at an early age, were brought up bowing down to unspoken group conformity and timetabled days. While I am writing this book, my mum will tell me how she never really had a sense of home, as she lived between boarding school and military bases, changing houses and countries constantly. As Lily Dunn writes in her memoir *Sins of My Father* in relation to upper-middle-class adults in 1970s cults, they replaced one institution for another, repeating the pattern and leaving the next generation of children to fend for themselves.

Yet collective living has been an aspiration for centuries. The nineteenth-century socialist philosopher Charles Fourier, who inspired Brook Farm, thought utopian life should be communal, based in a structure he named the 'Phalanstery' – 'a continual orgy of intense feeling, intellection, & activity, a society of lovers & wild enthusiasts'. Fourier defended women's rights and his ideas inspired Engels, Marx and Walter Benjamin.

Recently, Fourier's ideas are being revived. Across the world, people have lived through the deep isolation of the Covid pandemic, and our dystopian world propels us to seek out alternatives. Writers and thinkers such as Constance Debré and Sophie Lewis suggest we could 'abolish the family'. Lewis critiques the individualist nuclear family as an antisocial, anti-solidarity capitalist tool, recalling the words of Margaret Thatcher: 'There is no such thing as society. There are individual men and women, and there are families.' Lewis's analysis is thorough and pertinent. Yet when I read the alternative model she proposes, a communal sharing of tasks, of child-rearing and domesticity, I notice she doesn't once interrogate or reference research into child development or the experience of children brought up in collective models. Despite enjoying her book, I find myself longing for her to have asked this vital question: What does it mean and feel like for children to grow up in a crowd?

Sunday evenings are the one time in the week when there is no communal meal. In the morning, we have Sunday Cleaning. This is required of every inhabitant. Kids and Adults push dirt around. But on Sunday evenings, the rules dissolve. It's our allocated moment of intimacy. The crowd thins and the institution fades. No one eats in the Dining Room. David makes double-cooked chips in the deep-fat fryer. Their crunch is divine. People stand around snacking in the Kitchen. An American visitor makes piles of Navajo frybread. Deep-fried discs of wholemeal dough, puffed into delicious pillows, sprinkled with demerara sugar.

Often on Sundays, Alison cooks baked potatoes with grated cheese. The four of us take the meal to our Unit. Plates balanced on our knees, in her room, for a flimsy moment, we sit together as a family. Sometimes, she puts a plant pot on her head and we giggle when she sings 'I'm a Little Teapot'. In later years, plates balanced on our knees, we watch TV, often *Upstairs, Downstairs*, a period drama depicting the lives of a wealthy London family 'upstairs' and their servants 'downstairs'.

Alison passes around a jar of pickled beetroot. The beetroot juice dyes our meal, bleeding into potato and cheese. Hard as we try, we cannot stop the red juice flowing; it seeps into our food like the communal words and the lockless doors. Everything on our plates turns slowly pink and purple. Annie Dillard wrote infamously that 'how we spend our days is, of course, how we spend our lives.' Over fifteen years, until we leave home, Sunday evenings are the only moment of the week we all spend together with our mum. At the time it feels sufficient to make us into a family. But as I write this, I wonder whether it was enough, or whether it was outweighed by the seconds, minutes, hours, days, weeks and months when we were sucked into the group – the glorious, treacherous, beating river of the crowd.

7. The Roaring Voice of the God of Joy

'There was a kindliness about intoxication – there was that indescribable gloss and glamour it gave, like the memories of ephemeral and faded evenings.'
F. Scott Fitzgerald, *The Beautiful and Damned*

'Prepare yourselves
For the roaring voice of the God of Joy.'
Euripides, *The Bacchae*

If I run fast enough, I think I'll get up the stairs and into my Unit before the other Kids catch me. Brandy, Sunshine, Jason and I are playing a version of hide-and-seek, up and down the stairs, excited and scared. We're hoping to get lost, hoping to be found, and I love both these things and always will. As Donald Winnicott said, artists are people driven by the tension between the desire to communicate and the desire to *hide*. Except in our game, you shouldn't get caught, because then you play Bloody Knuckles, get the skin ripped off your hands.

My favourite hiding spot is on the second landing, inside a cupboard stuffed full of broken cameras, broom handles, bin bags of dirty clothes, velvet curtains, boxes spilling out papers, crushed glass, a torn cover of Pink Floyd's 'See Emily Play', and bits from the game Risk. The goal is simple: players conquer enemy territory by building an army, moving troops in, and engaging in battle. If you slip inside this cupboard, you can peek through the keyhole but no one can see you. From there, I can watch.

But I can't go to the cupboard now because I just found a letter in the Post Room, and need to get to my Unit. The envelope is clutched in my hands, my name on the outside, and I think it is to do with the short-story competition I entered. My heart is beating when I fall on my bed and look at the envelope, wondering if I should wait – as though if I open it, the envelope might explode like a bomb, and it needs instructions to be defused.

The competition was advertised in my local library: 'Write a short story. Maximum five pages.' I wrote my story in my notebook, by my timetables, then typed it up on Violet's typewriter, painting Tippex where I spelt words wrong. Now, I should have the results, and when I rip open the letter, I read 'You have won first place' and learn I will get a prize, a book token presented by a famous writer.

The joy shoots through me, and I run again, back down the stairs, calling 'Alison, Alison!' In the back kitchen, I find her talking to Barbara; one of the cows has mastitis. Its udder is swollen and red. When I tell them the news, Alison smiles. 'Well done.' Her eyes shine, and my mum is pleased, like she's glowing inside. But Barbara mutters, 'Writing is for the people,' and I nod because this means that I can't be too proud, and the happiness inside me shrinks. But when I tell Barbara the story is the diary of a child after the breakout of nuclear war, Barbara smiles and Alison smiles more, and I am relieved.

Then Jason, Brandy and Sunshine turn up, but I don't say anything about the competition. Instead, I run away, holding my letter. They call my name, but I ignore them, dash out of the house and head to the woods, past the burnt remains of the fire we built with the other Kids, under low-hanging branches, and through gaps in the bushes. When I get to a clearing, in the birch wood where the roe deer hide, I lie on my back in the soft, green grass. Quietness settles inside me. The winning letter in my hands, I look up at the trees. Leaves sway in the wind. 'I won,' I whisper to them.

In the community, being creative is good but winning is not the right thing, reaching a goal is not the objective. Hierarchy is a bad thing, and if you win you create hierarchy. Writing about 'Why Utopian Communities Fail', Ewan Morrison highlights this entropic side of communal living, where 'individual inner motivation and goal orientation are frowned upon, projects lose energy very quickly and are often even sabotaged by others'. He describes incomplete paths, abandoned machinery, spaces cluttered with half-finished projects. Yet, while the community house is full of discarded, cast-off plans, there are also creative moments in our year, where the stakes are raised and everyone is allowed to shine. When it comes to parties, the artists, film-makers, photographers, writers, cooks and musicians gather their skills to create gifts and experiences, gourmet banquets and pop-up feasts.

The parties are fantasy worlds. Go inside and you don't know if you'll get out alive. They are populated by spirits and mermaids, rumbles of laughter, dappled elderflower wine in sombre green bottles, hot summer nights, late evening tears, giant people dancing in purple clothes, decorations, candlelight, music and film. A cumulus of faces and bodies sit, talk and sway; big and small people, kind and nasty friends. Dreams come alive. At the festivities, I am six, seven, eight, nine, ten – I am tumbling all the way to twenty.

One day, in the atrium, the Adults take coloured balls of wool and tie, knot and interlace the strands, creating a kaleidoscopic spiderweb. Each Kid is given the end of a thread and we follow, unwinding the wool until we reach the treasure at the end. For birthdays, special cakes are made, colossal cakes to feed the masses; for football-obsessed Lawrence, the sponge cake is square, decorated like a television, and placed on a commode inside which is hidden a tape recorder commentating an imaginary match in which Lawrence scores a goal. There are cakes like cats with spaghetti whiskers, pirate cakes, strawberry cakes, number cakes, flower cakes, cakes for tiny children and for full-grown adults. Cakes are carried into the Dining Room; the lights are turned off. Forty people sing 'Happy Birthday', and when it is my birthday, I want to hide under the table.

The October parties are some of the best in the year. They are organized by all the people in the community born in October. Barbara, Eagle, Violet and Bill get together and plan a surprise. One year, at the start of the party, upstairs on the third floor, we visit a room transformed into a fairy world with candles floating in flowery water. Then, forty of us make paper hats using newspaper, scissors and tape. Once the hat is on your head, you are given a Tequila Sunrise (or a non-alcoholic version for Kids). Afterwards, Adults lead each of us on a blindfolded journey.

In darkness, I climb over mountains and smell the perfume of flowers. Led by hands, I travel through swishing fabric, am carried through a bewitching space. A violin plays, a voice whispers in my ear about dreams weaving a shade. There is a poem by a man called Blake. At the end, I am lifted up and up, and a voice says, 'Now you jump.' And I hesitate, and the voice says, 'You have to jump.' When I jump, I land on what feels like soft jelly. Pulling the blindfold from my eyes, I find I am on a red and yellow bouncy castle, inside the Yoga Room. Giggling, we jump up and down. Adults and Kids celebrate in the air. It is like a dream and I still remember this bouncing, revolutionized, playful utopian light. Utopian researcher Ruth Levitas writes that 'Utopia expresses and explores what is desired.'

Later, these experiences of play and making will influence my art-therapy clinical work with patients, and the sessions training health managers, international MBA students and hospital directors to use creative resources and play freely with ideas, thinking outside the box. Led by Louise Bourgeois, Jackson Pollock, Plato and Peter Slade, I will spend days encouraging people to tap into what play philosopher Eugen Fink calls the 'peach skin of all things'.

Play is a complex notion to define. When I ask my youngest daughter what happens when we play, she says, 'If all the children in the world play at the same time. It grows. It grows and grows.' Playing is like a dream, as poet Paul Valéry wrote in 1914, because 'we have a combination of EVERY POSSIBLE MEANS of diverse impressions'. When I explain this in training sessions, or in clinical work, I say working with play develops divergent thought, because like in a brainstorming exercise, we consider all the possibilities and produce as many ideas as we can. Later, we use convergent thought to choose which idea is best.

The communal parties of my childhood were filled with possibility and were also entirely handmade. In the house, I learnt to create something extraordinary from nothing, to make costumes for a cast, to write a song. Years afterwards, when I was running community arts projects, international collaborations, plays and performances, I decorated entire schools, made pop-up art galleries, organized immersive performances with people in bathtubs, and shot and edited films with little financial aid.

In the community we learnt to call, as Euripides wrote in *The Bacchae*, on the force of the God of Joy. And of all the times when the God of Joy was summoned in the community, it was at Christmas when it most ruled our world. Our Christmas was as tall as Mount Everest, a place to reach up to, where eagles flew and people prayed. It was the peak of our year – of the universe.

It is December 1982, three days to Christmas, and newspapers offer cures for dole queue blues, and adverts for

Zenith windows, and if you buy a festive TV you get a Free Remote Control. At the cinema you can watch *Superman II* and the newest James Bond. Christmas is a time for heroes. Venturing downstairs, I head for the Lounge. Normally, the curtains are closed and the space is dusty and brown, dotted with worn-out chairs, old settees and piles of abandoned paperbacks. It is only used for Friday Meetings, but at Christmas the Lounge comes alive.

When I push open the large wooden door, inside a log fire crackles. In the corner, Sunshine is sat behind the grand piano. The piano came with the house, and it speaks of better days – or worse. The black piano curves and shines. It is like a slippery gangster's car or the letter S. The lid is sometimes shut, and sometimes open. Today it is propped up like a gaping mouth.

As I get closer, Sunshine places her fingers on the keys; she presses down and chords travel through her hands. Her music wipes out the Friday Meeting Minutes, the Agendas and angry red faces, the insults and shrieks. The notes brush against spiderwebs in the dark corners where no one goes. Sunshine makes sound on ivory and coal. A coin spins in darkness. She is playing Beethoven's *Moonlight Sonata*, and she knows the piece by heart.

'Ace,' I say, when she has finished.

She whispers, 'I am skill.' We collapse into giggles and I plead, 'Can we play "Chopsticks" now?' She has taught me how to play this four-handed tune. Sunshine nods, but then the door bursts open. Barbara is saying, 'Get a move on, you lazy sod.' She is carrying a tree stump and Thomas grips the top. Branches spin out like giant's arms, waving to the day. Our celebration is slicing through winter. The tree shivers, and green needles sprinkle on the floor, carrying the sweet, sharp smell of pine.

'Let's get it up!' Barbara uses a ladder, and they heave the tree vertical. Needles brush against the ceiling's plaster roses. Our tree is four metres tall. It is four times as big as me, vigorous and strong. Two centuries earlier, across the Channel, the French revolutionaries gave trees a sacred status. Having abolished Christianity, during the Reign of Terror they invented new symbolism, replacing Jesus with the Goddess of Reason (the initial model for the Statue of Liberty). They built what they called 'mountains' on town squares and planted 'trees of liberty' at the top. These trees were seen as symbols of agrarian, popular culture. People sang songs round the branches, as the aristocrats and disbelievers got their heads cut off. In the community, myths and symbols intertwine, and the tree is appropriated for a Christian and capitalist celebration held in a semi-communist house.

'Should we leave it here?' Barbara asks Bill, who has just walked into the room. The tree is his job.

'Let's put it in the middle of the room,' I say, because I imagine us all dancing, spinning round the emerald branches. Barbara looks at me and raises her eyebrows.

'Just leave her there,' Bill says. 'She's a beauty.' Bill once worked as gardener for the Queen. A tree surgeon, he can make anything sprout from the earth. I know that the pine tree is not deciduous because Bill has taught me this word – like 'perennial', for plants that grow every year, not like annuals, which must be planted again and again. In Bill's arms are cardboard boxes marked 'Decorations'.

I look up at Bill, aligning swinging baubles in the green, pine sky. Bill passes through the outside, the edges of our lives. He does not go to school meetings, wake us up or buy us clothes. But he is at the centre of Alison's existence. Behind him the fire crackles, and he takes the decorations and slowly, delicately, suspends them from twigs.

In our Unit, we have a small, second tree. Our family tree. Every year, Mum takes out a cardboard box of decorations. There are tiny, painted wooden toys, a rocking horse and elves, miniature dangling candles and slim tinsel strands.

'Can I help?' I ask her. She nods her head.

At the top of our tree, she puts an angel made by Rachel from a blue-eyed plastic doll. If you jiggle the body, the doll's eyes open and close. She is an angel made by our dead sister. Her dress is a cardboard tube wrapped in silver foil. On her head is a golden crown, decorated with a single strand of red tinsel. Every year the angel is placed on the top branch of our tree. Rachel absent. Present. Absent. Present. We walk with her, living with our dead.

Three days later, it is Christmas morning. On Christmas Day, we are always with Alison at the community. We go to see Dad on Boxing Day. When we awake, the room is black, and I feel my stocking, heavy on my feet. The uneven weight is warm, like a living thing, a friend I am about to meet. Christmas morning is like talking to a stranger, the opening, not-knowing and sometimes-waiting is the best thing. The build-up, the list-writing, the imagining. Alison saves money all year, hoarding pennies, five-pence pieces and twenty-pence pieces in three different teapots stored in a white-painted dresser. We know Father Christmas does not exist; we have known for years. Mum makes Christmas magical.

Suddenly my light is switched on. My sister rushes in. She is wearing a long nightie, and I dream of owning a long nightie. Recently, our RAF granddad saw a photo of Claire and said she looked pretty. I was jealous of these things said by a man who we had only met twice. No one ever tells me I am pretty, especially now I have short hair. Nobody normally uses the word 'pretty' to describe us, or 'lovely' or 'cute'. Some of the community women and men, like David, call me beautiful, and clever and precocious, but secretly I would love to be called pretty because even though I have cut my hair short, this word is used for little girls.

I ask Claire quietly, 'What time is it?'

She whispers back, 'Don't know.' We have promised Alison we will not get up before seven. It is 6.45. But Claire says, 'Let's open our stockings now.' We pile onto my bed and stick our hands inside giant socks, pulling out wrapped packages. We rip off paper and find: a pencil decorated with cats, a rubber shaped like a house, a green notebook, a small plastic rabbit toy that can leap from a shelf, a fart cushion, a set of fake glasses, ears and nose, chocolate coins, strawberry lollies. At the bottom of each stocking is a tangerine. Twenty minutes later, our brother is awake, and the three of us run into Alison's room, each wearing fake glasses, ears and nose.

Alison's head pops over the side of her newly built pine

platform bed, 'Sssh,' she says sternly, 'Bill's still asleep.' She climbs down, dressed in a T-shirt. It sags out of shape.

'Shall I make Bill tea?' I say. She nods her head and I make Bill tea and add four sugars. I think that he likes it that way. Climbing the ladder slowly, I put the hot tea by his sleeping head, whisper, 'Here's your tea, Bill. Happy Christmas!' He doesn't answer. Bill is snoring. Face crushed into the pillow. Every morning, Bill must be woken. Claire, Alison and I take turns. Now, he is fast asleep.

I climb back down. We wait. Then Alison says to Claire, 'Just go up and ask Bill again. It would be nice if he were here to open the presents.' Claire nods her head. She climbs up the steps. That is our special job. Claire and I are told: 'Wake Bill up' or 'Go and see Bill'. When I am older, if Bill is depressed, Alison will ask me, 'Go and check Bill is OK. You are so good at making him laugh.' I always obey.

'Happy Christmas, Bill,' Claire says, at the top of the ladder. She continues, in a cajoling voice, 'Do you want to come and open the presents? Please . . .'

Bill snores, in the deepest sleep. Claire climbs back down. Sat on the sofa, in Alison's jungle of spider plants, the four of us wait. Outside, snow falls, flakes racing across an opaque sky. The world is stuffed with white like an eiderdown. It is filled with frozen water. The sky is tense. I look at the packages under our tree, at Rachel's angel with her golden crown. On the TV, I have seen Superstar Barbie advertised, and a Farrah Fawcett doll head. I could brush hair, make plaits, rub lipstick on her smile. I dream of battery-operated toys like Operation, the Simon memory game with four flashing lights, Hungry Hippos, or a Glo

Worm – a bright green soft toy that lights up your nights, a larva in pyjamas.

Eventually, Alison says, smiling, 'Why don't we sing to wake him up?' And we sing 'We Wish You a Merry Christmas' at the top of our voices. But Bill still snores. So, we open the presents, just the four of us. Mum has hand-made our gifts this year. When I open my parcel, there is a bag made from patchwork squares on one side and purple corduroy on the other. Mum has embroidered lilac letters in chain stitch: 'Susie's Bits and Pieces'. Inside the bag are a metal tin of coloured watercolour pencils, two sketchbooks and some bottled inks.

'Thanks, Alison.' I hug her tight, because the bag is beautiful, and I will paint pictures now. My sister has a similar bag, but she has been given tin whistles and a book called *Learn to Play the Tunes*. There is even the music to 'Molly Malone'. My brother gets a handmade bag too, and inside is a train carriage to go on his train set.

The three of us have also been given sleeping bags for summer camp. We started going away alone to alternative, ideological camps last year. The first few days, I got homesick, cried, and sat in a circle singing American folk songs. Then, I met a girl called Isa, and we became friends. During a rainstorm, we built a roundhouse with the staff and other children. At the top, we held swaying branches. Raindrops dripped on our faces and swam in our eyes. No one picked on me like they do in the community. When Alison came to collect me at the station, I told her, 'I met a girl called Isa. She's my best friend, and we're going to go away to camp together every year.' Isa becomes a friend outside of the community; her house will be a place where I stay with a 'normal' family. With Isa, I share idle summer dreams.

In Alison's room, we look at the sleeping bags, put camp thoughts aside, and leave our Unit. On the stairs, the other Kids are yelling 'Happy Christmas'. Sunshine has red moon boots on, walks down the stairs in slow motion like an astronaut. Jason carries a green puppet of Kermit the Frog that his grandpa sent him from New York. He tosses the green Muppet from the first landing, 'Let's make frog soup,' he shouts. We scream as the frog thuds on the floor. It is still snowing, freezing inside and outside the house.

In general, anthropologists identify festivals and parties as places for social development and experiment. They are also considered to be moments of protest and subversion. For example, during a carnival the peasant can be King for a day. In the community this means that we can, for a few days, embrace some of the things that people do on the outside – eat traditional food, celebrate Christmas. Our revolutionary stance is infiltrated by nostalgia. For a few days, our domestic life becomes the stage for a mishmash of 'old' and 'new'. In the evenings, we sing made-up satirical Marxist songs about growing cabbages, alongside traditional Christian hymns. There is the hustle and bustle of collective, institutional celebration. Everyone performs.

Downstairs, in the Kitchen, Barbara is dressed in a Ban the Bomb apron. It was handmade by the demonstrating women – who Barbara calls her 'sisters' – at the Greenham Common peace camp. They're protesting against the

British government and Maggie Thatcher's decision to let cruise missiles be stored at Greenham. Soon 30,000 women will hold hands and form a human chain around the nine-mile perimeter fence. But, in the Kitchen, a B has fallen off the apron. It reads 'Ban the OMB'.

Barbara teases Lawrence, 'Why aren't you wearing an apron?' She ruffles Jason's head, says, 'And you should wear one too.'

Jason smiles. 'Yeah, Barbara. And then you'll want me to make the feminist Christmas tree from tampons? I did it last year.'

Barbara bursts out laughing. 'My enlightened boy.'

Around them, one hundred potatoes are being peeled, Firefly is slicing carrots into mountains of orange discs, three of our turkeys sit in giant roasting pans. Violet has peeled three Brussels sprouts. She has never liked cooking. But when I show her my watercolour pencil set, she promises me that in the afternoon 'we can make art together, swirl inks into sensual flowers like goddesses'.

Claire comes into the Kitchen, and copying an upper-class accent I rush towards her, pointing my finger. 'I am a member of the Conservative Party, and spiffing good. Get Britain back to work!' But Claire collides with Lawrence and he spills his hot tea. 'Bloody piss off, Claire!' She mutters, 'Shut up, Lawrence!' Since India, Claire is often rude to Lawrence, but I want to keep the peace and get a cloth to clean the floor.

David is leaning up against a counter. He says, 'Oh god, Susie. What are you doing? Just looking for someone to marry you?' Everyone laughs. I blush, and Claire blushes too. The Adults roar with laughter, opening their mouths like Christmas lions.

Alison interrupts them. 'I am writing down breakfast requests.' She has a notebook in her hand and is wearing an apron decorated with Friesian cows. It is a present from Bill. She says, 'Today we are serving fried bread, sausages, eggs, tomatoes, mushrooms, tea, coffee and toast.' She giggles. Barbara smiles. Firefly says, 'Only the best for radicals!'

Bill walks into the kitchen. He is finally awake, hair tousled, mug in hand. He takes Alison into his arms and kisses her on the lips. David does a wolf whistle.

Alison says, 'Bill!' She blushes and the kitchen bursts, once again, into cheers.

In the Dining Room, exotic fruit platters have been prepared on silver trays. Pineapple chunks alternate with orange slices, pale yellow grapefruit segments and yellow mango fans, delicate towers built from pale pink lychees, black grapes, star fruit and kumquats. I have offered to be a waitress. I bring people their food.

1. Vegetarian for Eagle
2. A full but with scrambled eggs for Violet
3. Bacon and eggs for Barbara
4. Everything for Troy
5. Everything for Sunshine
6. Everything for Jason
7. Everything for all the Kids

After breakfast is the Christmas Photograph. Charles, a new member, and Lawrence take pictures. 'Come on,' they yell, as a parade of Kids, Adults, dogs and babies trudge in snow. It is one of the only moments when the entire community is together. We are recorded, counted and framed.

We skid down the steps. Brandy throws a snowball into Tina's face. She starts to cry. Charles says, 'Hurry up!'

At the end of the lawn, by a snow-covered stone semi-circular seating area, Charles places everyone into size lines: taller, tall, small and smallest. We become an angelic Christmas choir. Charles stands behind an old-fashioned camera, a black curtain draped over his head. He and Lawrence read the light, run back and forth. He shouts: 'Get yourself into the sun. Four point six. Is everyone there?' Lawrence says, 'Come closer. Move further away!' Charles is muttering, 'Let's get some atmosphere.' He has been to film school, and wants to work for Channel Four, because the radical TV channel has just been launched.

I am standing on the top row in dungarees. From here, the snow spreads out and covers the lawn. Yesterday, we built snowmen and snowwomen. 'You must have men *and* women,' I told Violet. 'They must be exactly the same.'

'Hark the herald angels sing,' someone starts singing, and we join in, glorifying the newborn king.

Charles shouts, 'Are you ready?' He begins a countdown and we all yell: 'FIVE, FOUR, THREE, TWO, ONE!' Click.

Barbara says, 'Let's make a radical gesture!' Firefly chips in, 'Yes, let's make a radical gesture.' We raise our fists to the sky. Claire shouts at me, 'You look like you're asking the teacher to go to the toilet.' I blush. Click.

*

It is time to go back inside for the Annual Present-Giving Ceremony. A month earlier, Eva (another new member) visited each Unit with a hat crammed with slips of paper. On each paper was written the name of a community member. She came into my bedroom, I pulled a slip, unfolded the paper and read the name.

'Now remember,' she insisted, for it was the first time she had done this, and Barbara had explained all the rules, 'don't tell anyone the name you have in your hand. You must make a present for the person on the slip. There is no opting out. The present must be handmade.'

In the middle of the Lounge, we take turns sitting in the chair for the Annual Present-Giving Ceremony. Bill and Barbara have built the Christmas fire. The ritual is a dream. It feels unreal and like I am there but then disappear. When I sit in the chair, I want to laugh and cry, run and hide and yet be there. Lawrence walks towards me, saying 'Happy Christmas', and plays me a tune on a wooden pipe. Everybody claps their hands. Then, I give a drawstring bag I have embroidered with a golden sun to Violet. Violet gives a framed hand-drawn map of the garden to David. David gives a handmade chopping board to Walker. Walker gives a knitted scarf to Sunshine, and Sunshine does a dance for Bill.

Over all the Christmases, during the Annual Present-Giving Ceremony I am given: a revised hippy version of the *Wizard of Oz* musical, a renovated black lacquered antique chair, a chocolate cake, a massage, a performance of a Dolly Parton song, an ugly wooden sculpture made from a log, a photograph of the house, a framed ink drawing of a tree, a sewing kit, a purple knitted bobble hat, a haircut, a set of Victoriana-style lace underwear, a handmade chess set and a voucher for a cheese sandwich.

Each time, the crowd hushes and waits. We are still before our shared joy. In the community, joy shoots through us like the burning fire, spreading from Adult to Adult, Kid to Adult, Adult to Kid, Kid to Kid. Like the blaze in the fireplace, joy sparks from the first match. In the Lounge, we are all inside the crowd, and some years, in the low-lit, winter days, fifty people celebrate, erupt from the depths of the year. The crowd is hot and strong, and I always run back to it, during breakfast, the photo and the ceremony, darting in and out, until the flames ignite me. As Nobel Prize–winning writer Elias Canetti noted in his study of crowd behaviour, *Crowds and Power*, at the fiery heart of the crowd it is so tightly packed the word 'individual' does not exist. A fire must be built, a group must be constructed. The fire-crowd will consume each person until only a group remains. Canetti meant that in certain crowds we are set on fire by a sermon, a speech, ignited by a belief. Individuality vanishes. In our utopian house, at Christmas, this crowd-fire burns.

But as the years pass, the magic of communal Christmas and the parties dims. The playfulness dulls – what play expert Eugen Fink describes as bringing light, or 'day-ing' the world, fades. As the Kids get older, the obligation of the Annual Present-Giving Ceremony becomes a constraint. It is complicated when you pick your enemy's name from the hat. It is difficult when you are a teenager and twenty-five

Adults examine your freshly made-up-for-a-party-face, or you don't want to pretend everything is perfect inside the house.

Years later, Claire tells me on the phone, 'I hated the Annual Present-Giving Ceremony, sitting in that chair, everyone staring as I waited for my present. Everyone watching me.' And I agree with her, because despite all the wonder, I now feel more like I was caught up in the fiery merriment, strangely bewitched, lost in the crowd. 'Christmas was so big. Too institutional. Maybe just too forced,' I reply, and I recall hiding upstairs in our Unit at later parties. By my late teens, I could no longer face the crowd, was no longer able to comply with big communal events. They exhausted and drained me. The sparkle and glitter felt fake. The sound of the roaring voice of the God of Joy became too loud, out-of-tune and deafening. After all, as Euripides teaches us, intoxication is dangerous; and everyone knows that if you play with fire you can get burnt.

I think about questions of celebrations and creativity a lot. In my work as an arts therapist or running team-building sessions and seminars, how to facilitate groups and creativity is a constant concern: the ethics, intentions, promises and practice.

Over twenty-five years of using play and creative tools in my work, I have developed two important rules. The first is that a leap in the dark requires trust. One must feel secure to play. Before practical sessions begin, with child/adolescent or adult groups, on flipcharts we write charters, invent our play conditions (these are not imposed), and ideas are debated:

respect, participation, confidentiality. In *Playing and Reality*, Winnicott underlines the importance of this safety, a framework meaning we can experiment with symbolic risk and failure without either anxiety or tyrannical compliancy.

Secondly, when I use play there is always a get-out clause, a possibility to opt out of the 'joy'. For the word 'creative' sometimes sits uncomfortably with me: its pop psychology connections, a corporate jamboree feeling, gurus in collarless shirts, sticking rainbows onto walls. As a play practitioner, I have deep reserves about formulaic, one-size-fits-all doctrines. I am very cautious about people being dragged along by the crowd. My work in theatre and drama and my upbringing have taught me about the joy of the group but also the danger of this fire. Play and making are intimate acts. Their force in change can be collective or emerge through a unique, person-centred process.

One evening, I try to explain to A that the Annual Present-Giving Ceremony was not like giving a present to a friend. As I reached adolescence, I realized that the love involved was random but unavoidable. Obligatory relationships were pulled from a hat. Our group Christmas resembled Soviet domestic spaces, where a lack of privacy was expected in order to transform personal relationships into 'proletarian comradeship'. The ceremony was a spectacle, and a demonstration. One by one, we *had* to sit in that chair, watched by forty people. When I look back, I feel a deep sense of vulnerability, that my small child body was sucked into this crowd, intoxicated by the beauty, lulled into a false sense of security.

*

The Christmases A and I have with our children are quiet and intimate. My three daughters always want the same thing; it is a ritual because 'Christmas is bigger than the rest', they say. Even the eldest, an eighteen-year-old feminist with a shaved head, wants Christmas done exactly-the-same-way-as-we-do-it-every-year: the stockings opened on the parental bed, the Christmas breakfast – a whatever-you-want feast involving English fry-ups, American pancakes and shakshuka – presents under the tree, and Christmas lunch at five. In the afternoon, A and I go for a long walk and the girls chill out in their pyjamas and watch TV. We try to balance between things being the same but also changing, so that the rite does not become institutionalized rote.

As I write these words it is nearly Christmas, and I am away with my toddler in a tiny Airbnb in a fishing village on the jagged Breton coast. I am here to work on this book. The poet Etel Adnan spent the last years of her life on these pink cliffs, writing, 'To look at the sea is to become what one is.' While I write, the toddler draws, and we often write and draw together, and I relish this making side by side. In the seaside town, I type and put pen to paper like I did in my notebook for the short-story competition, when I learnt to keep quiet about my achievements. I write and write, as I have done since I was a child, translating the experience of human life. Early evening, we go to see the Christmas lights, and then the toddler watches a cartoon mouse hip-hop dancing as I write some more. Bathtime. Bedtime. Then, I drink wine. More writing. It never stops.

Before I go to sleep, I make Xmas lists. As I am planning

the festive shopping, the toddler stirs. When I kiss her good night, she says, 'Maman, we are just two.' She is our third daughter, so her quiet mummy time is precious and rare. I whisper, 'I love you with all my heart.' Outside, the festive street decorations flick on and off. The roaring voice of the God of Joy whispers into my ear and I write into the night.

Throughout my childhood in the community, occasionally people from the outside come to our communal Christmas. One person, Cora, is always invited. A local woman, she limps through our double doors. A butte of flesh, Cora advances balanced on a stick, wrapped in old cardigans. Her swollen feet shuffle in split slippers. She is an aged moustached walrus covered in barnacles. Her face is blotchy, cheeks stained scarlet and yellow. Her grey hair is lanky, coated in grease. Alison says to me, 'Come and say hello to Cora.'

Cora has a sweet smile. It pulls at my heart. She can barely speak, just says 'Hello', 'Yes', 'No', 'Thank you' and 'Goodbye' in a voice like a child.

Alison says, 'Take Cora into the Lounge.' I help Cora to a chair, by the fire, to wait for Christmas dinner. Close up, I smell her odour emanating like a fog, a layer round her hillock: damp, old sweat and urine. Alison says, 'She lives in a flat with ten cats. People complain because she wets herself. But it's not her fault. She was in a mental hospital.' She explains, 'In the mental hospital they had to go to the toilet at a certain time of day. They had to eat at the same time every day, shower at the same time every day. It was real institutional living. Can you imagine?' I nod my head, and Alison continues. 'You know that Cora got shut up in the mental hospital when she was fourteen because she got pregnant. It's outrageous.'

Sometimes we visit Cora's flat because Alison volunteers and does her weekly shop. The smell hangs outside the front door. Inside, it is decorated with embroidered pictures, and what Alison calls 'antimacassars' on the back of the chairs. Cats roam everywhere. Shelves are piled with old, metal biscuit boxes. Cora points to me, and she means I can open them.

When I lift the lids, one box is filled with neatly folded, never-used handkerchiefs, embroidered with daisies and the letter C. Inside another tin there are postcards and souvenirs from seaside hospital trips to Blackpool, Brighton and Eastbourne. But most of the tins are crammed full of buttons. Buttons like boiled sweets. Buttons like stars. Cora has snipped these fastenings from old cardigans that she gets free from jumble sales. She unravels the cardigans into wool, sorts the balls of wool into colours, and crochets geometric shapes. Finally, she stitches the crocheted squares, rectangles and hexagons into double blankets. They smell.

As she does every year, on Christmas Day Cora arrives with a carrier bag. She hands it over to Alison, nods her head. Inside is a crocheted blanket made from pastel patterns, lines of apricot, pale yellow and candy pink. Bill exclaims, 'It's beautiful. Such amazing work,' and Cora blushes.

In the Dining Room, we serve Cora a plate of roast turkey, roast potatoes, carrots, mint sauce, gravy, Brussels sprouts and peas. As she cuts through a potato, Alison says to Barbara, 'Maggie Thatcher took people out of the hospitals, closed them down. No one looks after people like Cora.' As I pile peas onto my fork, I smile at Cora, and despite her stink, I like her. She builds worlds from cosmic wool.

Inside my Breton house, I still have Cora's tins of buttons (given to me after her death), and sometimes I sleep beneath her blankets. Our community welcomed Cora inside. As a child it taught me immense tolerance, humanity, and that art, like Cora's extraordinary blankets, is possible everywhere. Yet Cora was also a justification of our way of life.

When we pull the crackers, Cora puts a purple paper hat on her head. Around her Adults and Kids tuck into food, celebrating our post-revolutionary state – described by Mexican poet Octavio Paz as 'a releasing of so many ferocious, tender and noble feelings that have been hidden by our fear of being'. Inside our Dining Room, surrounded by fifty people, Cora is comfortable. For years, she ate dinner in the mental hospital. As Charles looks on, she spikes some turkey with her fork. He raises his glass and gravy dribbles down his chin.

8. Laps

'The body was a cage, and inside that cage was something which looked, listened, feared, thought, and marvelled; that something, that remainder left over after the body has been accounted for, was the soul.'

Milan Kundera, *The Unbearable Lightness of Being*

'I asked myself: "What could possibly be the connection between a common rape in a Leeds hotel room and what's happening in Bosnia?" And then suddenly this penny dropped, and I thought: "Of course, it's obvious. One is the seed and the other is the tree."'

Sarah Kane, on the genesis of her play *Blasted*

Since I started writing this book, I've been seeking out texts about utopias, communism and institutional childhoods, boarding schools, cults, children's homes, the military, hospitals and kibbutzim. Places with intentions, utopias removed from society. Some have too many rules, others no rules at all. I read PhD theses, memoirs, novels, history books and articles asking how organizations and groups mould existences, shape emotions and behaviour. How have people reimagined the social group, our human need to be together? In the thirteenth century, a monk, Salimbene Di Adam, recounted the infamous and cruel experiments carried out on infants by Holy Roman Emperor Frederick II. Fascinated by the origins of human speech, and reputedly wanting to know how language emerged, the emperor gave a group of babies into the care of nurses. They had strict instructions not to 'prattle or speak' with the children. They could be fed and bathed but were not to be given any affection. Tragically, Frederick never got an answer to his linguistic question because the children, starved of basic interaction, died. Babies cannot live without human warmth and contact. Darwin identified this as the source of all societies – our need for connection, communication, support.

Utopias prescribe new ways to communicate with and care for their children and young people, and this impacts everything. Early childhood experiences from birth to age eight affect brain development, and provide the foundations for all future learning, behaviour and health. The LIFE Study, following the lives of individuals over the course of thirty years, has shown that adolescence – the period in which we test the waves of adult life – impacts our self-esteem, productive life and subjective well-being, even during middle adulthood.

Recently, I learnt that between 1921 and 1922, 7 million children were abandoned by families under Stalin's USSR regime. Scrolling through Twitter, I read about a childhood in a cult, and come upon differences and similarities with mine. In *Slouching Towards Bethlehem*, Joan Didion ventured into the 1967 hippy movement, meeting a San Francisco psychiatrist who said, 'The themes are always the same. A return to innocence . . . An itch for the transcendental, for purification. Right there you've got the way that romanticism historically ends up in trouble.' Boarding schools, one author notes, are like prisons, run on emotional and physical abuse. Another explains that most socialist utopias, like the Bolsheviks, advocated removing children from parents, replacing the egoism of the traditional family with state-run rational love. Many of these organizations, in obliging children to be independent from an early age, install forms of parentification. Parentification happens when parents look to their children for emotional and/or practical support, rather than providing it.

The same themes spring out from all pages I read: children, trauma and abandonment. Yet as French writer Virginie Linhart, whose parents led the May 1968 student revolt in Paris, points out, 'No one ever tells the children's tales.' As we analyse and invent utopias, and experimental living projects, it seems essential – yet surprisingly rare – to distinguish between the impact on adults – who chose the adventure and have already been brought up – and the impact on children, who are in their formative years and may never know anything else.

I am ten and then eleven. Our father marries his girlfriend, and they start to have babies. The babies come every other year. My half-brother Alex is born and Claire and I feed the babies – as we have learnt to do in the community – and play with them like we look after the little Kids. Our paternal grandparents die, and at their funerals we cry with our Christian cousins who have posters of chimpanzees on their bedroom walls with the slogan 'God Loves You'. Bill stays in our lives, but we remain a Single Parent Family. Alison now works more hours at the youth club. She is good at her job, organized and dependable. We begin to rise in our status in the community, climbing up the egalitarian ladder, because Tripti and Lawrence are planning to leave and Violet and Eagle might be going soon. We are Founding Members.

Over the following year, a devastating miners' strike begins in the UK, Ronald Reagan starts a second term as US president, Chernenko leads the Soviet Union as General Secretary of the Communist Party. He announces Russia's intention to boycott the Olympics, and joined by eight Eastern Bloc allies organizes the 'Friendship Games'. The world advances in the shadow of the Cold War, small and big circles turn, and things happen to me, events impossible to date in time. They fix themselves outside the utopian calendar, float in the cosmos.

One September afternoon in the Kitchen, on the Cooking Rota, by 'Dinner' Firefly has dustily scrawled her name, the one chosen with her women's group a few years ago. For thirty-one years she was a good girl known as Brenda; now, she is a beetle, shimmering in darkness, she is Firefly. Yet in the communal Kitchen, anxious hair sticks to her brow and she frowns into a bubbling saucepan. Grey vegetables float in a muddy sauce. Firefly is cooking curry for forty, and she jokes her Northern mother only taught her to toast bread, bake hard scones and burn fruitcake. Pushing round, copper glasses up her slippery, white nose, Firefly turns the greasy pages of the *Moosewood Cookbook*. With a wooden spoon, she tastes her curry and shakes her head. Salt, pepper, ketchup, prunes and raisins are added. Sweat drips from her forehead.

In the corner of the Kitchen, on the lap of a Danish visitor, I am sharing a recent philosophical realization. 'I want nothing. But do you realize that can't make sense? Coz you have to want something. So, my sentence doesn't work.'

This word puzzle has exploded in my eleven-year-old brain. It is like the film *Harold and Maude*: it changes my way of thinking, expanding the mind. I have cracked open a brown rock and found a crystal inside. For days, this thought irradiates into my sense of language: something, nothing and everything. I walk round the house in a daze.

The man says, 'That is radical. You're so mature.'

As we talk, Firefly pours curry powder from a jar, mistakenly rubs it into her eyes. She begins to weep. 'I am too intense,' she mutters, and she begins telling us about her recent Rape Crisis meeting. She heard that girls as young as ten could be living with their rapist. Firefly grabs some toilet paper from a roll on the counter and wipes her falling tears. I wriggle on the man's lap, and he tickles me.

The word 'lap' is a curious thing. A lap is a component that covers another component – one thing overlapping another, as it were. You can also run laps, turning round and round, stuck ineluctably inside a closed shape. Finally, the word 'lap' means pudendum, the external genital organs of a female, the word from the Latin *pudenda*, 'to be ashamed'. Most days in the community, when I am a preteen, I sit on the laps of doppelganger dads. None of them are my dad, and their laps are homonyms, words that have the same sound but many different meanings.

I am drawn to these men. My dad is far away, surrounded by new babies, but there is always one of these men willing to spend time with me. In all the children's books I read, men are encountered and retrieved: long-lost uncles, grandparents, and trusted acquaintances. Men rescue children, liberate them and save the day. Kings can make everything better, and I seek out the nurses, the carpenters, the travellers, the computer scientists, the therapists, the musicians, the media wannabes, the dropouts, the academics, earnest socialists, and the unruly performance artist who spent twenty-four hours in a gallery smashing panes of glass. I make them gifts, stick two hundred lentils onto a birthday card, draw a picture of the woods, and bake them chocolate cakes. In their bedrooms and the Kitchen, while they gulp sweetened tea, instant coffee and puff on roll-ups, I talk to these men. Some of them are kind, and some are not. For years, they will be my friends. My best friends.

Middle childhood is ending, the preteens will soon begin. Hormonal signals are travelling to my brain, battling for metamorphosis. My body skids on the cusp, the verge. When I ride my bike and squeeze the brakes, pleasure rises from between my legs, spreading from my core, fizzing outwards to my fingertips. My winkle (I still won't use the word 'vagina') is suddenly warm like late-spring sunlight, and unexpected rays caress my skin. My hair stands out from my head, I am alive as the grass, and I ride down the country lanes.

Inwardly, despite my attempts to be grown-up, I am green and innocent, and trust the trees. I am green like unripe fruit, inexperienced, and this is a problem; I never get a chance to grow up. Naivety becomes my system of deterrence but it also makes me vulnerable, and certain things confuse me. In my bedroom, when I am getting undressed, Alison walks in. She looks at my body and tells me, 'You have inverted nipples. You may have problems breastfeeding.' Light hits my naked chest. Pectoral muscles and fatty tissues are expanding, and the pink tips of areolae top my tiny breasts. There is a pause, she walks out, and I dress hurriedly.

Sunshine has read a novel by Judy Blume about becoming a teenager in New York. The mothers file their daughters' nails, and style their hair with heated rollers. But in the community, we're given facts about bodies, menstruation, sex objects and 'inverted nipples'. Sunshine and I read an old copy of the *Power of Women* journal. It says, 'If you have a vagina you are defined as a sex object, not just by the whistles in the street but every institution that sees you as a woman.' These words/facts are weapons I do not know how to handle: 'inverted nipples', the book *Our Bodies Ourselves*, and close-up drawings of vaginas in *Spare Rib*, whose letters page includes titles like 'Not Solely For Fucking', 'Rape' and 'Methods of Abortion: Vacuum Aspiration'.

The French writer Henri Michaux wrote, 'We are not

alone in our skin', and inside and outside of each of us, different stories are told. This learnt language then translates our identities. When I am eleven, the different languages and identities fight it out in a mental boxing ring. I don't know why Mum is telling me about my nipples, but her judgement must be right. I store these facts away: I have inverted nipples and I am Not Solely For Fucking.

In *The Unbearable Lightness of Being*, Milan Kundera offers his character Tereza's experience of communism and bodies: 'When she lived at home, her mother forbade her to lock the bathroom door. What she meant by this injunction was: Your body is just like all other bodies . . . you have no right to hide something that exists in millions of identical copies.' When I read these words as an adult, I immediately recall the community's open doors, the relentless bombardment of information, the clinical language and the lack of gentleness. To be gentle in the sense of 'to take care of, respect'.

One day in the Kitchen, a man, Lionel, grabs me and pulls me onto his lap. We are special friends. His long hair tickles my face, gentle as a corn sheaf plucked from a field. He is dry and warm, safe as summer. Lionel is a new member. He says, 'Do you want to come and stay in my Unit tonight? I'll give you a massage.'

I nod, excited and thrilled. It's like going to Sunshine's Unit for a sleepover, or a tuck-box party at a boarding school (I read about these in my books) – jolly girls munching on currant buns. Lionel is a nearly forty-year-old man, a father and a husband. His wife is away for the weekend with their daughter. Lionel will be alone.

In the Cowshed I ask Alison, 'Can I sleep at Lionel's tonight? He wants to give me a massage?' Alison is milking a cow while telling a joke to a visiting miner's wife. Currently hundreds of miners in Britain are on strike, three-quarters of coal mines have been picketed, and we are providing relief for the families. They stay for weeks and weekends in our country home. Alison says absent-mindedly, 'Yes, yes. Don't forget your sleeping bag.' Kids often sleep overnight in other Units in the community.

I inform Saskia proudly, with a skip, 'I'm sleeping in Lionel's Unit!' She says, 'Lucky you. But I'm going to see Madonna at Wembley Stadium.'

Saskia's dad got them backstage passes. He's a journalist, and lives with a glamorous Italian woman with tinted glasses in a cool, tall house. Saskia's stepmum is a militant feminist. She has talked to Saskia so much about periods that Saskia is terrified of the prospect of telling her once hers start. Her stepmum explains, 'Don't worry, you can have sex when you have your period. Me and your dad just put a towel on the bed.'

Saskia tells me, 'It's disgusting.'

I answer 'Yuck', and we fall to the floor, curling inside the laughter that reduces her stepmum's strange words to ashes.

That night, I leave my Unit, sleeping bag in hand. I gallop up flights of stairs and down corridors, skipping past different doors. Our house is full of corridors, the word coming from the Italian *corridoio* meaning 'running place'. Corridors were a seventeenth-century architectural invention of the upper class, in order to avoid seeing servants, but were an important feature in Fourier's utopian dream. His 'street gallery', or communal corridors, would smash the bourgeois family, aid circulation and eliminate privacy.

As I run along to the end of a corridor, I think about how I have never slept in Lionel's Unit before. I am alone. In the community, intimacy is a rare flower, harvested by hand like a saffron thread – a thin orange strand plucked at dawn. Our waking moments are lived in a swarm, and as Canetti writes, 'The crowd never feels saturated. It remains hungry as long as there is one human being it has not reached.'

At the door to his Unit, Lionel greets me, his brown eyes deep with promise, his face patterned with a smile. 'Hello.'

'Hi,' I answer.

'Put your sleeping bag next door.' I do so, and when I return, Lionel says, 'I'll give you the massage now.'

I nod. His proposition is as logical as toast, or a jump into a skipping game at school, leaping into helixes of turning rope, feet pounding as the girls chant loudly: 'Cinderella, Dressed in yella, Went upstairs to kiss her fella, How many kisses did she give him? ONE, TWO, THREE, FOUR . . .'

'Take your top off,' Lionel says with a smile.

His floor is rough. He puts a towel down. Turning, I think I should undress. But I don't want to undress, and I do not know why I cannot take off my clothes. I have come for a massage, but something stops my hands.

'Take your top off,' Lionel repeats.

I blush, obey and undress. 'Sorry.' I go to lie on my stomach, stumble slightly, place my half-naked form on the towel. Head to the ground, my cheek is in floor dust, and Lionel straddles my little body, drips oil onto my back. His hands slide up and down. We are alone, and it is late, and I feel something bad happening. It is like sickness.

He says, 'Turn over now.' I turn and look up. But it is impossible to watch him pouring oil on my chest and stroking my breasts. I now know I should not be here, in this Unit alone, in this community. I should not be anywhere on this planet. I am eleven, and a volcano is erupting, there is a rain of stones. My eyes close.

'This is our secret.' Lionel's mouth is by my ear. 'This will be our secret. Don't tell anyone.'

His words scurry through me, travelling from the external ear, they reach my internal ear. His words carry a top-priority warning, an SOS for lighthouse people and emergency support, the police, ambulance crews and mountain rescue teams: blackout, immediate crisis shutdown.

I whisper, 'Yes.'

Our eyes meet for an instant, and I have nowhere to look when his hands move down my body. Where are the words? Even as an adult, I will have to look through the thesaurus, in the dictionary. Writing on victims, in his prize-winning work on the history of communism, Thierry Wolton stated, 'Terror is difficult, impossible to transcribe . . .The hardship of the ordeal, the shame of what we have known, the fear of awakening the wounds, the will to forget . . . The experience of inhumanity cannot be shared.'

I wait, and when he stops there is no relief. 'You can get

dressed and go to bed now,' Lionel says, and I get dressed and walk towards the door. In the other room, I put on my pyjamas and get into my sleeping bag. In the darkness, I hear a clock. Even now I remember the sound.

Sitting up, I grab a sock, a woolly hat and a scarf, and wrap the clock in these objects, one after the next. I am terrified Lionel will rape me; I have heard this word, 'rape', read the four letters. Yet I do not understand how this thing has happened. The clock keeps ticking, and I want time to stop, to abolish all cuckoo clocks, watches, sundials and Big Ben, to erase time from here, erase what has happened, and stop what is to come, stop the past, the present and the future.

My friend the archaeologist sends me an email from Pompeii. In AD 79, disaster struck the Roman town. Following a series of earthquakes, Mount Vesuvius erupted and hundreds of inhabitants were buried beneath a tide of volcanic lava. The mineral matter conserved the victims attempting to flee the river of molten stone. We can witness them today – women, children and men, their bodies stuck at the exact moment when trauma hit.

With his email, he attaches a photograph of a family, their bodies curved together, uncannily vital-looking, two parents and two children, as though they have been placed in safekeeping, motionless in life.

The next morning, I return to my Unit undone, and it feels like I sleep through the following weeks. Like the family in Pompeii, I have been stilled. Part of me is covered in hardened ash, cold lava, and I cannot get out. When I walk down the wooden stairs, my body is clunky and heavy, and I am terrified I'll cross paths with Lionel and terrified I won't. It is such an effort to get through each morning, each afternoon, each evening, each day and each night.

'Don't you love me any more?' he whispers, catching me alone in the Washing-Up Room. I bump into Lionel in the Dining Room when we celebrate saying goodbye to Lawrence and Tripti, who are moving away. 'Be free,' Tripti tells me, when I cry as I wish her goodbye, and she strokes my cheek. In the garden, Lionel applauds when Sunshine and Brandy roller-skate. I see him watching me; his smile tightens and my body contracts. I am elongated, stretched until I might snap. The bread is baked, the cows are milked, the sun rises in the east and sets in the west. Lionel's eyes twinkle. He is the sun, and I am a broken bone. Soon, I will disappear. 'Don't you love me any more?' he repeats. There are over forty people in the house, but I am alone, and I wonder – if we have broken down the nuclear family and Lionel is a parental figure – is what happened a form of incest because I am inside my home?

At night, I dream I return to Lionel's Unit to explain I still love him. Truly, I love him so much it hurts. Regularly, I begin to sleepwalk, leaving my bedroom and walking up our corridor, trying to get to his Unit. According to Soviet visionaries, all social encounters and activities should take place in corridors. The entire wall of our Unit's corridor is a series of windows overlooking the landing and the staircase. Glass squares in white-painted wooden frames. It is like something I learnt about at school: a panopticon, an all-seeing device. It is a nineteenth-century architectural thing, often used in prisons, so a watchman can watch over occupants without the occupants knowing. This is an odd thing about the community: how everything can be seen and yet stays hidden; how the openness, the facts and the bare skin cover our secrets. The lack of intimacy inadvertently produces an ignorance of abuse, a kind of rationalized blindness.

Bill finds me regularly sleepwalking in the corridor. Confused, I wake up, standing by the wall of windows. Each time he leads me gently back to my room and tucks me up in bed. Nobody asks why I am sleepwalking, and I continue. Yet, however hard I try, I cannot get to Lionel.

Trauma often leaves unspoken traces in the body, physical symptoms. Because trauma involves shock and surprise – it is something for which we were not prepared – the survivor is silenced, and what is not said evolves into a form of non-verbal communication.

In a workshop, in a hospital, I ask managers to walk around the room while another person walks behind them, observing how they turn, place their weight, angle their head. The person behind watches and tries to learn how the other person walks. The goal of this exercise is to realize the complexity of non-verbal communication; how everyone has a completely different way of moving their muscles and bones. Body language has a linguistic intricacy, a grammar and punctuation; it is as complex as a written text. In the face, forty-three muscles combine to produce 10,000 possible expressions. Often when I do this exercise it reveals upbringings, culture, childhood accidents, whether someone has had a military or artistic career, but participants also – even though this is not the objective – allude to moments of trauma.

Traumatic memories are like a huge world, and when something sucks you back in, the overwhelming terror means you cannot easily leave. When I work as a therapist, I never delve into a client's trauma without extreme caution. Even when, as in the exercise above, I am working with body language, I am very careful with participants and provide a get-out clause.

Years ago, in a Parisian psychiatric unit, I worked with a little girl called Marie. She'd had a traumatic upbringing, and barely spoke. In our drama-therapy sessions, Marie would sit immobile and wouldn't say her name. She was in a group with three other children. The sessions were run in a circle with six mats, and two children either side of the nurse and me. For weeks, the nurse and I racked our brains and tried different exercises. But Marie would not speak or move. Then one day, we decided to put Marie on a mat in between us, in a safer position, with the three children on the opposite side of the circle. That day, for the very first time, she smiled and said, '*Bonjour. Je m'appelle Marie.*'

After a few weeks, I think I should tell Alison about Lionel. I read in a book called *The Women's Room* that this is what people do. *The Women's Room* is a novel about the lives of three decades of suburban American housewives with cold husbands who penetrate them without care. It is the international bestseller of the women's movement. I have read this book dozens of times: five hundred pages of liberation and despair. Women get drunk on cheap wine and are raped in neighbours' bathrooms, turn insane from screaming kids and baking cookies. In *The Women's Room*, the woman-girl life is unbearable. Characters attempt suicide and are interned. Women walk in shadows, they always die. It is a litany of rage.

Last year, Dad saw this book in my bedroom. 'But you can't read that, you're only ten!' he shouted, and I shrugged because I'd been reading it for a couple of years. On his next visit, Dad gave me *The Complete Works of Shakespeare* and *The Collected Works of Dickens*. In the novel *A Christmas Carol*, Tiny Tim says on the final page, 'God bless us, every one!' Whereas in *The Women's Room*, I read that if an Adult touches a Kid inappropriately you tell your mum.

When I decide to tell her, Alison is with Eva. Eva is a single woman who has just moved here from Sheffield. Sometimes she and I play chess. Eva is no-nonsense, walks in shorts and boots. Her voice is clipped, her sentences cut as short as her brown hair. I open her door. Inside, Eva and Alison are drinking tea and I edge into the spartan room. There are stones in my mouth the size of whales. My feet drag at the carpet. I mumble, 'Hello, Alison. Hi, Eva.'

'Yes?' Alison answers, caught mid-conversation. 'What do you want?'

I turn bright red. 'You know when I slept in Lionel's Unit . . .' The words fall from my mouth incoherently.

Alison and Eva both say 'Yes'. They turn to me, expectantly, and I feel two pairs of pragmatic eyes travelling up and down my body. They stop at my face.

I say, 'Well . . . he massaged me and . . . and I didn't like it.'

Eva and Alison look at each other. They laugh. Alison says, 'If you don't like it, just tell him to stop.' Standing before them, I realize I must have said it wrong, and don't say anything else.

Instead, I walk slowly to the woods, and in a small clearing I stand by our fritillary. It is a fragile bloom, and we have been told, since we moved into the house, 'Be careful, this flower is a rare species and important to protect.' The fritillary grows, safeguarded by a small wooden fence, beneath an overhang of trees. We are not even allowed to touch it. Leaves rustle in the wind. Delicate white petals form a translucent bell. The flower head shivers in the breeze, and I think, *it had to happen.*

It is winter, early morning. Driving to an optician's appointment, I am thinking about writing this book. Outside, it is dark, and thick fog has descended. It deafens hedgerows and muffles streetlamps. The fog has stripped my route of familiar signs and landmarks. It is a soft, white blanket, blinding the landscape. All that is left is: road, fog, cars and light. With my landmarks hidden, I am bewildered. The only possibility is to follow the car in front, to stay between the markers on the road.

As I drive, I remember when, years ago, my mum was visiting me in France, and we went to a seaside town, a citadel. Seagulls swooped in the sky, and we walked around the ramparts, making laps, turning in circles on the stone. It was one of the only times I asked her about why she didn't react when I first told her about what had happened with Lionel. She looked at me with sadness in her eyes and said she was sorry and didn't remember that day. She explained she now regretted everything that had happened around the abuse, that it was such a different time then. On the ramparts, we stopped walking and looked out through an opening in the wall, a kind of window to the sea. In the distance, waves lapped at the shore.

On this foggy winter morning, as I remember our discussion, I get lost in the orbit of a roundabout I have driven round a hundred times before. I think about how conversations about the past are like ramparts. They involve systems of defence but we can get stuck inside, going round and round in laps, spiralling in a vortex, trying to find a way out. Trauma is like this, it pins us in time.

Yet, when I finally exit the roundabout, the fog starts to lift, and silvery tips of grass are caught in sunlight. It creeps into the sky. A new landscape, a fresh day on the cusp. As poet Etel Adnan said, 'Often we feel time to be linear, inexorable, suffocating. At other moments we find it oceanic . . . But there are also moments when time appears to be . . . both vertical and horizontal, both "single-minded", monotonous, inalterable, and multi-dimensional, infinite.'

In my car, I think all I can do is keep moving forwards, finding new perspectives in multi-dimensional dawns, laying the sentences down.

From now on, Lionel invades my days. In the Kitchen, or the garden, as soon as we are alone, he asks the questions: 'Don't you love me any more? Why don't you come and see me any more?'

However much I want to, I cannot return to his Unit, and I now jump, daily, between new skipping ropes: there is my loyalty towards Lionel, and the night in his Unit. I trip and fall between the cracks of these things and feel sick all the time. We talk in the English language about feeling at home in the body, but we can also feel uncomfortable in our own skin. When I am eleven, I feel stuck inside my own body, as though I am lost and terrified inside an abandoned, derelict building I entered by mistake.

Weeks later, I am at the pool with Lionel and his daughter. Despite searching, I couldn't find the words to refuse Lionel's offer to Alison to take me swimming. On the drive there, I end up sitting next to him. His daughter is in the back. His wife is not here. Lionel teases me as he drives the car. The road is lit in a haze of golden light. It bisects the countryside, cuts through lush green.

The swimming pool is freshly built, a modern pyramid of crystal glass, triangles filled with glaring light. High-pitched screams bounce off mosaic tiles. Kids are everywhere. The lifeguard blows his whistle, makes the swimmers obey the rules posted on the wall: do not dive-bomb; do not eat in the pool; no heavy petting.

The pool water is turquoise. The sky outside is button blue, and I am wearing Saskia's red swimming costume. Her costume is high-cut and made of a slinky material, like a scarlet snake. It does not fit me, and the costume slips off. My white wet breast is revealed, and a pink nipple. Lionel catches my eye. He gazes at my breast. Awkward and ashamed, I pull the costume up. 'Don't you love me any more?' Lionel's eyes twinkle. There are no rules to guide me against his words. For many weeks I am silent, a decaying silence.

It is mid-December, months later. On the radio, Band Aid, the supergroup of British and Irish pop musicians, are singing 'Do They Know It's Christmas?' to raise money for Ethiopian famine relief. In her bedroom, Claire and I play the Burning Down the House game. 'If the house were burning down what would you take?' I say. She looks over at me and gives me a superior smile, flicking a crimped fringe from her made-up eyes. Soft and dark browns have been stroked along her eyelids. Claire is so far above me I should be flat on the floor.

'If the house was burning . . . I would take my David Bowie autograph, all my records and my Billy Bragg interview!'

Claire's answer is impressive – she got to interview the singer Billy Bragg when we drove to Glastonbury Festival, travelling with Violet in our black cab. During the festival, Claire slipped inside the VIP tent and walked up to Billy, asked her questions face to face. She wants to be a journalist, to work for the *NME*.

'So . . .' Words trickle from her mouth; gloss picks out her bottom lip. 'What would *you* take if the house was burning down?'

The answer is on the tip of my tongue, and I race to tell her. 'If the house was burning down, I would take my secret box.'

Claire looks at me with disdain. 'But you haven't got one.'

'But I'll get one for Christmas.' I am convinced of this.

Anytime I am asked what I want for Christmas, I tell Alison, Eva, David, Bill and Sunshine: 'A secret box.' The idea of this thing makes me happy – a small wooden box with a key. My secrets inside.

'No, you won't!'

'I will.'

'Won't. And get out of my room now!' Her eyes crush me into place. I slump from her room, trying to hold my head high and failing.

On Christmas Day, I receive a box with a key. Over the next few years, I keep various things inside:

- An autographed photo of Brian Cant, a kids' TV presenter who I see live on stage
- A photo of Lionel, the man who sexually abuses me
- All the diaries that I will eventually write over the next three years
- A collection of bits of my body: scabs, toenail clippings, tufts of my hair, and folded sections of my sunburnt skin that I have delicately removed in paper-thin sheets

The latter are gruesome personal relics, and when I think of them now, they remind me of the religious practice of keeping body parts – like King Saint Stephen's thousand-year-old hand in Budapest cathedral. Inside my wooden box was a child's holy hoard. It was my treasure chest. Often, I wonder what it is that makes a trinket, or a body part, an object bound for worship, the incinerator or a museum display. How do we attribute value and meaning to things?

Freud believed that one of the reasons we collect is to regain control.

I kept my secret box for decades. After a while, the body parts were discarded, but the diaries and the photos stayed inside. Yet the box was not a museum; more like a cold storage from which objects could be brought back to life. These animistic things contained a certain power, and it was as though the bits and pieces that I kept were landmarks in my wild childhood wood. When put together, the stuff formed a kind of map or trail, like in 'Hansel and Gretel', a scattered line, and when I followed the path, it led to a place called home. A few years ago, I put the box up for sale on an antique stall, and it was such a joy when it was gone.

Over several months, I work with a Franco-Spanish client in the South of France. The woman has been hospitalized following a nervous breakdown and cannot stop speaking. She jumps from one subject to another in a form of hypomania. When I introduce the first exercise, I say, 'An artist called Schwitters said that art is making new things out of found fragments and the treasure we find by chance.' To begin, I take two folders containing various pieces of paper, and put them on the table. One folder is marked 'Words' and the other 'Pictures'.

'This is an improvised spontaneous exercise. You can choose as many images and words as you like. But try to take at least three from each side. There are no rules, no right or wrong. You're the boss. Take things you like, that catch your eye.'

She talks about a fire engine she saw on her way to the unit, about a friend, and about what she'll eat for her dinner. I suggest we work in silence so she can focus on selecting her images and words. On the table, there are pictures of a collapsed robot sculpture, a series of white marble jars, flowers, a black-and-white photograph of New York, a statue of a Roman emperor (possibly Caligula), snow-capped mountains, a mountain river, an aboriginal dot painting, seven geese flying across a pink sky . . . On other slips of paper are printed dozens of different words.

After a period of quiet thought, she takes two pictures: the mountain river and a photograph of flowers. From the piles of words, she takes a selection. I say, 'Right. Next week, we are going to try and put all this together.'

During the next session, in between more energetic conversation, she places the photo of the mountain river below the image of the flowers and puts the words together into a text.

The opening lines read:

The unopened flower, comes alive
From nowhere, if you're looking
see, the water flows

What I immediately sense in her work is an intellectual deftness, a subtle grace and flow, a sharp contrast to her disorganized communication. These contradictions are telling, for what is kept inside in contrast to what is revealed, what we keep safe and what we show to the world outside, are often defining signs. A lot of my person-centred clinical work is based on identifying and reinforcing inner strengths. These are often hidden, have been buried during traumatic events.

Freud wrote of art as a process of sublimation where unconscious conflicts are transformed into symbolic, cultural forms. Art therapy can be extraordinarily empowering, as inner stories emerge in a language that is unique. It gives voice to the person, inspiring interest instead of apathy, and raging beauty can replace despair. Over the next months, following my client's initiative, we explore art focused on flowers and botany. The woman begins talking about her life, scraps of conversation about her difficult past are caught in the morphology of flowers – corolla and petals, stems and whorls. We visit a botanical garden together, sketching rare rose blooms. Before she leaves the unit, stabilized and having found a job, we collect all her paintings, drawings and collages in a hand-bound artist's book that she entitles *The Language of Flowers*.

I am with Claire in her bedroom at the community. We have just got back from summer camp. For the second time, I went away with my friend Isa and camped in Wales. Because we are mature, Isa and I were put in a group with older kids, and I bought fags and smoked. Every day, I wore a scarf over my face, covering my mouth and nose. I felt awful, but I didn't tell Isa about Lionel because I didn't know what to say. One of the staff – who had met me the previous year – kept asking, 'Why are you wearing that scarf? Are you OK?' I always replied, 'Everything is fine,' because I have kept telling myself that, even if my stomach hurts constantly, I will win the fight. Yesterday, I smoked in a bus stop with Saskia, and this is being grown-up. But it feels like who I am is falling apart.

Claire puts on lipstick and ignores me. She's wearing skintight jeans and a black mohair jumper. I am wearing old beige trousers, bought from a jumble sale. With my V-necked woollen top and oversized pink plastic glasses, I am twelve but look like I am going on forty. When I see photos of me then, it is as though I have aged prematurely: there is a dimming of the lights, a kind of atrophy.

I say, 'Claire, you know Lionel?'

My heart beats, and I smell sweat. Out of nowhere, I have decided I should tell Claire what happened. Lionel has left the community now. When he went, I made sure I wasn't there to say goodbye.

'I was sexually abused by Lionel,' I tell Claire, and this is how I will tell people calmly for years to come. Occasionally, I laugh. I do not mention the clock, the sleepwalking or the months of Lionel's questioning. I might be twelve, but I am not a div, and that means I am not stupid. When I finish, I hear a plastic click as Claire returns her lipstick to its tube. 'You have to tell Alison.' Her words are underlined. There is something like horror in her eyes.

'But why? What for?'

'You have to tell her,' she insists.

I don't understand. Months have passed, and I have sorted things out; I put my terror in a bottle and threw it away. Since it happened, it is like I established my own government and my world is what Barbara calls an 'autarchy', meaning I am alone. It's taken a while, but in my mind I have a judge to deal with law and punishment. My judge has read R. D. Laing – who says the family makes people mad and who thinks communal living drives people sane – and feminist books by Kate Millett, and *Spare Rib*. Paradoxically, in the context of the utopia, what I conclude from these feminist and anti-psychiatric texts is that *these things happen*. It happened to Claire. Adding two and two together, I rationalize: the problem is society. This is the story that I tell myself, and there is no need to bother Mum.

Furious, Claire repeats, 'You have to!'

A few days later, I am in the van with Alison heading to the shopping centre. Apart from the Cowshed, the van is the only place we are alone. She reverses into a parking space.

'You know Lionel, who used to live in the house?'

'Yes.' She is checking mirrors.

'Well. He sexually abused me, he touched my breasts and . . .'

When I look, I see Mum's face has crumpled. All of a sudden, she is saying that Lionel is a shit and shouldn't have done that to a little kid. Mum never swears. She sounds angry. We undo our seatbelts and get out and walk into the shopping centre. Mum doesn't ask me any questions and I say no more. The conversation is over because conversations with Mum are often short. I am relieved because I have told her. Once we are inside, she unexpectedly takes me out for French pancakes. They are surrounded by a smooth lake of melted chocolate sauce. It is an unheard-of treat. Afterwards, she buys me a grey thermal vest, with wide shoulder straps. That night, I write in my diary, 'Alison is an amazing mum, I love her, not just because she buys me things, but because she is Alison.' She survived Rachel and Dad leaving. These are the hardest things, and I believe in her; my love is immutable.

I read in the newspaper about an English violinist who, following the trial of her sexual abuser, committed suicide. She was forty-five, with children and a successful career. Her friends said, 'She was dynamic, had no fear.' The heart of this story touches me. I want people to live, and I begin to wonder about points of resistance. In therapy, we can describe resistance as the technique a client uses to avoid addressing their issues. However, what I am describing here refers instead to the medical definition of 'points of resistance', being any characteristic of an organism that lessens the effect of an adverse environmental factor, such as disease or infection – resisting harmful influences. These are inner strengths.

In identifying my own points of resistance, I think of covering the alarm clock with socks, and I wonder, was I trying to get control of time, was a part of me refusing to submit? Resistance is different to resilience. In psychological terms, resilience describes the capacity to remain calm during crises and to move on from the incident, supposedly without long-term consequences.

In the occidental mental health field, resilience has been popular since the seventies, lauded by psychiatrists such as Emmy E. Werner and Boris Cyrulnik. Yet to me, resilience often feels more about crisis management: 'Keep calm and carry on!' Being resilient, I think, is a useful skill shared by professionals who work in care and disaster. Disaster expert Professor Lucy Easthope explains that after disasters the 'demobbing' is the toughest part of the gig – trying to fit back into family life. This is why resilience is not enough for individual victims of trauma, because, as Easthope describes, the hardest part of working in disaster 'is going home'. Resilience helps you work and survive but it does not teach you how to 'be'.

In comparison, resistance is to make an internal or external stand against; to oppose. In my clinical work, resistance is often a source of pleasure or curiosity for clients. Frequently we begin our art-therapy work from a person's points of resistance, translating their strengths. In this way, the Franco-Spanish client chose flowers, while another middle-aged woman I worked with revealed she had been a majorette in childhood, and during sessions we restaged her routines. An illiterate man had once been in a school play, and this gave him the confidence, years later, to perform with other clients, acting the part of Oberon in *A Midsummer Night's Dream*.

Resistance also means a covert opposition to a ruling power. Resistance is often hidden. The word 'resist' comes originally from the Latin *stare*, 'to stand', and *sistere*, 'to stop'. Aged twelve, I was an obedient, willing and well-behaved child, yet despite my clear adherence to community values, something inside me stood firm.

When we're in our twenties, Claire explains the horror she felt when she discovered Lionel had abused me. She says, 'I thought history was repeating itself. I didn't want you to be tarred with the same brush after what happened to me in India. You were so innocent. I didn't want you to be soiled.' As we sip tea, she continues, calmly, 'You know, for years afterwards, I wondered how to retaliate. I decided I would take self-defence classes, find Lionel, and then I would disguise myself, wear a wig, make-up, and a sexy dress. I would meet Lionel, seduce him, and then humiliate and hurt him.'

Claire laughs lightly and runs her fingers through her hair. Years later, with her permission, I turn her idea into a short story. While, of course, I am not advocating physical violence, it was a sweet form of revenge: a tale of resistance.

9. I Want to Break Free

'The likelihood that your acts of resistance cannot stop the injustice does not exempt you from acting in what you sincerely and reflectively hold to be the best interests of your community.'
Susan Sontag, *At the Same Time: Essays and Speeches*

'Where there is power, there is resistance.'
Michel Foucault, *The History of Sexuality, Volume 1: An Introduction*

Every week, from the age of seven, I walk the twenty minutes to the local library, and I borrow four books. My path takes me past the greengrocer's, the newsagent's, the butcher's, the baker's, the bank, the post office, and across the town square – where the bad fox hunt meets every Sunday. The library is tucked behind a multicoloured, striped house owned by the local 'mad' man. Dressed in pirate's clothes with silk ribbons plaited in his hair, he nods at me when I go into the library, and I smile back but not too much. It is always better to keep a distance, even if we are both aliens, skirting on the rim of this country town.

Inside the library, high walls are lined with books, and when I've read all the Children's section, the librarian lets me take the Adult books, but only the Classics. Back in my room at the community, I read for hours. Reading is one of my forms of resistance. Most of the Kids are preteens now, and I should be playing snooker, or fighting over the Atari – a treasured possession provided by Sunshine and Troy's grandparents – to play Pac-Man, or pairing up to imagine secret signs for the card game Kemps. But instead I have a new book, *When Hitler Stole Pink Rabbit* by Judith Kerr. Jason calls me 'four-eyes' because I have to wear the ugly free NHS glasses – and it seems I read too much. But I cannot stop. Books are my home, and when you turn the cover, you close one door and open another, moving to imagined worlds. My reading takes me into Frances Hodgson Burnett's *A Little Princess* and Carlos Fuentes's novel *Aura*, a paperback I find in the Lounge, about a beautiful woman decomposing inside her dilapidated house.

Brandy roller-skates through my bedroom, and I don't even notice when I am inside rags-to-riches tales like *The Railway Children* or *Ballet Shoes*, where poor, talented girls chance upon old, bearded men. Encounters change fortunes and decent girls avoid tragedy because sacrifice means you get redemption. In a good book, when the words join up like the carriages of a train, you feel the words become a story.

In Laura Ingalls Wilder's books *Farmer Boy* and *Little House on the Prairie*, there is ice cream stored in a haybox, a dugout house, and apple pie. At the time I am reading them, the colonial racist pioneer narrative has not yet been questioned and instead I drift into stories of new beginnings, and people hand-milking cows like Alison does.

Because of this book, I drink mugfuls of raw milk with every meal, until it makes me sick and I stop. In between, I reread *The Women's Room*, and Andrea Dworkin's essay 'The Rape Atrocity', stories of women's bodies and abuse. Then mythical books: *The Dark Is Rising*, *The Brothers Lionheart* – because it has dead siblings – and *A Wizard of Earthsea*, where I learn about good and evil, and the importance of naming, of the words we choose.

Sometimes I read so much I cannot tell the difference between what has happened to me or to a character. Me and the reading become one thing. John Berger spoke about how our images of an alternative life 'call out to us wherever we go, whatever we read, wherever we are . . . They come with us everywhere, we take them away in our minds'. We see them in our dreams.' Books are mirrors I permeate.

My daughters do this too. 'Who are you?' they ask each other, having watched a film, a TV series, or read a book. When you are a child, it is important to decide which character you are. They identify and inhabit these imaginary worlds. 'Which House are you in in Hogwarts?' my daughters ask, when they respectively read through the seven Harry Potter volumes. This House question will obsess them, and all their friends, because the House that is chosen for them by the hat will be the home where they belong.

'As this is your last year in primary school, children, you will be taking secondary-school selective exams.' Our teacher explains that pupils who pass this exam will get a place at the state grammar school.

The exam tests how we think. Thinking and imagining

are some of the things I like best. Imagining is, as Gaston Bachelard writes, 'not the capacity to make new things but to transform our perceptions of the world outside'. With imagination, you can do anything, and I imagine the grammar school will be different to my life in the community, as well as my primary school. This is a point of resistance.

At school, I now barely have any friends. At playtime, I look after the little children and we play. In the classroom, I sit on my own, and Mary and Paul no longer talk to me. There is a gap between us, we are no longer friends, and Brandy and I are also often apart. At weekends, I write to Isa and tell her what I am doing: reading, rehearsing for plays, or riding my bike with Sunshine. But at school, people call me weird, and it is strange, this solitude, because a child's solitude is a stone. In the palm of your hand, it is insignificant. A stone is a small loneliness, but it contains the history of everything.

That autumn, the IRA try to assassinate the Conservative cabinet in the Brighton hotel bombing, and in big letters newspapers shout: 'A calendar of carnage!' Margaret Thatcher escapes, but five other people are killed. Bombs from the Troubles explode every year for years, and there are nail bombs, kneecappings, and the British Army shoot the innocent. Claire sings 'Sunday Bloody Sunday' by U2, which is about the British military killing protesting women and children. The Brighton bomb blast brings down a five-ton chimney stack, which crashes through the hotel floors into the basement, leaving a gaping hole in the hotel's façade, and I will remember the arc of this ruin and the ragged edges exposing the inside. The smoke, the disaster, the flashing lights.

The world is always ending somewhere, but at school I am usually top of the class. The teacher tells us we will begin practising for the exam, and we fill pages with triangles and cubes, complete patterns with straight lines and curves. Sequences are established. Logical conclusions. The exam tests what they call non-verbal reasoning. If A stands with B and then marries C, has 2.4 children in a mortgaged semi-detached house, eats processed food, votes Thatcher, and works nine-to-five, should A have an affair with the neighbour because s/he takes antidepressants, and their way of life is oppressive?

If I pass the exam, the logical conclusion is that I go to the grammar school, wear a blazer with a gold embroidered pocket, am tutored in Latin and Greek, and get to Oxford. In this future, I can be like Grandma Bella even if she is dead, because she is the only person in the family who I think is like me. I understand things too quickly, and it is not easy being like that. Claire hates me for it. 'Clever clogs,' she says. She failed the exam, and fights with Alison all the time, whereas I am a 'good girl'. Claire says she hates the community, but I tell her it is like anywhere else. I fight with Claire and she pushes me against our Unit corridor wall, gripping my wrists, and it hurts.

Recently, she got caught shoplifting and she is 'going through a bad phase'. She has mixtapes with Duran Duran's 'The Reflex', 'Relax' by Frankie Goes To Hollywood, and songs by Queen. When Claire and I are getting on, we sing a Queen song together, 'I Want to Break Free', about lies and things being real, because we both know about reality. But passing the exam would mean I could become a child who succeeds. The thought is as exciting as falling in love. This could be my real life.

When I get home, in the Kitchen, I tell Alison the exam news. But Barbara, Eva and Charles join in our conversation and it feels like the Adults speak as one. They criticize the exam system as biased because the children who fail go to the local comprehensive school, and must leave school at sixteen, and if you are a girl you are told to be a secretary, and if you are a boy a mechanic. Claire failed the exam and has not gone to the local comprehensive but to an alternative comprehensive thirty minutes' drive away. This radical school has over 2,000 pupils. It is radical because you call the teachers by their first names, the school trips are to India, and anyone can get in, even pupils who have been expelled.

Barbara is stirring lumpy parsnip soup. 'The local system is inegalitarian and sexist. Everyone should have a chance. And boys can be hairdressers. Girls can mend cars.'

Eva is kneading bread. 'You cannot predict a person's future based on exams taken at twelve.'

Charles adds, 'The system discriminates against children, is elitist, sociologically orientated to maintaining the class system.' Charles is divorced, and his tennis-playing son, Karl, is at private school. At the community, most of the Adults were privately educated. They went to boarding schools, read Homer, played hockey, and ate lunch while speaking French.

The days pass, and I wait for the exam but I hide my excitement, tell no one my plans. Since the events with Lionel, I've packed parts of myself away. My phosphorescence is fading. It lacks bright light. There is an outer coating of brutal pragmatism growing around my skin. I repeat to myself: *I will be reasonable, and accept whatever happens.*

Often, when I work with patients who have been sexually or physically abused, I see this kind of hard resignation, a shoulder shrug towards reality. It is easier to imagine the worst and talk about it stoically; it is a handy defence mechanism against the pain. A few years ago, in New York, I worked in a psychiatric hospital with an exceptionally talented young man who had suffered physical abuse during his childhood, and had chronic agoraphobia. He brought me his notebooks so I could see his drawings, some of which were of imaginary, complex buildings reaching into the sky. He blushed when I turned the pages offering compliments. I asked whether he'd thought of studying architecture, as I knew he came from a financially stable family who could help fund such a plan.

'Of course not. I'll never come to anything. I'm too unstable. But anyway, I can look at architecture books instead.'

'But what about all the people you'd meet, and the stimulation, and the time to work,' I replied. 'I am playing devil's advocate, but I think you'd thrive.'

When I said this, there was a sudden small light in his eyes, because another person's belief in our unique potential helps set us free.

*

When I am twelve, my teachers and the mothers at the gate tell me, 'You will easily pass the exam.' And I know I can, and I could wear the blazer, and get in the bus with other children who like books. But inside me, there is a battle between hope and functionality, dream and machine, me and society.

'You can do anything,' Tripti told me before she left, and it is an odd paradox in the utopian community: we are told we can do anything. This anything feels like it can be everywhere and be all things at all times. But this anything is held inside the walls and does not include everything. The house is tinged with an anti-intellectual strain, and achievement is not acceptable because it means you are different to the collective. There are certain things, like winning short-story competitions, that mustn't count. All selection is vilified.

Despite this, over the years I continue to enter all kinds of competitions, often covertly, as if to test my luck. Secretly, I am possessed with ambition, determination, and a raging curiosity to find my place in the world. That summer, I enter, for the last time, the County Show children's classes. In a huge field, decorated with bunting, cows are inspected, dogs are groomed, and I go into a white tent and display the things I've made:

1. A miniature garden on a tray with moss, tiny trees, flower petals, and a small lake fashioned from a mirror
2. A potato man in a pirate costume
3. A flower arrangement
4. A poem I wrote about spring
5. A fruitcake

For the fifth consecutive year, I win the trophy, engraved with the words 'Bequeathed by Lord and Lady for Overall Winner in the Children's Classes'. But that day, I walk in the sun for too long, without sun cream and in blue shorts that are a size too small. The shorts – which I found under the stairs – cut red lines into my legs. I eat five Lemfizz ice lollies bought from an ice-cream van because they are the cheapest thing on sale, walk the three miles home, carrying my silver cup, and then vomit, repeatedly.

One of the challenges of finding a way out of the community was that the doors to this world were closed. This is one of the issues with the utopian model; not the idea of change or of inventing new social models, but the withdrawal. Inside utopias the need to conform can become intransigent. Recently I talked to an American psychiatrist friend about this, and she said to me, 'When you are a child growing up in a close-knit intergenerational dysfunctional family, or a group like you did, you conform to survive. It can take years to acknowledge what went wrong, undo behaviour and relearn how to be yourself,' and she referred to a patient whose family were in a survivalist cult. 'During therapy, it was as though she had to relive the different stages of childhood to finally grow up and become her adult self.'

Surrounded by a changing cast of forty other people, finding my way in the community was difficult, and I think this is one of the reasons it has taken me years, after leaving the house – and not until I have had my own children – to confront what happened there.

*

When I talk to my partner about his own points of resistance inside his home, I expect him to respond with ease. Instead, he describes the difficulties of growing up inside a suburban house where his mother ran a hairdressing salon next to his bedroom, and his father installed a tailor's workshop below.

In the morning, he would wake up to the hum of his father's sewing machine, and then have to face the clients in the hairdressing room. There was a constant to-and-fro of customers, and as the two businesses concerned hair and clothes, everyone had to look their best. I picture him, a teenage boy having just woken up, being summoned by his mum to greet clients, edging into the hairdressing room, the stink of ammonia in the air. In the mirror, he'd see the customer's head, his mother and himself reflected. He says, 'There was such a lack of privacy. It was awful sometimes, like living in a shop.'

I wonder, if this is what now makes us both a little *sauvage*, wild – in the French sense, meaning slightly antisocial. For even though I love groups and am a 'people person', in our home, A and I are reclusive.

That spring, a TV journalist comes to the community to interview us about what is now called 'alternative living'. She has red lips, sleek black hair, and wears bug-eyed shades that she never removes. Gliding between rooms dressed in vampish clothes, like a punk Isadora Duncan, the journalist directs romantic scenes. In the Lounge, Sunshine plays the grand piano. Notes of Debussy's *Suite bergamasque* float in the dusty air. In front of the camera, when asked about our life, I say, 'Living here has its good points and its bad points. It's like any way of life.' For fifteen years I always say the same thing. This is our 'newspeak': a term coined by George Orwell in *Nineteen Eighty-Four* to describe propagandistic language characterized by the elimination of certain words and the use of abbreviations. The goal of newspeak is to reduce language and narrow the range of thought. Over the years, we learn, through a kind of slow osmosis, from overhearing the Adults and repeating their words, that our house 'is like any home' and 'living here is normal'. It is an understandable attempt by the Adults to counter the marginalization, or stereotypification, of our utopian way of life. But it is also a lie.

The day of the exam, papers are distributed. Brandy and I tick, draw and write. I am nervous but I enjoy it; the logical conclusions, the playfulness of speed. Mary sits in front of me. Her black hair swishes right and left. After it is over I want to talk to her, but in the end I say nothing.

The test we take is based, I will later learn, on the research of a man called Cyril Burt, who claimed he had proven that identical twins, separated at birth, would still maintain the same level of achievement. His research appears to show that intelligence is something you are born with, not something that is learnt. Environment doesn't matter. The community Adults don't agree, and later Burt's evidence will be shown to have been falsified.

We wait weeks for the results. In June, they finally arrive. In the Post Room, I tear open the envelope, and I have passed.

This is my chance. Through newspapers, novels and the TV, I've learnt grammar schools are elevators, escalators, a way to break free. That evening, in our Unit, Alison congratulates me, but then she tells me I'll have to go to the comprehensive because we don't believe in the selective process or class inequality. She doesn't ask me what I want, and there is no discussion. As she talks, I don't know what to say. It feels like the world is breaking into tiny pieces. In her room, everything turns to floating dust: the platform bed, the spider plants, and the books on the shelves. Despite all the communal discussions, I thought I stood a chance of passing the exam and going to the grammar school. When I walk out of her room, I am so disappointed. The verb 'disappoint' comes from the fifteenth-century *disappointen*, meaning 'to dispossess of an appointed office', or else from the Old French for 'to be removed'.

Yet even as my dream is disappearing, as the hours pass I need this disappearance to make sense. That evening I try to find a rational explanation: Claire failed and so did Brandy, Jason, and Saskia; I am the only child at the community to have passed. But things cannot be different for me. It would be inegalitarian. We must take a stand against the system.

Dad does not agree. On the telephone, incredulous, he asks, 'But, where will you go to school?'

I repeat what Alison has told me, that I am going to the alternative comprehensive, and he sighs. Claire goes there already, and when she hears that I have passed the exam, we fight like cats and dogs; she calls me a 'lord' because I am a snob to have succeeded, and I start to call her a 'peasant'.

So I try explaining to Dad, and I think it will help but it

doesn't when I say, 'It's biased.' Finally he sighs again and says goodbye. It is as though he lost the right to oppose Alison's decisions when he walked out the door all those years ago. That night I can barely sleep.

At the school gate the following morning, the mummies hiss like geese: 'Well done! You and Mary are the only pupils to succeed. You clever girls.' I mumble, 'I won't be going,' and they ask, 'But why?' They come closer, surround me with their pecking beaks. I say, 'My mum doesn't believe in the system. It's an unfair way to decide children's futures.' But inside me, it hurts to say this thing. My script was written by someone else. I'm saying a thing I believe in, but don't believe in, and betrayal is happening twice. The Look spreads among the mums; outrage and gossip light their smiles. But I feel like my words are shameful. Sartre said shame happens the day we become aware of the look of the other.

That evening, Barbara jokes to Alison, 'If we are really looking for equality, all the Kids at the community should go to the local comprehensive. They should leave at sixteen and become hairdressers and mechanics.' Alison laughs because I'll be going to the alternative comprehensive, and even if we reject the grammar system there is no way any of the community Kids would go to the local school. But I feel sick inside.

At this moment, there is no differentiation between intention and impact, between the intention of justly protesting against an unfair system and the impact of a parent seeming to prioritize politics above their own child. As parents we constantly make complicated, life-changing decisions for our children that they often passively accept. Yet what was different in the community was that politics *and* group compliancy ruled. We were told to consciously renunciate the self, and submit to the collective good. When I think of what happened around this exam, it reminds me of what a leader from the Khmer Rouge once said: 'Zero for him, zero for you, that is true equality.' Possibly the most damaging impact on me was believing I came second to the crowd.

In *The Life of the Mind*, Hannah Arendt explored the problematic area of how we are led to take the wrong decisions. Thinking (for example, what we believe to be right and wrong) must be flexible and based on experience, which prevents it from becoming ideology. Ideologies divorce thinking from experience. Ideology removes people from the present, and even well-meaning actions become senseless. According to Arendt, thinking allows us to give meaning to our lives. Thinking can be what makes us act, it can be what makes us love.

In my own house today, our three children have been educated at different schools, according to their interests and needs. These differences have extended to their after-school activities. All three are musical, but one had classical French training in a conservatoire, the second attended a local 'rock school' and plays in a band, the youngest was taught by her two elder sisters. When they were babies, as I'd had voice training, I sang to them as I breastfed, dressed them and changed their nappies. Today, our house is filled with music: trombones, rap, ukulele, Benjamin Britten, and songs from all the Barbie cartoons. Over the past ten years, my daughters have sung a cappella together. During Covid, they performed over Zoom for international cabarets; they sing at local events and for family and friends. Their three different voices join: one deep and earthy, the second clear and pure, and the third steady and calm. Each is differently trained but they are complementary. Sometimes they do mash-ups of tacky princess animation songs, and their three voices are one.

During that summer break after primary school, I dream of the grammar school incessantly. On hot days, I lie in an ocean of grass, and imagine things being different. My sister teases me in the corridor, and I shout 'Peasant!' Brandy and I grow closer, and we talk about Sunshine behind her back. 'She is so fake,' I tell Brandy. 'Thinks she can play the piano. So posh.' We giggle, and I know I am being mean, but I do not stop. While I am away at summer camp with Isa, I picture myself carrying a leather satchel, wearing my knee-length uniform. Isa is going to an all-girls school, and I wish that I could go to a school like hers. Even if it is politically wrong, every night in our tent I imagine myself at the grammar school.

That summer, my 'self' is overwhelmed by all the contradictions between what I want and what is happening. The philosopher Jacques Derrida didn't believe in one true identity. We are all made up of different threads, and sometimes it is complex to gather them together. But if our different selves are too polarizing, too paradoxical, we struggle to find a coherent shape, a 'home' self where we can stretch out and daydream.

As July turns to August, I am overwhelmed by these oppositions, and experience an odd, silent, solitary, desperate wishing. It happens on the front lawn, and by the redwoods, and when I help Walker pick buckets of sweet strawberries in the garden. We eat them with fresh whipped cream from our Jersey cows, and Tina is there, and when no one is looking I pinch her. She cries, but when she blames me, I pretend that she is lying.

Up until the very night before the new term starts in September, I truly believe Alison will change her mind, will turn to me and say that of course I can go to the grammar school, and grow inside this world I have fabricated in my mind.

But when I wake up it is my first day at the experimental comprehensive. My grammar school dream is abandoned. That morning, I put on jeans, a T-shirt, and eat homemade brown bread. For thirty minutes, in the van, we drive through the countryside, until we reach the dual carriageway and then the new school. When we arrive, all the community Kids separate in the car park, and I am no longer with Brandy. As I walk through the swinging doors alone, I think that I can reinvent myself. I put the smart blazer and the Latin books away in my dream attic, and I decide this is a new country. I will not give up. Here, I will become someone completely different. Someone else.

10. The Gong

'In the case of sociology, however, we are always walking on hot coals, and the things we discuss are alive, they're not dead and buried.'
Pierre Bourdieu, *The Sociologist and The Historian*

'It is the worst of community that it must inevitably transform into charlatans the leaders, by the endeavour continually to meet the expectation and admiration of this eager crowd of men and women seeking they know not what.'
Ralph Waldo Emerson on utopian communities, in *Historic Notes of Life and Letters in New England*

Often, I wonder about why we need to imagine utopias – perfect families, societies and lives. Yet spend time with any group of Western liberal people, and eventually someone will joke about 'moving to a commune'. It is a popular fantasy, and very appealing: to live off-grid, escape the rat race, and share the burdens of life. For centuries, thinkers, artists and writers have experimented with these ideal worlds. In the mid-nineteenth century, in America, Ralph Waldo Emerson toyed with joining the Brook Farm commune, but finally declined as 'solitude is more prevalent and beneficent than the concert of crowds'.

Frequently, I feel torn as I read and research, as I believe in equality and collective responsibility. I am also motivated by people inventing new ways of being, and I understand Anna Neima's belief that utopian movements are inspiring because they 'refuse to accept the shortcomings of the world and the impossibility of change'. Utopian worlds lay bare what is wrong with the real one.

Yet etymologically, the word 'utopia', I remind myself, means nowhere, and 'nowhere' is core to utopian communities' identities. They often strip themselves of history, refuse to learn from what came before. In 1872, Samuel Butler wrote a satire called *Erewhon* – an anagram of the word 'nowhere' – about the utopian aspirations of Victorian society. His book also inspired a 2017 episode of the science-fiction TV series *Doctor Who*, taking place on a planet where robots only communicate using emojis. Everyone must be happy or die.

Thoreau questioned this blanket idealism in Brook Farm members, and wrote in his journal: 'As for the communities I think I had rather keep bachelors quarters in hell than go to board in heaven.' This is perhaps the underlying weakness of any utopia – not the values it upholds but the tyrannical drive for success.

Charles has made what he calls 'whore's spaghetti', spaghetti alla puttanesca: pasta coated with tomatoes, olive oil, garlic and olives. When Charles is cooking, we always sign in to meals, writing our names on the board, because his food is edible. I've just come down from Mia's Unit. She recently arrived in the community with her football-obsessed brother Peter, her mum, and Max, her new stepdad. In the last few weeks, other Kids have moved in; our number is spiralling, multiplying. Ophelia has a bedroom which is so rarely cleaned she has a colony of escaped gerbils inside. Sally (and sometimes her brother Ruskin) has come to live with her dad, Jim, the therapist. Little Sally wanders freely round the house for days, dressed in pink pyjamas. She gets lost and cries for her daddy, and Jim often tells me, 'Adults do things because of what happened in their youth, in their past. It is a very damaging time.' Karl moves in to live with his dad, Charles. He only stays for a while, like Margaret, an American girl who calls the community home for half a year, and later writes me letters from Detroit, always signed, 'Margaret, still a virgin'. A while after, Sasha comes, and others who I don't remember, and in the back corridors the Adults start to groan, 'There are too many Kids.'

In the Kitchen, Charles says, 'Do you want to ring the Gong for dinner?' I take the Gong from under the stairs, and walking around the house, I hit it.

Traditionally, gongs are percussion instruments originating from Asia. Flat metal discs, they are hit with mallets, other objects, or hands. In certain cultures, such as the Central Highlands of Vietnam, gongs are part of spiritual practice, connecting humans and divinities. In the Central Highlands, each household owns a gong and gongs are linked to the cycle of time. Usually, the gongs are played collectively, accompanying marriage ceremonies, celebrating pregnancy or the building of a new house, welcoming newborns, or announcing the departure of a dead person's soul. In some groups, each instrument is believed to contain the spirit of a god. The gongs sound the world.

I am wearing a knee-length skirt and my enamel rainbow-cat brooch. Sunshine gave me the brooch for my thirteenth birthday. Sunshine never goes to school, and I miss her when she travels with Eagle and Troy. Recently, we went to a Scottish cottage together, and in the evenings we meditated, imagining rainbows around the house. I told Sunshine that Brandy said she was 'posh'; I lied, but I don't know what else to do. The lying rises inside me. At the cottage, Eagle cooked us dinner, and talked to a visiting friend about AIDS, the new disease that has killed Rock Hudson, and how homelessness is on the rise again. On a shelf, I found the book *Mister God, This Is Anna*, the story of a four-year-old runaway and her friendship with the author, Fynn. The book deals with spirituality and religion. It also suggests that most people will be blind to the beauty you perceive; they will not understand your meaning in the world. To live is also to be alone. When I read it, it makes me cry.

Six months have passed since I took the exam, abandoned the grammar school dream, and started my new school. It is about two years since what happened with Lionel, and I have a short, pageboy haircut, like Princess Diana. But my flick will not hold, and will never hold. The new school is in a new town, where everything shines bright and there is a shopping centre. 'It's a plastic and concrete town,' we joke at school, because the town emerged from nowhere like an oasis in the desert. In the new town, they built the radical school. Some teachers are motivated, but others are weird.

At our school, everyone is a 'casual'. That is the style, and you have to fit in. In the papers, they write about the Cambridge 'Main Firm' football supporters: smartly dressed thugs, eighties casuals in expensive sportswear. At a recent match in Luton, eighty-one people were injured in a riot when boys in Pringle jumpers, with baseball bats, threw bottles, cans and nails. When you dress like a casual you can be like a yuppie, trading in the City, or you can be in a bottle fight.

Despite everything, I'm trying to make friends here and to be a casual, but I need hairspray, blond streaks, a white jean jacket, frosted lipstick, and a zillion other things that I do not have, like hot water and an iron. My body is gawky, and I constantly stoop, but I bang the Gong anyway.

Erik Erikson proposed a theory of psychosocial development consisting of eight stages of development of identity and personality, from infancy to adulthood. During each stage the person experiences a psychosocial crisis, which can be positive or negative in terms of personality development and the formation of identity. According to Erikson, development of a sense of self or identity is the central task of adolescence. Being a teenager is like living in a home that is constantly evolving, as though you wake up in the morning and all the rooms have been moved around and you get lost inside yourself.

At the radical comprehensive, the teacher asks us to make a Retrograph, documenting backwards from 1985 to our birth, including personal and world events. We are learning sociology instead of history, so we will understand we are shaped by society and that what happens to us is because of the world. We must link outer events to ourselves. In sociology, it feels like what happens outside is more important than the inside, the group stronger than the individual.

Major Events

1985 The miners' strike ends.	My baby sister was born.
1984 Los Angeles Olympics. Goverments paid extra attention to Third World.	Dad gave us our grandparents' old Mini.
1983 Curfew in Sri Lanka.	My grandma and granddad died within months of each other. I took the secondary school exam. Another documentary was made about our house (*the community*). My baby brother was born.
1982 Martial law in Poland. Earth tremor. Falklands War.	My cat got run over. I stopped Brownies.
1981 Brixton riots.	My dad married again. We bought a dog. The cat ate the gerbil. I started acting lessons, was in a play.

1980 Russian Olympics (boycotted).	My sister bought a gerbil. My mum got a boyfriend.
1979 Russians invade Afghanistan.	My dad got a girlfriend. My dad moved again and took Minnie (the cat) with him.
1978 Dustmen strike.	Our family moved to the community. My dad moved to a flat.
1977 Undertakers' strike.	I was the Queen in a school play.
1976 The vast drought.	I learnt to swim. We bought a cat called Johannes. Started school.
1975 End of Vietnam War. Sex Discrimination Act introduced.	We bought our cat Minnie. I started playgroup. I stayed in Moorfields Eye Hospital for three weeks for two operations.
1974 Miners' strike. Two general elections.	I caught pneumonia and nearly died. My dad and mum got divorced. My brother was born.
1973 Britain enters EEC.	I said my first sentence: 'Where has it gone?'
1972 A state of emergency is declared by the prime minister because of the miners' strike.	I was born in April. After four months, we moved. My sister died, a brick wall fell on her. Her name was Rachel.

As I wander down the corridors, hitting the Gong, hormones whizz round my body. The vibrations are like the changes in my body, radiating into my core. Gongs typically produce not just sounds but also 'soundings' – that is, sounds that extend in time. A gong continues to reverberate after it is hit and gradually softens into silence.

This is like the rides at Alton Towers, an amusement park. It is the first one in Great Britain, and I've never been. Claire went, and she told me she was in a rollercoaster seat with a metal thing that went over her head. The car went slowly up and then there was a fall. I imagine her, the pit dropping in her stomach, and Claire plunging, hair on end, screaming with terror and joy. When you are a teenager, being alive is electric. Everything reverberates.

By the Dark Room, I stop as the light is on, and I wonder if David is inside because he is often here. You can't walk into the Dark Room but must knock on the door. It is one of the only rooms with this rule, because negatives are made into photographs, and if you open the door at the wrong time you destroy the process. Inside, red bulbs light the darkness; from trays of wet chemicals, slippery pictures are born. David says, 'The photograph is a weapon against fucking oblivion.' There are pictures of us in the woods, of picnics on lawns; the Christmas photos pile up in the corner. The pictures catch the present, and we look at them in the future while we try to remember the past.

On the blank side of the photographs, David writes down names. 'Who was that?' he asks me. Men, women and children are identified. First, in black-and-white, Lawrence in dungarees, Barbara in flares. Everyone has long hair, drapes of hair pulled back with leather bands. In the snow, people lean like trees in thick knitted jumpers. Cameras focus on Bill's boots and Thomas's beard. Click. Outside, the Falklands War rages for two months. Protestors march against Thatcher and nuclear weapons. Peace women say: *Shoot us if you dare.* Tripti has a baby on her hip. Saskia smiles. Tina cries. The European Court of Human Rights rules that schools in Britain cannot allow corporal punishment against the wishes of parents.

In the Dark Room, David laughs, says 'Do you remember when . . . ?' There is a photo of Thomas and a visitor dressed up for Christmas as pantomime dames, with frilly skirts and fake breasts. Meanwhile, in the Hyde Park and Regent's Park bombings, the Provisional IRA kills eight soldiers. The first compact disc goes on sale. In the next photograph, some people have left and others have arrived. Walker has short blond hair. Lawrence's dark curls are cut. Charles wears sunglasses and smokes a cigar. Punks appear. Colour photos. Derek has hedgehog spikes, and what he calls 'fuck-off eyes'. Saskia's blue hair is shaved at the sides. She wears skin-slick trousers, and a black-and-red-striped jumper. I am twelve, in a silk evening gown and heels found at a jumble sale. David tells me, 'Lucky I control myself, I just want to fuck you.' Click. That year, the miners strike against government plans to close twenty coal mines across Britain. Five hundred people stampede for one job. In London Zoo an upside-down elephant dies trying to stand up, the pill celebrates its twenty-fifth birthday: the answer to every maiden's prayer. More photos, and the Kids are older, the Adults plumper.

Currys sell colour TVs with video machines. Riots in Birmingham escalate, leaving two people dead. Then, we are teenagers; a crowd, an awkward gang by the photo's edge.

I hit the Gong harder and harder. A teenager with a Gong is a mighty force. Bang. Gongs became part of domestic life in Britain during the Victorian era, echoing the colonial and class divisions present at that time. Gongs were part of the colonial tradition of collecting (or stealing) objects from other cultures. In Victorian homes, where timekeeping was paramount, gongs were rung by maids and butlers, signalling dinner and dressing-hours for members of the upper class. In the community the Gong has been given a socialist meaning, in the way the Soviet revolutionary habitats appropriated old things to accommodate new meanings. There is a superimposition of old and new hierarchies. The past reverberates into our present, even if we pretend otherwise. In the pages of Samuel Butler's anti-utopian *Erewhon*, in each perfect household there is no music, but rather 'half a dozen large bronze gongs, which the ladies used occasionally to beat about at random. It was not pleasant to hear . . .'

In the community, it is often the Kids that ring the Gong, and I walk up the stairwell, and glance through our Unit's windows towards my bedroom. Inside are my books, secret box, and clothes. Since I opened the doors and ran into my new school, I have shapeshifted. I've started going to parties, and buying *Just Seventeen*, fingerless gloves, and cigarettes. At the new school, I've made friends, but I flit between groups, between the 'nice girls', the 'maths boys' and the outsiders. On weekends, I call Isa and sometimes I get the train and go to stay at her house. It is a special friendship, outside of everything. Regularly, Saskia and I puff cigarettes in the bus stop. We have become occasional mates. Saskia is trying to get me to bleach my hair and sniff poppers, because these drugs make your heart crash. Your body jumps round a room.

Beside my bed is a new book, *Slake's Limbo*, about a desperate kid living in the New York City subway. The bird of fear flutters in his throat, but Slake scavenges enough trash to decorate the tunnel's forgotten construction room. He befriends a subway driver who dreams of being a shepherd. Slake inspires me, because I like the idea of finding stuff, and making beauty from what has been lost and broken.

This book is like the survival books and novels I used to read, about children living alone in the mountains, lighting fires, eating wild berries and building homes from branches: temporary shelters from the storm. It is important to know how to survive, but now I read teenage books about plagues and nuclear bombs instead of savage seas. There is still a Cold War, missiles could strike, and at school I want to start a protest group and go to Upper Heyford air base. Bang. Downstairs, I hit the Gong harder.

Every day, I obsess about the parties I get invited to, or not. At our school, people have birthday discos in rented halls, and I don't know what to wear. I am trying to fit in with everyone else. My body needs to be shut in and to run out. It morphs constantly. There are hairs on it, and I don't know how to shave or even if I should, because it is a symbol of oppression. In the community, women are hairy. Barbara, Eagle, Alison and Eva all say 'Shaving is bad'. But shaving must be done to fit in at school. There are dark hairs growing on my legs, under my arms. My hairs stick out the sides of Saskia's red swimming costume, and it is so embarrassing.

In the purple communal bathroom, I find an old, blunt razor left by someone in the dirty sink. Anxiously, I rub the blade on my armpits, legs, and around my winkle that now has no name. Later, I will discover Claire does the same thing. She finds the discarded blunt razor in the purple bathroom and scrapes her dry skin. It burns and cuts. But we will do anything to conform.

At school, the other girls in the class tell me constantly: 'You look a mess.' These girls eat free strawberries at Beefeater steakhouses, own curling tongs and cans of deodorant, and wear ironed trousers with straight creases running down each leg in perfect lines. At the parties they look bright in pastels, and I want to be like them. Since I was ten, I have done my own laundry, cramming dirty clothes into the communal machine. When the cycle is finished, I put the wet crumpled garments haphazardly over the wooden racks. Afterwards, I do not fold or iron, and my clothes are dishevelled, slightly curdled. I do not bath or shower regularly. I don't have any deodorant or know that you must wash before you put deodorant on. No one has explained.

When I was a child, and now as a teenager, the feel of dirt is cosy. A warm protective layer like a coat: mire on my skin, last week's clothes, furry unbrushed teeth. It is as ordinary as banging a gong and it takes me a while to realize how feral I am. When I am eighteen, I tell Claire, 'I've decided not to bother taking make-up off at the end of the day. I'll just put fresh stuff on in the morning.' Astounded, she snaps, 'But you have to clean your face!'

A few years ago, I met a female friend at a wedding who had visited the community, and – to my astonishment – she said, 'Your house was so, so dirty. I had never seen anything like it.' At one point, when we were small, all the Kids caught ringworm and the infection meant one of the Canadian twins began to lose their hair. When I am in my thirties, a member of my family finally admits, 'When you were children a relative once met you at a station and was horrified at how dirty you were.'

The communal dirt was a mixture of Marxist ideology, the glorification of physical labour, and a hippy back-to-nature fantasy. Yet while communists traditionally valued cleanliness and hygiene, our dirt stayed on our bodies and walls. In his essay 'The Great Relearning', Tom Wolfe focused on the San Francisco hippy movement in 1968 and its relationship to dirt – how it encouraged people to share cups, toothbrushes and beds. Wolfe described a local doctor's shock at the lack of hygiene and the return of fungal diseases. The hippies disregarded the basic practices of cleansing alongside certain ethical laws.

These days, I shower daily, and it still feels new, like something I have been offered late in life. A small gift to be clean; a gentle, daily practice. It has taken me a while, but I like a clean house and luxuriate in all forms of bathing, untangling and soaking. A cat wash. A long soak. A three-minute shower. 'One of my greatest pleasures in life,' I recently told my middle daughter, 'is beauty products.'

'Why do you like them?' she asked.

'Because it feels so nice to take care of myself.'

When I get out of the shower, I wrap myself in a towel and put on body lotion. My sister-in-law calls this 'robe time'. Cleansing lightens and heals. It is not a covering-up of natural smells, or a refusal of my body. It is a quiet resistance, a great relearning of my skin.

Recently, I spent a day in a German sauna, a modern red-brick building by a lake. A Dutch writer friend took me. 'It's a women's day, but everyone will be naked.' She looked me up and down with frank eyes. 'Will you be comfortable with that?'

'I think so,' I said, but I wasn't sure. Because of my childhood I am wary of certain situations.

I discovered an indoor pool, children wearing swimming costumes in a family area. In the changing room all the women, mostly middle-aged and plump, were naked or in robes. Dotted round the complex were different saunas and steam rooms. Dozens of naked women milled around. Outside, they relaxed on chaises longues, catching the spring sun by magnolia trees, a lake, and a little red-and-white-striped lighthouse.

It felt strange at first to be naked in a crowd, but I was quickly put at ease because no one was interested in looking or being admired. The women chatted, and as I don't speak German I imagined them discussing successes or worries at work, husbands or wives, darting between subjects as women do, unpacking family secrets, telling jokes. I thought they must be nurses, doctors, teachers, parents, secretaries, lawyers, shop workers, and journalists. Everyone was welcome and the atmosphere was quiet and gentle. It felt so different to the nudity I had encountered as a child; softer and less performative.

In the last sauna, my friend and I placed our towels on wooden benches around a pit of hot coals. An employee entered, banging a small gong. Then, she took a bunch of beech leaves and walked round the coals, beating them with the leaves. Smoke and beech scent filled the air. Then she took another bunch of beech, attached it to a rope and began spinning the leaves over our heads, and we were caught in waves of hot smoke and beech oil. It was intense, almost overpowering. When it was finished, the gong was sounded again.

Outside, the sunshine had gone and it was pouring with rain. 'Let's swim in the lake,' I said, and we ran in and dipped our hot naked bodies into the water, happy to be alive. All around women were taking time for themselves, their bodies and their friends. It was wonderful. As we returned inside, by the door we saw a small crowd had gathered, and when we looked back, a rainbow stretched over the lake. Each end of the rainbow was falling into the water, framing the distant red-and-white lighthouse and, in the centre, a blooming magnolia tree.

In the community, I leave the grimy bathroom behind me, the scum-ringed sink and the blunt razor. Walking back downstairs, I hit the Gong, but 'hitting' is not the right word because I am banging with all my might. In the entrance hall, I open the door and the front garden gives way to the woods, where spring bluebells are growing, foxgloves and honeysuckle. The new member, Jim, waves. He's wearing a T-shirt with the words 'No one is to blame'. Jim works in co-counselling, what he calls 'life-changing' therapy, which comes from California. We're used to having therapists in the house but their number is increasing. The Adults have been on weekend courses, retreats, and have trained for a couple of weeks, being led down enlightened corridors. They don't talk so much about Marxism any more, and some of them are members of a new political group called the Social Democratic Party. It is, a new member says, 'more reasonable'. What is happening politically in the outside world infiltrates our walls. Eagle – who supports the SDP – holds a rebirthing group with a man dressed in an orange velvet cloak. When they rebirth, from under a blanket in the communal Lounge, the sound of them screaming travels up the chimney. We hear them in the fireplace in Alison's room. When it's just the two of us, Claire shouts down, 'Shut up, you fucking hippies!' and we laugh and laugh.

As I bang the Gong, I hear a telephone. I wonder if it is for me. Some days, I giggle hysterically with Isa on the phone. She calls me, and we play telephone games where we tap songs onto the receiver and get the other person to guess the tune. We joke we are best 'telephone' friends. Other evenings, when we are in our Unit, Alison does a trick. In her room, beneath the platform bed, hangs a pair of heavy, navy curtains. Alison puts her head in the middle, slides it up and down and pretends to be a zip.

Other days, I am filled with anger – anger towards my dad because I don't fit into his life, anger towards Jason for calling me 'four-eyes'. I hate my NHS glasses and Troy tells me I have a 'zit face'. I've started getting spots every day, and cover them with toothpaste because I read about this in a magazine. But the red and yellow pimples emerge anyway. 'You're ugly,' Troy says, 'really fucking ugly,' and I feel so small.

Standing with the Gong, I try to erase this memory. Erasing memories is easy. You fold the bad time like a sheet of paper, again and again, until it is a wedge, a scrap. I do not need to remind myself that 'we are lucky to be here' and it is different from society. Our house is a utopian island.

Opening the double doors, I step back inside, the scent of garlic and tomato sauce floating in the air. I am still banging the Gong. As I stand under the stairs, mallet in hand, Ed walks towards me. He's been a member of the community for a couple of years; he moves between the house and Scotland, and has a Mexican girlfriend with unwashed hair. She always looks resigned. Ed reads Gabriel García Márquez and is bald with a pot belly and a beard. He doesn't like the Kids, everybody knows.

Ed is getting closer, twitching, treading swiftly as a rat. In his hand is a brown glass mug, filled with water. I am banging the Gong. Suddenly, he shouts, 'Stop making so much fucking noise,' and throws the water in my face. I stop, mallet in hand, and the water from the mug drips over my eyes, my cheeks, it slides from my skin onto my clothes. I want to run and cry, burn and think. But I cannot move, and the water drips onto the floor. After a while, I hang the Gong back under the stairs, with the stuff nobody wants but that is never thrown away; the chipped, tarnished, stained and useless things.

Ten minutes later, we're eating in the Dining Room. I am at the table with the Kids. Word has spread about Ed, and their eyes are on me. The Adults are murmuring. Behind us, Jim is talking to a visitor, Gabriel, about transpersonal psychology. Alison is laughing, but with him not at him, 'because therapy is serious'. The pasta dish is good, but I feel sick, and all I can look at is my mug of water and the table.

All the Kids are eating the whore's spaghetti. Strands of pasta dangle from Tina's mouth. Red sauce is splattered all over her face. I push back my wooden chair. Sunshine glances up, smiling at me nervously. I am feeling sick again, but I take my mug of water and walk towards Ed. I stand in front of him and throw the water in his face. The water slides down his bald head, over his cheeks and nose, drips into his beard. It catches in the dirty bristles like diamonds.

It is suddenly quiet in the Dining Room. As though someone turned the lights off. Eva looks at the bare walls, swallows pasta and coughs. A baby whimpers. Charles places his cutlery beside his plate; fork on the left, knife on the right, plate in the middle. Adult. Child. Parent. Neighbour. Friend. Facing Ed, I stand for a second. Our eyes meet, and a banshee leads a thousand marching feet.

Justice. Justice. Justice. I walk out of the room, exhausted. Later, Alison says to me, 'Well done.'

I have been a strong woman, defended the cause. Mum does not need to speak to Ed. I have done the work. At the following Friday Meeting, and in the corridors and on the stairwell, the Adults start saying, 'The Kids are out of control.'

Parenting during adolescence is no easy feat. Adolescent brain development is characterized by an imbalance between the limbic reward system and the not-yet-developed prefrontal control system. Teenagers get very emotional and want things, but haven't yet got the capacity for reasonable thought.

If I were to make a Retrograph of the following months and years, events line up. While in the Vegetable Garden, Barbara, Jim and Thomas discuss the SDP and Labour Party leader Neil Kinnock suspending the Liverpool District Labour Party amid allegations that the Trotskyist Militant group is attempting to control it, and no one seems to notice us hit puberty. As swiftly as the Gong is rung, one bang after the next, we transform from pastoral Rousseau children into a gang of utopian teenagers left to our own devices. In the community we have been impacted by outside events, shaped by society. Yet what is specific in our social experiment is that our upbringing happens en masse. The weight of our small differences is ignored. We have broken what Jean Baudrillard called 'the boundary markers' of the symbol known as 'home'. Bang. The Adults repeat: 'The Kids are out of control.'

In China, gongs were used to announce danger and war. In the community, the vibrations are felt throughout the house and the Estate. Beneath a redwood, the timid roe deer raise their heads, gaze up at the trees with dark eyes, but no one inside is listening. Bang.

11. The Labyrinth

'Maybe there is a beast . . . What I mean is maybe it's only us.'
William Golding, *Lord of the Flies*

'Threads snap. You would lose your way in the labyrinth.'
Oscar Wilde, *The Picture of Dorian Gray*

None of us stays the same forever. It is a November afternoon in a child psychiatric unit. Five teenagers, a nurse and I are sat in a circle. A thirteen-year-old girl looks me up and down. 'Next month, I can't come to the group. I am going to see Woons Deerecion.'

'Who are Woons Deerecion?' I ask.

She and the other four teenagers laugh. The girl, who was adopted from Rwanda at the age of five and has witnessed atrocious scenes of war, articulates each letter; 'W-o-n-s D-e-e-r-e-c-t-i-o-n are a boys band.'

'Oh, One Direction,' I say. Everyone laughs at my British accent, and I notice another girl giggling. She barely spoke when we began the therapy sessions, and for the first three weeks cried on entering the room.

I ask, 'What's your favourite One Direction song?'

The girl raises her eyebrows. 'You wouldn't like it.'

'You never know, I might just love it. Why don't you bring a CD next week?'

'Maybe.'

The five teenagers each say goodbye and we pass a drum from hand to hand. We always finish the same way, a ritual departure. The nurse and I smile at each other. Words spilling from our mouths, we take notes on anamnesis, laughter, phobias, relaxation, anorexia, imagination, addictive behaviour, acting and improvisation. This drama-therapy group has been together for a month. The individuals and group are starting to emerge. In my clinical notes, I separate what I have observed about the group dynamics and each patient.

The nurse and I plan the next session. Each sequence takes part in a different space in the room. There is a welcome space, a circle for the warm-up, an open space for improvisation, and then at the end of a session we re-form a circle. Theatre and drama are intrinsically linked to ritual, and ritual involves an architectural organization of space. Theatre director Peter Brook, in his seminal book *The Empty Space*, showed that what makes theatre is the drawing of a line between the actor and the spectator. In a drama-therapy workshop, spatial organizations contain emotions. They help define a beginning, a middle and an end.

The next week the girl brings the One Direction CD. We listen to her favourite song, 'What Makes You Beautiful'. The week after that, I propose, 'We're going to imagine we're at a One Direction concert. The band are about to walk onto the stage. Lights are flashing, and we call out their names.'

In our circle, the nurse, the five teenagers and I scream at the top of our voices – *Niall, Zayn, Liam, Harry, Louis* – and collapse into giggles. One of these five teenagers has a serious eating disorder, one self-harms, and one – despite being a straight-A student – suffers from school phobia. A boy with autism can only join improvisations if he first mimes a radio quiz, shouting out, 'We have a winner, we have a winner.'

Over the following months, the teenagers develop stories and scenes. We form and re-form our circles. One week, we spend the session improvising a Spanish package holiday, and the girl from Rwanda rides an invisible donkey led by the young woman with school phobia. We send imaginary postcards, get sunburnt noses, and swim together in the sparkling sea. At the start of each session throughout the year, we shout out: *Niall, Zayn, Liam, Harry, Louis*. The last session, before the school holidays, we sing 'What Makes You Beautiful' together. The teenagers have navigated the therapy sessions, confronted fears. One girl says, 'It was like being in a labyrinth, but I found my way out.'

'Adolescence' is a term derived from the Latin word *adolescere*, which means 'to grow into maturity'. The first use of the term appeared in the fifteenth century. Yet almost two millennia earlier, both Plato and Aristotle proposed sequences in life span. Aristotle even described three successive, seven-year periods (infancy, boyhood and young manhood) prior to adult maturity. In Shakespeare's 'Seven Ages of Man', the adolescent is stage three, 'Sighing like a furnace'.

For a decade, I work with teenagers, in psychiatric inpatient and outpatient units and special schools. It is some of the most challenging, and enriching, work of my career.

The adolescents thrive on intense drama, accompanied by incessant laughter. In one unit, we devise a play about the tragic story of a lost potato-masher, 'a missing object', where all the teenagers act roles based on kitchen equipment. It is a comedy about loss, deception and abandonment. Many of the teenagers have suffered abuse and are in foster care. The play is narrated by a lonely wooden spoon, who appears on the evening news requesting information, and is finally reunited with its potato-masher friend.

In the workshops, physicality is intense. During drama games, the teenagers adore getting very close, but also need to be kept far apart. Spatial organization is key. With one group of five, I am accompanied by two co-therapist nurses as we often have to break up violent fights, and we have a cooling-off area. The emerging and vibrant sexuality present in adolescence means we always have strict guidelines about what kind of touch is allowed. In a workshop for young people with learning difficulties, masturbation during the session is banned. The trick is to neither ignore nor forbid sexuality but to acknowledge rules and societal norms. We need to make our space safe, and therefore it has to be clearly structured and defined.

The teenagers' extreme behaviour reflects the quantum leaps they are making in their lives. In Tony Wolf and Suzanne Franks's bestselling guide to living with teenagers, *Get Out of My Life*, the authors explain how during adolescence we reach from our childhood home towards adulthood, yet simultaneously want to be our nurtured, baby selves. As we turn from family and home, emergent sexuality amplifies our focus. The world is new, but this newness is volatile.

As the Kids in the community become teenagers, we continue to lead two lives: inside and outside utopia. At the comprehensive, we are separated because the school considers us like siblings or cousins, family members who should not be in the same class. As there are two thousand pupils, we rarely see each other during the day.

In my class, girls and boys send notes to each other, gossip about snogging, getting off with someone and then chucking them. Unlike in the community, school friends don't talk about the end of the miners' strike, the Handsworth riots, or social discontent. One clever girl mentions the new Equal Pay Act, allowing women to be paid the same as men. But everyone ignores her. Instead, we chat about who fancies who, and things are either 'wicked' or 'disgustingly sick'. On Saturdays, and after school, the best thing is going to the shopping centre. It's a laugh, and one weekend, a girl invites me, and I get dressed like a casual, and someone from the community drives me there in the van. At the shopping centre, the girl and I share a Coke. She tells me that when her boyfriend comes to her house she has to keep her bedroom door open, because 'my mum doesn't want us doing anything'. I laugh, but I don't tell her about what it is like at the community because no one mentions doors being left open or closed. Everything is different there.

In the research paper 'Architecture and Anthropology.

Working in between Concepts'. Anda-Ioana Sfinteş explores how we understand any built space and its use. She focuses on the meaning of delimitations and separations through walls, windows and doors. Describing the relationship of two neighbours over the garden fence, she shows how boundaries enable interactions because they frame and define, separating things that need to be distinguished. In the community these definitions are hazy. The only firm boundary is between our world and the one on the outside.

Claire says, 'Don't tell the Adults. We're all meeting at the Hayloft in five minutes, idiot.' She thumps my back. Her big-sister rocket fist redresses the slant of my spine. It's after school, and I follow her out of our Unit. I know the Adults have banned us from playing in the Hayloft. Fuck Claire, and her know-it-all posturing. My fingers slide along the cool, mahogany banister. As I walk down the stairs, my feet are magnetized. I am drawn by the Hayloft, and the pull of the Kids. The terrifying bliss of being together. It's June, nearly the summer, and the Hayloft is calling.

As I head down the main stairs, I spot Eva. A striped towel folded neatly over one arm. She strides towards the communal bathroom. Uncomfortably, I think of Alison. Yesterday, before I went to bed, she said, 'Eva told me you looked awful at dinner. I noticed everybody staring at you!'

Last night, I was trying to dress like a casual, wore a pale blue miniskirt and a pale pink crumpled shirt. Half of my eyelid was shaded pink, and the other half electric blue. My eyelashes were coated in bright blue mascara. It was hard to walk into the Dining Room. At school, my friends get told off by their mum or dad. But we are judged by over twenty Adults, and last night Barbara snorted, 'You're growing up,' and David grinned, 'They all fucking are!' The new therapists in the house mentioned breaking patterns. Alison hates my clothes, make-up, and the clouds of hairspray I swoosh on my short hair. But everyone at the comprehensive wears make-up. At breaktime, they swing cans of hairspray around their heads to fix their flicks in place.

Alison and Eva keep their faces bare, and clothes functional. Two years ago, Eva and I were friends. We played chess together in her room, and I studied moves on black and white, and she congratulated me when I called checkmate. But the axis of my planet has turned. I fell from the flat edge of my previous world. Lionel happened, my new school happened, and Ed.

Jeanette Winterson wrote that 'sanity is the thread through the labyrinth of the Minotaur. Once cut, or unravelled, all that lies in wait are gloomy tunnels unfathomable by any map.' As a teenager in the community, it's like I've entered a tunnel; it's exciting and terrifying to be at school and with the Kids, but I cannot see the end.

On the staircase, I count the thirty steps. Soon, we'll be playing our Game. The Kids do different things together at the community now, and one of them is our Game. On the ground floor, Sunshine waits for me, green eyes darting. 'I'm hungry,' she says, but I don't offer to go to our Unit for toast because private food and money have become an issue. We are ravenous teenagers, and all the Adults are skint, and each Unit has a fridge but if we eat the food inside, we get in trouble. After school, Alison yells, 'Don't eat the food.' We often say to each other, 'Just give me a bite,' and recently I have started making sandwiches piled high with pickled beetroot, peanut butter, gherkins, cheese and mayonnaise, because then no one ever wants to share.

Sunshine has just got back from New York, and she's telling me about the film she saw, *The Breakfast Club*. 'They're teenagers in an American high school: a weirdo, a nerd, an athlete, a rebel, a princess.' I've seen the trailer, and secretly would like to be the princess, but I think I might be the weirdo. 'They kiss at the end,' Sunshine adds, and I blush. The thought of kissing boys always makes me turn red. Giggling, we shimmy through the Washing-Up Room, sinks packed high with dirty plates and encrusted cutlery.

In the Kitchen, the bread mixer is brimming brown. The mixer paddle turns. It is as big as my arm, churning dough for thirty soon-to-be-baked loaves. Max says, 'Hi!' and pours a sticky stream of molasses into the dough; swirling circles of burnt sienna.

'Hi!' we answer. Max's bread is always bad. But we smile, friendly, so Max won't ask us where we're going, and we won't have to mention the Hayloft. Max is Mia's stepdad, a divorced computer scientist. He's working on a new project for a thing called 'mobile phones'. Max is my friend, and he teaches me DOS programming. Sometimes, the Adults do these middle-class things, and we read Penguin paperbacks, eat organic sunflower seeds and understand the concept of imperialism. But we also have free school dinners, wear cheap clothes and free NHS glasses, and grow up with people using the words 'shit' and 'fuck'. Our cultural and economic capital do not match up. Often, I notice this strange mishmash at school because I speak 'properly' but find I don't fit in with the 'nice girls'. I breathe easier with anyone on the outside looking in, people who know what it is like when you run through life and keep crashing into invisible walls.

Max has shown me how to program his computer and make the words 'Happy Birthday' undulate on a flickering screen. One day, he also introduces me to ELIZA, the first computer Rogerian psychotherapist. For hours, I type questions and ELIZA – the therapist – answers. Sentences emerge in light. I write, 'What is fuck?' And ELIZA responds, 'Don't you ever say hello?' I write 'Hello', and she responds, 'How are you today? What would you like to discuss?'

'Love.'

'Tell me more.'

I have nothing to say, because I just want to fall in love, like in the magazine *Just Seventeen*. Love makes the world light up with a glow. In *Just Seventeen* there are also articles about sex which Sunshine and I read, and don't always understand, like: 'The morning after: what to do when you've gone too far'.

On the computer, I type, 'Hate.'

ELIZA answers, 'Tell me more.'

'I know someone who hates someone.' I am thinking of Ed, of Lionel, of our dad, Claire, and Troy. Recently, I have been fighting with Troy. Suddenly, he is a tall teenager, and comes into my room. He stares at me while I read on my bed. Things like this always happen at the community because everyone can go wherever they want. There are no clear boundaries, or defined spaces. Last week, Troy got on my nerves, and I snapped, 'All men are potential rapists,' as I'd read it in a feminist book. Troy told me I was a crazy, ugly girl. But Barbara said, 'It's true. All men are potential rapists.'

'What do you think?' ELIZA interrupts my thoughts.

'Hate is bad.'

'Do you have any psychological problems?'

In the Kitchen, Sunshine and I glance left, right. Yeast fumes infiltrate the air.

'Do you want to get past?' Max shuffles gently, folding small, shy arms and legs. Through a doorway, we enter the Back Kitchen. Ed is peeling potatoes. A haze of fury surrounds the mud and skins. It's like we can feel the words seeping from Ed's pores, like he's thinking: *Fuck women, life, this community and the Kids.* My heart thuds. Since the day of the Gong, I have been keeping a distance. We slip past his dark form. He's better to avoid. Suddenly, we hear a voice from the Laundry Room. Is it Alison? She can't know where I am going. These days, I often hide from my mum, turn inside myself. Sunshine and I speed up. We skid out of the back door and finally get outside. Eight doors connect the inside of the community to the outside. Getting out undetected is always possible.

Our school friends socialize with their own age groups. In the shopping centre no one mixes with people outside our school year. But the community Kids are together regardless of age, and our group spans seven to seventeen. We look after the little ones, and grow up with a sense of responsibility, knowing how to care for others. But when we become teenagers the stakes change, and yet nobody questions our blur of ages and needs. Instead, we self-regulate.

At weekends, when we're not in the Hayloft, we watch TV in someone's Unit. Everyone has their own TV now, and some people have video players. Fifteen of us bundle on a sofa, and we put on horror films like *The Omen*, or the musical *Tommy* where a man inside a sarcophagus is injected with heroin. Other times, we hang out in the Yoga Room, bring sleeping bags and spend the night. The Adults don't check up on us, and as the full moon hangs dangerously bright in the sky, we edge closer together, like normal teenagers. But there is no navigational system guiding our flight. Hands brush against breasts and over bodies. This happens with the Kids we grew up with, who the school considers to be like our family.

Michael, Jason, Brandy and Claire are sneaking out through the stained-glass double front doors. Mia, Troy, Karl and Rainbow wait on the steps next to the Gardener's Toilet, by the yellow scum-lined sink with its cracked bar of soap, like a tea-smoked egg patterned with hundreds of lines of time. I have never used it and I never wash my hands. Peter sits impatiently by the step to the Chicken Yard, rolling his football back and forth. Here, we once watched the brown mush of orchard apples being alchemized into juice. The Chicken Yard is where Thomas chopped a bird's head off with an axe. Charles took black-and-white photographs and we watched as the headless chicken strutted over the cobbles, blood shooting into the sky.

Sunshine and I cross the slope of the courtyard, meet a shadow.

'Where are you going? You're not allowed to play in the Hayloft.' Barbara is scowling, pitchfork in hand. Blue boiler-suit on, she is mucking out the stables. Delicate wafts of straw linger on metal spikes. 'We've told you dozens of times. You could kill yourselves.'

Sunshine and I are steady in the force of her glare. 'We're going to get our bikes, Barbara.'

I use the voice that makes people believe. In my drama lessons, Mrs Neel taught me methods of simulation. I underline my chosen words. 'Maybe we'll *ride into town*?'

'Or go and see the *donkeys*?' Sunshine bounces lies like tennis balls.

I say, 'Yeah. Brill. *The donkeys*,' and glance up at the Hayloft, a dream of bricks and promises.

Barbara trudges back to the Cowshed. We walk towards the Bike Shed, double back up the secret staircase by the Carpentry Workshop, past the metallic ring of spinning saws.

Here, you can cut a leg, or chop off a hand. But when the Kids have accidents, it always happens out of earshot, out of sight. In the thirty-one acres and the sixty rooms, it is easy to break a leg or an arm. Last year, Tina lost half her finger in the sausage mixer. An Adult wasn't looking and turned the handle too fast. Also, little Helen caught on fire from the circle of candles we lit in her room. Her pyjamas burnt bright in a polyester blaze. Seven or eight of us quivered when the ambulances came. We were shepherded away, taken back to our Units. Everyone hushed to bed.

As we have hit adolescence, the Adults have alluded to physical danger, but nobody mentions psychological risks, or sexuality. No one offers advice. The implications of not having a defined family group, or a safe living space, spill over into the reality of our lives. We become teenagers in a utopian space, cut off from the outside world.

In the community, I run up the Hayloft stairs, and Sunshine follows. 'Slowcoach,' I whisper, pushing her, because Sunshine is one of the only people I can push. At the top are lofty rafters, naked bricks and wooden floors. Shadows stir on a back wall. In the middle of the loft is a strange dark box filled with sour grain. If you put your foot inside you fall a slithering slide to hell. 'Never go in there. You could die,' the Adults say. At the other end of the room is the haystack. It is ours.

Sunshine giggles and Jason mutters, 'Shut up or they'll hear us,' and Troy turns around. He's grown so tall that he's taller than Jason. Troy gives me a stare. But I giggle too, and laughter bursts out of Sunshine and me, like the farts we make at the community yoga class when the Adults – in tight sweatpants and stained T-shirts – place themselves in lion pose, arching claws and roaring.

Sunshine doesn't like her brother. I think he's good-looking but I am also scared of him, and of the gossip that now goes from Unit to Unit, spreads from Kid to Kid. Whispering and giggling, we are scandalized. In the last few months, peeping at naked bodies has become a Kid thing. The house has many balconies and roofs, cramped spaces with access to windows. Our utopia is revolutionary but heterosexual, and the boys spy on girls. There are rumours and secrets, lies and truth. Sunshine tells me she caught Troy watching her undress and says, 'The boys look at us when we have a bath.' One day, through the smudged communal bathroom window, I see two figures. Pulling clothes over my damp, floundering body, I leave hurriedly.

In the Hayloft, Claire snaps at me, 'Shut up, posh girl.'

Troy grins, 'Yeah, shut up, posh girl,' and he looks me up and down, and I turn to Mia for support. Mia is my new friend, a jolt of sun in this strange year. We hang out together in the community, but are in separate classes, and I don't see her at school. Secretly, Mia and I do each other's homework. I write her essays and she illustrates my projects. Both of us get A grades. But in the Hayloft, Mia is edging close to Karl, and she doesn't notice me stare. Her little brother Peter bounces his football as she smiles at Karl, flips her hair. Amongst the Kids, everyone now fancies each other, saying who is fit or cute. Mia fancies Karl, and I think he has beautiful eyes. He wears ironed Lacoste T-shirts, smells of soap, and strangely insists on showering every day. My stomach lurches when Claire calls me 'posh girl' again. Usually, my revenge is to call her 'peasant'. But I cannot say 'peasant' in front of Jason and Troy. I will lose the battle. Every time.

Michael says, 'Shut up. I'm going to make the tunnel.'

For twenty-five years I work professionally with groups: actors, clients, students, children, managers, teenagers, nurses, social workers, human resources departments. Groups, teams, gangs, classes, families, companies and organizations. There is a point when a group can become a mob. A stadium crowd has supporters or hooligans. Mirror neurons program us to learn through social imitation, duplicating tasks and behaviour. But a team can turn into a machine, cohesion slipping into tyranny. Blind obedience. Excitement can transform into bacchanal chaos. Actors can be manipulated into following a director. Teenagers want desperately to be the same. Copy. Follow. Like sheep. A herd. People are easily tricked into a sense of belonging. Hating and loving as one. Look at a stadium. Yet, there is always a turning point, a fulcrum. At this juncture, a group can be cooled, watered down, accompanied back to being a collection of individuals. A group can be harmonious, with everyone playing different instruments like an orchestra. A group can exist together, experience belonging and a sense of home. But groups need to know who they are and what they are doing; any uncared-for group can become out of control . . .

We stand in front of the haystack, silent now, preparing for our journey. The haystack is a square construction built from dozens of bales. We harvested this hay together in our fields. Two by two we carried bales to the trailer. Sweet, rich hay is our summer gift for winter. Harvested hope. Food for our cows and sheep. At Friday Meetings, the Adults say, 'Self-sufficiency. Working outside the system.' The hay was once grass, and that means that you reap what you sow, and that the past influences the present. We are teenagers, the product of the exploded nuclear family. At the start we were small green blades shooting up from the earth, and the Adults cultivated our bodies and minds. They were the Adults, and us the Kids. Now we are the hay that once was grass, brought up as one big family.

During a seminar in Paris one rainy October, a clinical psychologist explains to us about adolescence, sexuality, family structures and the customs of exogamy, developed throughout the world, which refer to mating or marrying outside one's social group. She explains that incest is the opposite of exogamy, involving sexual relations between closest kin: mother/son, father/daughter, brother/sister. In a gloomy room, we take notes on anthropologist Claude Lévi-Strauss, who wrote that the taboo of incest is crucial to our species because it prohibits inbreeding and means we form new social groups. The psychologist in Paris insists that as family structures evolve, become blended and include stepfamilies, we need to be attentive to the need to protect children and young people, as situations can become confusing and potentially damaging. When she speaks, I think of the ambiguous relationships between the Kids in the community. It all depended on how long you lived in the house, whether the other Kids became like siblings, felt like brothers and sisters – one big, blended family.

In the Hayloft, Michael yanks two bales out from the stack, and then disappears into the dark hole. Back in view, he pulls out another bale. At school, Michael hangs out with *Back to the Future*–style geeks. On Saturdays, he claims, his friends put on lab coats and pretend to be deliverymen to steal washing machines. He says, 'They just wheel the washing machines out.' Claire says, 'That's bollocks.' But Michael's older than us so we listen, even if everyone fancies Jason and Troy. Lizzie, a new teenager at the community, says Troy looks like David Bowie. We are drawn together, moving like moths to light.

Now, Michael digs a tunnel with a black mouth. He removes bale after bale. Troy orders us, 'Susie and Sunshine, go keep watch.'

We obey and stand by a large open window, on the lookout for Adults, twenty metres up. Outside, a rope dangles from a hook, a snake swinging in the breeze. The rope and the hook are for hauling hay. A couple of months earlier, Troy stood by this opening, claiming, 'Boys are stronger than girls.'

'No they're not,' I said.

'I'm going to slide down that rope.'

'I'll do it first,' I boasted, even though I am not sporty, can barely climb the ropes in the school gym, am the kind of girl who is last in each school running race. Looking out, I grabbed the rope, wrapped myself round the coil, and leapt. Legs clenched tight around the twisted cord, I slid fast. Quick. Swiftly. I fell faster than the wall that killed my sister Rachel, and quicker than the bricks that crushed my pram. I hit the ground. Rope burns on each finger, burns between my thighs.

Afterwards, in the Dining Room, Alison whispered, 'You could have died.' David told me, 'You're crazy, but so brave.' That evening, I was a winner.

*

Now, in the Hayloft, Michael has finished, and we enter the tunnel, one by one. The hay crackles, tiny strands smack and tap against us. Explosions of dry grass bend and snap. With a crunch and rasp, I slither on my tummy. Inside, the tunnel is a gritty, moonless place. A one-way track. Troy says, 'Hurry up.' We crawl into the gloom, pull ourselves forwards with our arms. We could be buried here, eaten by the stack.

Inside the tunnel, the golden light of June harvest days is distant. The haystack labyrinth gives birth to a creature. It has eleven heads and twenty-two legs. We squirm forward, seeking our path out of childhood.

A labyrinth is an exercise in time. From the thirteenth-century labyrinth in Chartres Cathedral to Arizona's native O'odham people's Man in the Maze, labyrinths have symbolized movement from one moment to another. According to O'odham oral history, their labyrinth depicts the journey of life.

Mummified inside the haybales, our bodies squash together: arms, legs, heads and feet. A sliding mass of skin and hair. Hair in mouth. Knee on breast. Squealing and sniggering, our bodies brush against each other, and some of us long for each other. It all depends on our age. I want someone to kiss me, and for us to talk and laugh, and experience the romance of finding 'the one'.

Troy says, 'Let's look.' He lights a match, and we observe our chimera: half-human, half-beast. Everything yellow and black. The monster draws our eyes and appals us. Our Game is dangerous, made of gunpowder; it just requires a spark. Troy puts the match closer and closer to the hay, until Claire tells him, 'Stop.' In the tunnel, Troy blows out the match. The Game is over.

At the library, I read that Theseus ventured into the labyrinth to kill the Minotaur, to confront chaos and death. In André Gide's retelling of this Greek myth, Daedalus meets Theseus about to go into the labyrinth, and gives him Ariadne's thread, saying, 'This thread will be your link with the past. Go back to it . . . for nothing can begin from Nothing.' The thread in the labyrinth symbolizes Theseus's link with his history; inherited knowledge helps him find his way out. But, in the community, our threads have been cut. Each stalk disconnected. No thread can lead us out because our connection with our families and history was broken when our utopia left the past behind.

When the Adults found out we'd played in the Hayloft, they repeated, 'You will die.' Then, they shrugged and retreated, but we returned to build our labyrinth. Architecture needs boundaries to create a feeling of protection, to enclose areas for certain activities, establishing levels of privacy. Human groups need boundaries to live together healthily. Even love requires limits, as Anne Carson articulated: 'Eros is an issue of boundaries. He exists because certain boundaries do.'

Inside the community, architectural and psychological boundaries were missing. Since we were small, we roamed through open doors, growing up without parental guidance. Yet all the discussions about rape, bodies and bombs mean we thought we understood everything. We were overexposed to a constant utopian light, blinded by 'truths' thrust in our eyes. Poet René Char wrote in *Leaves of Hypnos*: 'Lucidity is the wound closest to the sun.' Looking back now at how we veered between adulthood and child-like innocence, I see that our knowledge was as precarious as the bales of hay balanced around us. As an adolescent I was naive, green as uncut grass, going deeper and deeper, trapped in our utopian labyrinth.

12. The Trees Are Not to Blame

'Wild is a word like "soul". Such a thing may not exist, but we want it, and we know what we mean when we talk about it.'

Kathleen Jamie, in the *London Review of Books*

'God has mercifully ordered that the human brain works slowly; first the blow, hours afterwards the bruise.'

Walter de la Mare, *The Return*

It is August 2016. Spain. We're on a family holiday: A, the girls and me. For hours, we've been driving through a desert landscape dry with dust, crossing pit-stop towns where girls walk in fluorescent flip-flops on roads spotted with potholes. The pit-stop towns feel like nowhere, not places to grow up in but zones to drive through. 'Zone', from the Latin; a geographic girdle. These places are belts, fastened with cheap buckles.

Finally, we reach our destination. The town is a neat anthill, a citadel surrounded by plains of olive trees. Inside the town walls, intricate forged-iron balconies are bedecked with burnt-orange flowers and lush, tumbling succulents. On doorsteps, old women with gold crosses, red lips and ironed slacks linger in the shadows of beaded curtains.

Our accommodation is squeezed into a steep street, so narrow that at the top the houses on each side almost touch. Inside, the four small floors are decorated with farming objects. The house has thick cool walls, uncomfortable red sofas and chintzy tablecloths. We've been renting this holiday place for years, and somehow it feels like home because we've repeatedly done happy things here. Time has passed, and the girls have turned from children to young people. The owner, the local postwoman, welcomes us with homemade walnut wine and giant watermelons from her garden.

Later. It is siesta time. While everyone sleeps, I write. In this house, I always work on the ground floor. Every year, I install a makeshift office here. It is quiet and cool. Outside, the heat is a dense, monumental construction. It stills clocks, and forces bodies into languor. Nothing moves, and no one talks. Far away, a dog barks. A radio crackles. The heat produces an eerie gap. It is a speechless moment in the day. During siesta time, I think of what Jules Michelet says, that we must *faire parler*, make the silences of history speak.

It is summertime at the community, and the English sun is fixed in the sky. In the greenhouses, red, yellow and green tomatoes glow next to purple aubergines and dark, arched green peppers. It's the morning and I am in David's room, on the edge of his bed, where I always sit. He's talking about an ex-girlfriend.

'She won't let me fuck her any more.' He is outraged, and I nod my head in sympathy. It must be difficult, someone not wanting to fuck you. Despite what happened with Lionel, the word 'fuck' is far away. Yet, I put on 'fuck' like a mask, and nod again. On his bed, David looks me up and down, 'You know, you wouldn't believe what's happening with the community Kids!'

My stomach twists. He keeps saying this to me when we're alone, and his voice is kind of titillating, and perhaps it's a warning but I'm not sure. Each time, he shakes his head and seems to measure out the words. My stomach shifts and I pull at his duvet. It feels like he thinks I am innocent and need to be informed. Maybe, I think, he's talking about the peeping the boys are rumoured to be doing, but maybe not? Anyway, I don't know what is 'happening' so I barely listen. It makes me feel uncomfortable. I am confused.

That August morning, I go back to my room, and take my new hardback diary; it's from the county council, where Dad works. Bound in red fabric, the embossed gold numbers read: 1985. Stretched out on my bed, I write: 'I miss Isa. The camp was so good.' By the campfire, Isa snogged a boy. As their lips stuck together, I turned away, jealous. Before camp, I stayed at Isa's house. She lives near the tube station and to get to her house I have a special ritual. When I exit the station alone, I pick leaves from a hedge. As I walk, I rip the leaves into little bits and scatter the green shreds along my path. The leaves must last the exact distance from the station to Isa's red gloss-painted door. Every time I visit, I leave a green trail behind me.

This summer, we went to a market to buy Isa a tie-dyed

dress. We got lost, or rather I lost her, but almost on purpose because then I was free among the rockabillies, punks and Rastas. In the market crowds it felt like I could do whatever I wanted and be whoever I chose.

In the diary, I write, 'It is nearly the end of the school holidays, and nearly all the other Kids have gone away to Scotland.' Pausing, I chew my pen, write more: 'Maybe I should have gone, but I am staying here.'

Only Troy and I are left at the community. Troy is still not my friend, but in the last couple of days he has been behaving differently. I write, 'It's ace mucking about with Troy. I hope I will see him later.'

When I open the door, the sky is perfect blue. Violet once told me when she was painting in the garden, 'The sky is a celestial dome, a sphere divided into constellations.' Above in the sky are bright stars and beyond them is the Kármán line. It is sixty-two miles above us, and the beginning of space. But when this day begins, it has no end, like all summer days when there is nothing to do but to be thirteen and yourself. There are beginnings, and daisies in the grass. White-fringed petals and yellow hearts. Outside on the lawn, I lie in the grass, in new green shorts and a striped T-shirt. Green on green. The sun is warm. Heat on the back of my shins and thighs, soft in the creases of my knees. When I look up, I see the path to the woods.

The woods are my outside home; the trees, paths, bushes and leaves. It is like being swathed in a sea of green. An emerald blanket that never falls from your bed. When I am in the woods, nothing matters, and I listen to the birds, lie on the earthy floor, and feel the beat of the roots. Everything is connected. In winter, I trudge through the snow, and the bare branches make black lace in the sky. Sometimes I come here alone and sometimes with someone, and sometimes we build fires and camp. The woods are always there and always being themselves, swaying and falling, dying and growing. Time is determined by flowers and fruit. In winter, there are snowbells. Daffodils and bluebells mark the spring. Sweet cherries arrive in summer. In autumn, apples and pears hang from the branches of the ancient fruit trees. The orchard skirts the edge of the woods. The lawn, garden, orchard and woods are layers of tamed nature, like concentric circles radiating out from the house, each section taking me closer to the earth.

On the lawn, Troy is suddenly next to me. Lying by my side, he flicks blond hair from his face. 'Hello.' His green eyes glint, and he looks like Sunshine for a second, or David Bowie. We start talking about the summer, Live Aid and Ethiopia. Then, he laughs when I say, 'Ed is a fascist.' He listens when I say, 'Black berets are cool.' For once, he does not insult me, and I am grateful, surprised. Normally, Troy ignores me, or he calls me ugly or Zit Face and bullies me. Usually, I am the butt of his jokes. But today, I am thirteen, three months and seventeen days, I feel pretty. I so rarely feel pretty.

'Boys and girls should be able to be friends,' I will scrawl in my diary that night.

'Let's go for a walk,' Troy says.

We walk towards the edge of the woods, to the end of

the path where garden meets wood. Concrete gives way to wild grass, and then wild grass gives way to undergrowth. We are beside the Herb Garden, by hooped paths encasing rosemary, thyme and basil. A joining of wild and domesticated space.

Later, when I am studying Drama at university, in my final year I will write a short solo play, and use a line from Hermann Hesse: 'Trees are sanctuaries.' The word 'sanctuary' comes from the Latin *sanctuarium*, meaning a sacred place but also a private room. The woods are where I take refuge, but they are also a place where I brush up against holiness.

Troy runs after me. We leave the garden, and dart around the orchard, where unripe fruit hangs in trees. The apples are formed but not ready to pick. If you bite into them, they are sour. Troy catches me by a tree trunk. His arm brushes against mine. 'I've had sex,' he says. I stop running and stare at the fruit trees, lean against a narrow trunk. I don't believe him. Troy is lying. Sex for a Kid is impossible. We're too young.

I have separated myself from what happened with Lionel, and recently I said to Claire, 'It wasn't that bad at all.' Pieces of me run in parallel lines, and with scissors I cut those days away, snipping and clipping until we are apart.

Since I was twelve, I have only ever kissed one boy. In July, we had a party at the house, the adults put a tree trunk between bales, and we had to knock the other person off the log with a pillow. There was a barbecue with sausages, and I met a French boy called Jerome. His Parisian parents were interested in experimental living. Experimental means it is a test. A test implies you're trying to find something, make a discovery. Jerome and I got talking but I didn't like it when he put his tongue in my mouth. I told him, 'No Frenchie, no Frenchie!' because kissing with tongues is what we call 'French kissing'. But the French boy didn't understand.

I stare at the apples, delicately nestled in each tree. When they are ready in the autumn, you must twist them. Green globes land in your hand with a snap. What Troy calls sex is different to a Frenchie. Sex is written about in books and in *Just Seventeen*. Even then, you go to First Base, then Second and Third. Sunshine and I read about it in Judy Blume. In the book *Are You There God? It's Me, Margaret*, they play a game called Two Minutes in the Closet: First Base is snogging and then Second Base is a hand under a bra. Third Base is touching below the waist, through clothes.

In the orchard, I laugh. 'Troy, you haven't had sex.'

'Yes, I have. Loads.'

'You haven't.'

'And other Kids have.'

'They haven't.'

I am writing part of this book during a residency in a Scottish castle surrounded by woods. Each day, I walk along a tree-lined river path. After a while, I get attached to a certain tree, and I climb the tree, and sit on a moss-covered branch. Often, I imagine all the poets, writers and translators who have come and worked here. Listening to the river, I feel complete, and experience an out-of-myself relationship with nature that I haven't felt since I was a child in the woods. In the castle library, I come across a passage by British philosopher and writer Iris Murdoch, exploring transcendent experiences with nature, which she calls 'unpossessive contemplation'. Murdoch describes the experience of 'unselfing', where nature lifts us out of ourselves. At the community, the woods were my torrent of green.

The sun is on my legs. Heat on skin. I am wearing my new green shorts. Our science teacher told us that, 'The skin is our largest sense organ. Stretching over two square metres, it distinguishes hot from cold, contact from pain. The sense of touch covers all our body.'

We walk away from the garden, through the rows of bent fruit trees towards the woods. Troy grabs me, singing 'Stand and Deliver'. It is a song by Adam and the Ants about highwaymen. I look into Troy's eyes, and then pull away. He carries on singing, and grabs my arm again, and says, 'Your sister has done it too. It's been going on for a while.' My fingers scrape the tree bark, rip off apple leaves. This is impossible, even more impossible than his first words. Troy's fifteen. Claire is only just fifteen. I am thirteen three months and seventeen days. In my hand, the apple leaf is green. The summer light is perfect, and it should not end, and I tear the leaf into tiny parts.

'I don't believe you!' I snap.

His smile radiates. It spins from his eyes, and flies into

the clouds. A toss of blond hair, and his words lull themselves into my skin. Is he lying? Inside my stomach, hundreds of butterflies flap their wings. Vivid scales quiver. He adds, 'I like my women to be faithful. Even David says that women should be faithful.'

I nod, bewildered. Troy's words are utterly untranslatable because the word 'utter' means what is most on the outside. They are far away from me. I sit under the apple tree and look up and into the woods, trying to fathom Troy's words, some of which – I will later understand – are true, some exaggerations and others lies. Inside the house, and in the thirty-one acres, things can happen without anyone noticing, or people just catch a glimpse, the blur of a Kid going through a door with someone else.

Later that afternoon, he leaves a note in my bedroom. It is handwritten, printed in childlike letters, because like Sunshine, he rarely goes to school. 'Meet me in the Mattress Room at nine.'

In my bedroom, I can't decide if I should go. It is hot outside and I twist and turn. I don't know what's in the Mattress Room, and it is like with all the unlocked doors. As I don't know what is behind them, I always want to open them, and no one has ever explained that some doors are meant to stay shut. I am thirteen and everything is possible. 'Something happened today,' I write on a piece of paper, placed in my diary later that night.

When I touch tree trunks, I always feel something soothing. As an adult, I spend many years living by the sea, and there is something about the green of the trees and the rush of the waves that always brings me a certain truth. Surprisingly, I get the same sensation when I am alone in a city crowd, and maybe it is about letting go – the humbling unselfing Iris Murdoch described. Perhaps these are places where I let myself confront mystery, a lack of control. Inside houses, it is a different matter, for when I am in a room I often need to be prepared and organized. The poet Etel Adnan writes that it would be good not to have known, to dream against the flow with your eyes wide open.

The Mattress Room is situated to the right of the main staircase, in a corridor, next to the Kitchen. It is in the middle of our house, in the middle of where we all started when we made our utopian home. My hand grips the handle, and I push open the door. Inside, the room has no windows, and is lined with deep shelves, and they are piled high with old mattresses.

Troy is waiting in the dense black. He lies beneath the bottom shelf, on the floor. The room has a sour odour. Old sweat. Horsehair. There is the smell of all the people who have slept on these beds. It is hot and dark. I lie down and Troy pulls me towards him, sticks his tongue inside my mouth. It is wet. Odd. There is a taste of unbrushed teeth and sour garlic. I say nothing. I am stilled. Frozen like I froze with Lionel. Like a deer blinded by car headlights, my body stops. This is a situation for which I am totally unprepared.

Troy does not drape a heart-shaped locket round my neck. We do not travel gently, and First Base does not go to Second. He pulls off my new green shorts and my striped

T-shirt, puts his head to my breast and sucks. He sticks his hands between my legs, places his fingers inside. Things enter and withdraw. It feels disgusting. He tells me I am lying where my sister lay. I am lying in her empty place.

After some time, Troy perches himself on top of me. His penis is hard, and I squeeze my legs shut. He puts his hands between my legs, tries to push them apart. But I whisper, 'I don't want to have sex until I am sixteen.' It is the only defence I find. He tries again, and I repeat, 'I don't want to have sex until I am sixteen,' and eventually, he gives up.

In philosopher and psychoanalyst Clotilde Leguil's post-#MeToo book about consent, she describes the state of stupefaction, a distinct sign of trauma. Drawing lines between sexual aggression, rape and traumatized soldiers, she explains how victims anticipate and expect things will be different – whether they're a soldier experiencing the full horror of war, or a rape victim who thought they were going out for a friendly drink. When something unexpectedly brutal, psychologically and/or physically violent occurs, and it is so radically different to a victim's expectations, the only solution is to disassociate. The person is reduced to ashes.

Writing about dissociation is a difficult task but it involves a feeling of being very far away. That day, it is like I finally pack up my dreams, Oxford, books, Grandma Bella. It is my fault, and it's time to go, to leave the Mattress Room, leave myself, and I prepare an imagined flight, a spacecraft for lift-off. Launch pads are installed, and life-support machines. Valves open and close, and my crew starts the countdown. There is a rumbling, a blast and lift-off, and we travel at 17,000 miles per hour. The house, the lawn and the woods shrink and disappear. There are clouds, then darkness and stars, and I cross the Kármán line, leave my body, and float without gravity. In free fall.

I belay. To write about this day, I must belay. 'Belay' is a mountaineering term referring to the paying out of rope. The belay device creates friction, which allows the climber to fall safely, and to live to climb again. Belaying allows time to breathe because, as Leguil writes, the words we use to describe trauma must be invented. They are different from one person to the next – and I see this with patients, and during clinical meetings. If we want to understand the impact of a specific trauma, we have to examine how the specific trauma impacts the specific individual.

Leguil writes about this difference in relation to the #MeToo movement. Solidarity and collective support are part of the initial revolt, but she insists that individual trauma must subsequently be approached individually. If not, we are expecting all women to have experienced the same, identical version of trauma, as though there is a uniformity in cause and effect. We risk a totalitarian approach. Her words cast a sharp light on my own experience of the collective in the community, which felt as though only a single story was available. In the community's homogenized, feminist wave, it was as if my experience was irrelevant.

*

I have three daughters now. From the age of ten, when they tip out of childhood, they tell me their nightmares about boys, bullying and drugs. Over breakfast, we talk about the scary and new things: starting secondary school, wearing a bra, drinking, going to a party, somebody holding you tight. Swearing. Suicide. Fights, periods, and the word 'rape'. Four small letters that send me – inwardly – to the ground. But, I explain, 'Rape is when someone forces another person to have sex.' Preteen, one daughter tells me about a dream she has where she is walking with a boy, and I am shouting to her, 'Wait, wait, wait.' From the age of eleven, they long to go to a thing called a nightclub and yet still play imaginary games with dolls. They cuddle us, and cringe if there is sex in a film. I tell them gently, 'Your bodies are precious. They are your private, precious things.' I say, 'You can always talk to Mum and Dad.' Between ten and eighteen, each age brings a different maturity. These are fierce, delicate and irresolute years. Sometimes, within months, they suddenly change. Our daughters run into their futures, and their dad and I put up moveable barriers and try to hang giant safety nets. Often, my daughters talk about this state of being in-between, sometimes being a child and sometimes not, and I say, 'Take your time. Let it be your time.'

Later, I put my green shorts back on, and walk back up the staircase to my bedroom. Silence spreads around the night and it envelops our Unit, and all the bricks that built the communal house. In my bedroom, I take out my diary, and I write, 'It is one in the morning, I can't get to sleep, I do not know if I will survive.' On a separate piece of paper, I write an account of what has happened, using words I think are right: 'licked me up', 'jack off', 'fingered' and 'sucked'. They are the only words I have but they are not mine. In between I write about God and hope and 'whether there is something up there', and: 'Tonight, I have grown up ten years mentally not physically.' Afterwards, I write about my death, and include a teenage will, detailing my bequests for my posters, pens, stage make-up and two red caps. I leave Alison 'my plants' and my dad 'my book of Shakespeare', and I specify that all my other books are to go to the local library. I sign, date, and put this letter in an envelope, sealing it with glue and tape. I attach it inside my diary with a paper clip. On the outside I write, '*To be opened at a real and true time*'. I put my diary inside my secret box. The box is locked with a key.

This is the first week I write in my diary, and I keep writing for three years without missing a day. I buy a second book and a third book, and they contain daily outpourings, drawings and words, charting the years 1985 to 1987. It is interesting with a diary what is left in and what is left out. Recently, a friend asked me whether I wrote my teenage diary for myself or for someone else. It was both and neither of these.

The book is filled with school, friends, rehearsals for plays, and everything is 'fucking excellent', 'brill', 'ace' or 'crap'. In my fourteenth year, writing becomes *plus fort que moi*, as they say in French; it is stronger than me. Sometimes, I write before thinking, just to feel my fingers grip the pen. It is not a delicate holding, because I grasp and scrawl until there is an indentation in my finger, a red curved notch. I also finish more short stories, poems, plays, and win more competitions. But I write the diaries daily, and there is much teenage talk.

Years afterwards, I finally find and open the sealed envelope, and read the letter. It is insistent and private. Chaotic and clear. Sentimental and authentic. The small missive was hidden in the pages of a diary with a warning, buried in a locked secret box. It is a time machine which I wanted *to be opened at a real and true time*, as though when I was a teenager I hoped that in the future I would understand things better.

Later, when I move into the Breton stone house, my dad brings my paternal family diaries. Boxes of them detail colonial missionary activities, two wars, studies at the Royal Academy of Music, and I think of Iris Murdoch's words about the individual as 'full of private stuff and accidental rubble'. One diary is kept from 1901 to 1980, with alternate entries by a husband and wife. He begins, 'she seems immature but should make a good wife'. Several diaries detail my granddad's school years at Marlborough, a private upper-class British boarding school. Aged sixteen, in March 1920, he wrote: 'Glorious sun. Letter from Daddy. Homer all morning. Hockey match versus Magdalene College. Organ recital.' As I write this book, I compare the contents of our diaries, what daily events we chose to note, and the spaces from all the things left unrecorded.

It is 1985, nearly the end of the summer holidays. I've just got back from Dad's house. I felt sorry for Dad and my stepmum because both babies were sick. Dad said, 'You must be good.' He is often telling us to be good.

Now, I'm with Mia in her bedroom. I didn't tell her about the Mattress Room, and I haven't told anyone because then it is like it never happened. It is easier if it never did, and if you wipe things away then they never existed. Instead, I'm wondering if I should stop being a casual, because Mia has just shaved the sides of her head. Punk is calling me and Kirsty MacColl sings 'A New England', and I'm looking to become another girl.

Mia says, 'We all slept in the Yoga Room on Saturday. It was brill. We stayed up until three. There was Saskia, Lizzie, Troy and all the Kids. Lizzie told a ghost story about a serial killer in the Black Forest. Everyone was there, and . . .' Mia pauses. 'Troy told everyone he'd had sex with Claire and tried it with you. And Claire was better.'

Mia's phrases are said lightly, perhaps she is testing the water, but my stomach hurts. At first, I don't reply. All the Kids in the house know. It is awful, awful and I feel so small; a stupid, ugly thing in the corner of a room. Stripped naked, I am in the cold dark with Claire, and I close my eyes and Mia waits for my reaction. But I throw on a smile, shoulders back. 'Oh right.' All I can think is that I must tell Claire, to protect her, even if she is older than me. There is no other choice.

Leguil talks about a kind of double punishment in traumatic situations where an individual has not given consent. In the case of rape or sexual aggression, not only has the person been forced to have sex but they also feel as though they have forced *themselves* to do something they didn't want. This second forcing is obviously not the victim's fault, coming from disassociation and the immobility of trauma, but it is from here that guilt rushes, with the questions: 'Wasn't it my fault?' 'Why didn't I stop them?' 'Why didn't I say no?' As a consequence of this second forcing, individuals will often find themselves, in their day-to-day lives, developing a general pattern of forcing, a strong sense of obligation and sacrifice. It can translate into self-harm, addiction or overwork. This imagined but very real sense of obligation becomes a matter of survival.

The next day, I choose an odd location for the discussion with my sister: the glass-walled corridor in our Unit. There is no privacy. Whatever the cost, the Fates whisper in my ear, 'Your destiny lies before you and it must be fulfilled.' The Furies know Claire and I are bound together now. They have sketched us trapped in sea-purple darkness. Waiting by the glass door, I feel terrified and ashamed. 'Shame' is the word describing how you feel when bad things happen in awful places with the wrong people, involving your sister. Telling Claire is nuclear-bomb level, the world no longer as it was before. I wonder how to tell her Troy betrayed us. He undid me, trampled on me, one hundred million times over. And I betrayed Claire. I did. But before I have time to think, she walks into the corridor. I stutter, 'Claire, I have to tell you something.'

She glances at me haughtily. My stomach fills with bile. 'I got off with Troy in the Mattress Room. And last weekend he told everybody that he'd had sex with you and has done stuff with me. All the Kids know.'

We stand in the corridor like two fence posts in the

wilderness, holding nothing up and keeping nothing in. The wind whistles around us. She turns and I turn, and she does not respond. This is the first and last time we ever mention what happened.

Looking back at these dense years in the community, the Adults seem to have veered between abandonment and denial. Belatedly, they'd realized things were out of control. But they turned a blind eye, and did not ask too many questions. There was overlooking, a glossing-over, and a denial of responsibility. We were left alone, stuck together, trying to cope. But when I turn to archive documents from the seventies and eighties, it seems this troubling permissiveness invaded much of the Western world. There was a confusion between the recognition that children had a sexuality and the idea that sex for minors was acceptable. In Europe, intellectuals such as Barthes, Derrida and Beauvoir signed petitions calling for the decriminalization of sex between children and adults. The London-based National Council for Civil Liberties became affiliated with the Paedophile Information Exchange, a group actively promoting sex between children and adults. The 2022 Independent Inquiry into Child Sexual Abuse report states: 'In the 1960s and 1970s, some malign influences advocated to reposition child sexual abuse within broader societal debate about sexual liberation . . . In the late 1980s, those involved in political, legal and social-work spheres mooted that some responses to child sexual abuse were "*over-zealous*", or constituted a "*moral panic*" or a "*witch hunt*". Such narratives minimised the scale of the problem.'

It also seems that one of the underlying problems in the community, rooted in the idea that the personal was political, was that it entailed driving underground everything that failed to square up to the political ideal. The politicizing of the personal meant that, for fear of criticism from each other during meetings or in corridor discussions, the Adults never dug beneath the surface. They never opened the doors to our inner lives and faced what was happening.

In the 1950s, Albert Camus finally rejected communism, because he believed it enforced a dangerous submissive compliancy. In his book *The Rebel*, he argued for moderation *and* the act of rebellion, never losing his conviction for social change. Differentiating between revolts and revolutions, he wrote: 'Our criminals are no longer helpless children who could plead love as their excuse. On the contrary, they are adults and they have the perfect alibi: philosophy, which can be used for anything – even for transforming murderers into judges.'

Days pass and there is a crack inside me. It gets bigger as Claire and I avoid each other. She begins the process of remaking herself with new well-spoken middle-class friends, scrambling fast to get somewhere else. They discuss socialism and the Fabian Society. My sister is still arguing with Alison, but pulling herself into the sixth form, and towards university. Meanwhile, I am writing in my diary.

The silence around this time remains. It is a vast architecture of nothing, invisible and yet so strong. To my surprise, the silence never reaches the woods, which remain themselves, somehow still growing in my mind. Hesse wrote of trees, 'Whoever knows how to speak to them, whoever knows how to listen to them, can know the truth.' Whatever way I look at it, the trees are not to blame, and it is important to see what stays untouched, beautiful and alive. That August, night falls on the woods. Owls swoop between the redwoods' branches, screeching towards the dark sky, and part of me is floating up there, drifting in space, beyond the Kármán line.

13. And the Stars Rained All Over the Sky

'non est ad astra mollis e terris via'
('There is no easy way from
the earth to the stars')
Seneca the Younger

'Talk of solitude . . . It is the last resort of
the civilized: our souls are so creased and
soured in meaning we can only unfold them
when we are alone.'
Virginia Woolf,
from a letter to Vita Sackville-West, 1927

At the back of my Breton desk drawer is a fragment of a meteorite. It is a small, black ball, densely dark. It glitters, and is marked with small craters and dents, traces of its high-speed burning passage through the atmosphere. This 'space rock', a solid piece of debris, was a gift from my archaeologist friend. The day he gave it to me, he told me three things about meteorites:

1. From the dawn of history to the present there has probably never been a day when, somewhere

upon the globe, someone wasn't worshipping a 'sky stone'.

2. Experts estimate that between ten and fifty meteorites fall every day. According to the American Meteor Society, only sixteen have been found in Norway.
3. In the Hebrew language, meteorites were called *betyls*, an equivalent to the Greek *baitylia*, meaning 'the residence (or home) of God'. Meteorites house our higher beings.

It's September. The summer is over. 'Hurry up,' Charlotte says, and I follow her to the back of the class, two rows behind the 'nice girl' horde, dressed in pastels, swishing in the scent of Harmony hairspray and Soft & Gentle deodorant. In the front rows are the nerdy 'maths boys'. Last year, I sat with these 'nice girls', who want to work in banks and go to university. But this year, I am at the back. Charlotte is my new best friend. She is petite and pristine, with long, blond hair, wet-gelled round an angel's face. Her plump lips glitter with frosted lipstick. She wears a white T-shirt and a thick gold chain.

That morning, dressed in a purple cardigan and a skirt, it took me twenty minutes to shade my eyelids in mauve and silver, paint Poncho Pink on my lips. Streaks of fuchsia blusher complete my look. But despite my efforts, when I walked into the classroom, a mean girl said, 'You look a mess.' The mean girl always tells me the same thing, and I never reply. It is like I am numbed. Charlotte says I should tell her to fuck off, and I wonder if I should become a punk.

Charlotte and I grab seats next to our friends: an Afro-Caribbean British kid and a white boy, the fourth member of our gang. He's cheeky and has nerves coiled tight like springs. He says, 'All right? All right. All right. All right.' At the front of the class is a small, pale-faced man in a creased corduroy jacket. Our new teacher has greasy hair, and we heard he just qualified. 'Please everyone sit down. My name is Ariel.'

'You have the same name as the washing powder, sir,' the white boy says. The class bursts into laughter.

The teacher blushes. 'No, my name is French. *Ariel.* Now, remember the school policy is that we call teachers by their first names. So, call me Ariel, you don't have to bother with "sir".' He says it boldly like we're going to be friends. In our experimental school, the teachers want to be close to the pupils. It is like being in the community, and I say, 'Fine, Ariel.' Looking him in the eye, I challenge his stare, because I know how to call adults by their first name.

'Now, I am your form teacher, but I will also be taking you for Shared Time. This year we will be studying Youth Culture. But we're going to begin with a project: Personal Identity.'

Charlotte groans. In front of us, a boy has rolled paper into a ball. He throws it up and down, and his straight fringe flips from side to side. In our school we study neither History nor Geography, but Sociology and a subject called Shared Time which means everything is combined. We have access to a sports centre and a working professional theatre. As a result, as an adult I will have extensive knowledge of Marxism, Weber and know how to set up a lighting rig for a play, but will have to teach myself the names of countries, capital cities, basic grammar and history.

'In the Personal Identity course we will be exploring who you are as a person. First, we're going to write down ten things we are, and then ten things we hope to be. Then we will write down our ambitions. Any ideas?'

'I hope to be out of this stupid classroom, sir.'

'I hope we'll get a new teacher, sir!'

Ariel blushes again. 'Well, that's a good joke. But take out your files and write at the top . . .' He writes instructions on the board: *I am . . . I hope to be . . . My ambition is . . .*

Charlotte draws Ariel naked. I giggle. Charlotte whispers, 'Ariel's so boring, do you know what I mean?' I murmur back, 'I am so bloody bored, do you know what I mean?' She says, 'And he's so ugly, do you know what I mean?' I say, 'He deserves a good slap!'

Ariel snaps, 'Girls! Concentrate on what I am saying.'

'Susie was just explaining to me about her Personal Identity, sir,' Charlotte replies.

'Call me Ariel, not sir.'

'It's fascinating,' I say, and he doesn't know whether I'm being sarcastic. But I am testing out being rebellious.

Hurriedly, the teacher writes on the board about the difference between expectations and hopes. 'An expectation is something that you feel will happen to you. An expectation is something we think we can see in the future, from the root of the word *spectare* in Latin, also linked to the word "scope", meaning "room to act". We can differentiate between this word and "ambition". Ambition is a desire for honour, it's something that you want to achieve.' Some people begin listening and writing. Two girls check their lipstick, and the nerdy maths boys begin whispering about telescopes and how the twentieth NASA Space Shuttle has just returned to earth. In front of us, the boy throws and catches his ball of paper, waiting to see when the teacher will react.

Suddenly, I decide that it is time. I have been thinking about this moment for days, turning the scene over and over in my mind. I say to Charlotte, 'You know, this summer something happened to me.' My voice is quiet. Charlotte is writing, putting hearts instead of dots above her i's. 'I was at the community, and Troy was there. All the other Kids were away,' I stammer. I am sure that I should tell someone what happened, even if I am terrified. 'Troy told me something about my sister,' I whisper. Then, I regret mentioning Claire. But I carry on talking, and now I have started, I don't know where to stop. Camus says to name things badly is to add to the world's disasters. But I do not own the vocabulary to describe a long, perfect summer's day stretching past the Kármán line. The Mattress Room.

To get it right, I would have to invent new words, be a Greek *onomatourgos*. A visitor at the community told me about them one night: how Socrates described these ancient crafters of names, makers of the universe. They were also lawmakers, and this meant the one who told the story, who invented a language, was in tune with justice and how the stars aligned. The visitor said that each new experience requires new words. Language is a living thing.

At the back of the classroom, my only lexical resource is the letter I put in the sealed envelope. I say, 'And we got off and then he made me . . .' and I repeat the strange words I wrote that night about licking, jacking and touching. It is like something I looked up in a dictionary, and after the list, I stop and laugh. In front of us, the boy throws the paper ball and it lands on one of the nerdy maths boys' desks. The maths boy looks around confused, as though the paper ball fell from the sky. Charlotte turns towards me like I slapped her face. Under her blond curls is something like shock, and I did not think that Charlotte would react like this. She lives in a new-build house on an estate. Family photos cover the walls. Her dad works in a factory, her mum is a cook, and I think her parents support the National Front. In her bedroom, everything is decked out in lace. Her home is nothing like mine.

She whispers, 'You don't tell other people that kind of thing at school,' and frowns. I swallow and blush, ashamed. It is a situation where I have misunderstood the codes, mistaken right for wrong. I start copying from the whiteboard. The words drift around, and I wonder about my ambitions, my expectations. The teacher says 'to expect' means what you know will happen, and I think about being inside a house and which rooms you expect things to happen in.

At breaktime, Charlotte and the others go outside, and I sit in the classroom, not sure what to do. In front of me one of the plump nerdy maths boys is explaining to a skinny boy with glasses that during the summer he saw the Perseid meteor shower. The plump boy giggles, and then farts. Despite the stink, I laugh, and begin talking to them. They explain that meteoroids are objects in space, and that when they start to travel towards our planet, those that burn up become meteors or shooting stars. The bits that manage to land on the earth are meteorites.

That day it feels like I am falling through space, travelling uncontrollably from what the skinny boy calls the exosphere, into the thermosphere, which burns at 200 degrees, down into mesosphere, the coldest place of the earth's atmosphere. Finally, I reach the stratosphere and then the troposphere, where hot-air balloons fly. Everything keeps happening at once, and I can't stop anything. It's like I have come from outer space, and I am a utopian alien speaking the wrong language, doing the wrong things. The maths boys keep talking. 'Only a few meteorites survive the journey to earth,' the plump boy says, 'but if you look at them closely, at the craters on the surface, they are marked by each thing they touch.'

Later, at lunchtime, I escape from the classroom. There are no school dinners because Maggie Thatcher cut the funding. A local church sells baked potatoes, but I am not hungry. The maths boys are debating the size of meteorite it would take to flatten our school, and I wonder about going back to the 'nice girl' crowd, trying to homogenize. It is difficult to feel at home, and often I bounce between people like a ball bearing flipping in a pinball machine. But this lunchtime, I return to Charlotte because I want to undo what I said.

Outside, Charlotte's boyfriend is waiting, his long easy figure balanced against a wall. 'All right, Charlotte?' he asks. She fingers the bracelet he gave her for her birthday, a tiny gold-plated star on a delicate chain. 'All right,' she answers. He is tall and blond and would be perfect on the cover of a magazine. He is a top casual. Knotted around his neck is a pure wool scarf, nicked from the shopping centre. The tough casuals compete to steal as many scarves as they can. They are like scalped heads to be displayed on a pole. Baby blue. Primrose yellow. Pale pink.

'Coming out later?' he asks. 'Nah,' Charlotte answers. I say nothing. I want to join in, but I am waiting, further along the wall.

'Look,' he murmurs. A gaggle of girls approach. They are gunslingers, with handbags draped over their shoulders. White stiletto heels click, sharp on the concrete path. 'It's Nicky Tucker, the Mars Bar Fucker.'

'Shut up,' Charlotte tells him.

The girls come towards us, as a crowd of kids rushes past, bellowing: 'Fight! Fight! Fight!' A little boy with a shaved head in a shellsuit screams into my face: 'FIGHT!'

Charlotte's boyfriend says, 'Hurry up!' and we break into a sprint. Behind the main classrooms, near to a place we call the Drains, a broken fence backs onto a housing estate. Litter is scattered in the grass, a milk carton wedged in a hedge, crisp packets like polka dots in the weeds. There is a crumpled poster for the racist MP Enoch Powell. At a Conservative Party meeting Enoch recently declared, 'What sort of country will Britain be when the capital city and major cities and areas of England consist of a population of which at least one-third is of African or Asian descent?' Because of people like Enoch there are riots everywhere.

The Drains is next to a main road, a place for smoking

cigarettes, drug-dealing and fights. As we get closer, twenty or thirty kids jostle in a ring, chanting, 'FIGHT! FIGHT! FIGHT!' The piled, tangled circle almost tumbles, almost falls.

In the middle are two top tough casuals, well-dressed bully boys: one short and stocky and the other tall. In the winter – someone told me – they spike snowballs with razor blades. The smaller boy's cheeks are flushed, and the other is pale and dark. A hand slaps a face. Next to me Charlotte's boyfriend yells, 'FIGHT! FIGHT! FIGHT!', every nerve in his body electrified. 'Kick his head in!' The tall boy punches the other's stomach hard. Arms like pistons. One. Two. He falls, doubled-up. The tall one is winning. The stocky boy is on the floor, curled tight like a baby. A punching bag. Then the tall boy kicks and kicks, until blood runs over the round-cheeked face. Suddenly, two girls arrive, shrieking, 'Teachers coming!' and Charlotte and I walk away. She casts a protective shield around herself, and I shelter inside.

You cannot hear a meteorite fall, I learn one day from the nerdy maths boys. It is a silent descent from sky to earth. But research has shown that the electromagnetic energy from meteorites is absorbed by other objects, specifically trees, leaves, fine frizzy hair and dark clothing. When a meteorite falls, these objects heat up and expand. This means that when a meteorite descends to earth, before it lands we hear strange sounds – crackling, rumbling, popping, hissing and swishing. The song of a falling star.

*

That evening, in the community, our Unit phone rings. I pick up, praying the call is for me. We all share the same telephone number but have incoming-calls-only phones in our Units. When you answer, often you walk around the house calling the name of the person loudly: 'Eagle', 'Violet', 'Saskia', 'Firefly. Phone!' On the top floor, there is also a phone box where you can phone out and leave coins to pay for your call. Nobody pays, and there are rows about this at the Friday Meetings.

'Hello. The community.'

'Susie?'

'Charlotte?' We burst into giggles. I am surprised. Charlotte rarely calls me.

'I can't stay on the phone long. I've got to work in my uncle's chip van this evening. I just wanted to talk to you about what you told me.'

I don't know what to say.

'He's not your boyfriend, is he?'

'No. And I hate him now.'

'Then stay away from him, and don't ever go back.'

I can hear her mum calling 'Charlotte!'

'I'll see you tomorrow.' She puts the phone down before saying goodbye, and we never mention it again. Our conversation is awkward and painful, but Charlotte places a compass at the centre of my life, and she guides the landing of my scarred meteorite.

Over the next few years, I visit her house often, going from the community to her lacy bedroom, where a collection of teddy bears wear T-shirts saying *I Love You*. This house becomes a kind of part-time home, like my camp friend Isa's house – which has paintings on the wall, pine floors and rugs – and later I'll enter the homes of my friend Natasha and another pal, a first boyfriend, and more. In these houses, I eat, sleep, smoke, drink vodka, throw up, talk, impress, deeply embarrass myself, and do homework on the floor. Most of these people, following the pattern that has been established since Mary stayed at the house, rarely come to the community. We move in one direction.

During these teenage years, I learn to stay in other homes, and I am constantly being someone else somewhere else. Later, when I work in child psychiatry, I learn that certain teenage patients with little parental surveillance are often described in French as *électron libre*. This means, in physics, an electron which is weakly linked to the core, and I recognize myself in this description: whizzing around, alone.

In France, when our daughters reach adolescence, my partner and I try to keep an open house. I get to know my children's friends (and their parents), and often adore them. Over burger feasts or soup dumplings, we have discussions about feminism, fashion and books. Of course, sometimes, when my daughters are bullied or meet the wrong person, I long to build barriers and prevent the madness from entering our house. Yet a person and a home must have doors and openings. If we close the doors to our inhabited spaces, they become totalitarian and segregated.

Interactions with the outside allow us to transform. As sociologist Erving Goffman stated, gated communities, isolated social housing, prisons, nunneries, utopian communes and psychiatric hospitals are all potentially at risk of becoming hermetically sealed. When I attended the seminar about sexuality and incest in Paris, the psychologist also explained why we need to keep institutions open, as closed groups become sectarian.

Historically, psychiatric units are classic examples of closed institutions. Even in today's evolved psychiatric care, when patients stay inside too long – often through lack of outpatient care – we talk about these individuals becoming institutionalized. Over time, people lose cognitive skills and can develop behavioural problems. Recently, a young man told me, 'I feel terrified when I am out on the streets after two years inside the hospital.' Patients become highly vulnerable, lose the ability to read social cues. One of the ways psychiatric hospitals have of counterbalancing this phenomenon is to keep their doors ajar.

As an arts therapist, I organize events in psychiatric hospitals, inviting artists, musicians, and film-makers to work with staff and patients, inside and outside the institution. These projects have rigorous guidelines, but they allow people who would never normally meet to spend time together in the company of art: a psychiatrist and a young man with schizophrenia discuss a bagpipe concert; a woman with a severe personality disorder talks about Dadaism to a documentary-maker; a nurse, an artist and a patient paint a spring landscape together on a giant canvas. When I think of Hannah Arendt and her ideas for activism in *The Life of The Mind*, it seems open doors root us firmly in the political present because we are constantly bumping up against new people and ideas. A home, a house or a hospital must be safe, but none of them should be a cage.

As riots break out across UK prisons, fifty inmates escape and mattresses are burnt, and in the mornings and evenings I am often to be found in the communal Post Room. Here, I pick up my letters from Isa, from new school friends I see every day, from distant friends and my paternal great-aunt – who has kept in touch – from strangers whose adverts feature in the back of *Smash Hits* magazine: 'Wanted: pen pal. I like cats and Sylvia Plath.' I will write to anyone, anywhere, and inside my envelopes my letters soon include collages made from ripped fashion magazines. Tearing glossy faces in two, I use metallic stickers, fluorescent pens, car spray paint, Tippex, nail varnish and lipstick. My envelopes are decorated, and sometimes I kiss the paper, leave the outline of my lips.

Letters are another way to make friends, a link with the outside world. When I post my envelopes, it is as though I launch them into the sky, and the replies come back from all over the cosmos – from Germany, America, Japan, London and France. Later, as an adult, connecting with people on Twitter or Instagram will feel like this. There is something temerarious about a friendship with a stranger. Emily Dickinson wrote, 'A letter always seemed to me like immortality because it is the mind alone without corporeal friend.' These letters are one of the ways I keep my doors open, when I am bullied at school or in the community. They resist loneliness.

It is an odd feeling, to be lonely in a crowd. For I am lonely inside and outside the community. There is no lack of people, or of friends. The loneliness comes from my constant movement, an inability to dwell, safely somewhere, and be myself. In *My Life in Orange*, Tim Guest describes his childhood loneliness in the various communes of the Indian guru Bhagwan Rajneesh. 'Loneliness was like frozen water, like falling into a pond in the dead of winter and turning blue with cold. Loneliness was like stepping on a live rail.' It is the loneliness of the meteorite.

It is too cold to get out of bed, but through my bedroom walls comes the blaring sound of Dire Straits. A new member, Gabriel, moved into a room next to our Unit. I want to tell him to turn the music down, but tucked under my duvet I write in my diary instead. 'There's a party tonight. I think it will be brilliant. Charlotte is going, and all the class.' That afternoon, I can't find anything to wear because I have grown again, elongating out of control. In my drawers, the clothes are too small and the colours are faded, because when I do my washing I don't sort dark from light. For tonight, Sunshine lends me her new fake cricket jumper and I have a new lipstick, Heather Shimmer, bought with money nicked from the communal washing machine. Yesterday, when I did my weekly laundry, the coin drawer hung open like a treasure chest and the coins begged to be taken. I have started to get money from here regularly. The money is my due.

Later, when I am getting ready, Claire pushes open my bedroom door. 'Are you wearing that tonight?' She examines the jumper on my bed. I am trying to style my hair, checking my reflection.

'Yes, I borrowed it from Sunshine.'

Under Claire's steady gaze, I fumble as I backcomb my short hair, trying to tease my fringe up and around. My dream is to look like a magazine model, with a fringe curved like Hokusai's *Great Wave*. But when I check in my mirror, everything is drooping. Disappointed, I get my Heather Shimmer, and Claire takes my place. She pencils in her eyebrows, and next to her I apply the lipstick. In the mirror, we are reflected, two sisters. She pouts, I pout, and giggle at our matching lips. Claire almost laughs, but then she frowns.

'You just want to look like me! You want to do everything like me!'

'I don't want to look like you,' I say, trembling, even if I wish I was as pretty as her. But Claire thinks she's fat and that I am skinny. Sometimes she gets angry and gives me her old clothes. 'I am too fat,' she shouts, and then she takes all the clothes back again. We're constantly fighting and making up. It is like we are too close and too far apart.

Now, she snaps, 'Yes, you want to copy me. All you ever do is copy me. If you're not careful, I'll put your hand in a liquidizer and flip the switch on.'

'You and whose army?'

'You think you're so tough. And your make-up is minging!' She slams my door, and her anger stays in my room. I shout, 'Fuck off,' hoping she can hear, but in my mouth the words are awkward, like 'wanker', 'shit stain', 'wicked' and 'do you know what I mean?' Now, I finish most sentences with 'do you know what I mean?' because I am trying to speak like a tough little casual girl.

Before I leave my Unit, I sneak into Claire's room. Spotting her new necklace, a tiny Yin and Yang on a silver chain, I grab it, slide out of her room and hide the necklace behind a basket. Fuck Claire!

Downstairs, in the Washing-Up Room, Thomas is washing two cups from a pile of dirty plates, and arguing, loudly, with a weekend visitor. The journalist has come from Liverpool with his wife to discover communal living. Earlier, I took the couple around the house, gave them the usual patter.

'We are a non-income-sharing community, but everyone contributes to maintenance and running the household.' I also tell them about the new Space Meetings we've been having; the discussions about boundaries, norms and rules. They are run by some of the new Adults, like Jim and Gabriel, who are therapists. They talk to us about co-counselling, where people take it in turns to be counsellor and client. It requires no experts trying to help people, and this is good. Emotional outbursts are encouraged as 'discharge'.

The co-counsellors often pry and poke. 'Tell me how you feel! Look at me! Tell me!' They ask questions and stare. The Kids laugh at them, and we call one man Tetrahedron behind his back, because he's counselling so many women and in multiple love triangles. Yet despite our laughter, I hate it when they try to get us to look at them, and I get lost in the vortex of their stare. My stomach hurts when I talk to the co-counsellors, and I write in my diary: 'Why do they insist on all these questions? I am only a kid.'

But earlier, I didn't tell the visitors about the questions and love triangles, and instead explained, 'We have cleaning on Sunday, and everyone joins in, even the Kids.' I laughed at the word 'cleaning' as we all know cleaning is pointless. The man nodded, but his wife looked with dismay at the broken furniture and stained bedding in the Visitors' Room where the couple were sleeping. 'How interesting!' she said.

Back in the Washing-Up Room, the visiting journalist looks intense, and Thomas's roll-up jerks as he says, 'The miners were only on strike for a bloody year. They shouldn't have gone back to work in February. The world was ready for a revolution. Look at the riots this year. This is real action!'

'Yes, but the miners had to go back to work.'

'Yes, but what do you think happened in Russia?'

The journalist snorts. 'Come on, everyone is questioning communism now, you don't seriously want –'

I butt in. 'Thomas, when are we leaving?'

Thomas is supposed to be giving Troy and me a lift to the party. I don't want to be with Troy in a car. But I don't have a choice. The two men glance at me, and then laugh at a private joke. I know it is something to do with me.

My new face has a mask. Eyes blue and black. Lips flushed. Hair sprayed. But the clothes are useless. When they stare, I feel naked. Thomas winks at the journalist. 'We'll leave in about ten minutes.' Anxiously, I look at my watch. Thomas says, 'Just piss off now!'

In the Kitchen, David is making bread. He wolf-whistles and I stand awkwardly. 'Very nice. That skirt is short. If you were any older, I would . . .' David breaks into laughter, and says to no one in particular, 'They all still want to marry me.' At the stove, Eva is stirring a massive pot of soup. She sniffs. 'You're wearing an awful lot of make-up.'

I say nothing. Suddenly exhausted, I think I won't go and see Alison in the Cowshed before I leave, because she'll probably say something about my make-up, and I wonder if you can see my knickers if I bend over. Claire says that is the test. Ten minutes later, I stand outside the stable block and call out a 'goodbye' as I hear the regular squirts of milk hitting the plastic bucket.

In the car, Troy and I barely speak. 'I hate him,' I will write in my diary that night. 'He should find a prostitute to satisfy his needs.' Thomas drops us off at a suburban house. In silence, we walk through a wooden gate and up a path. I get to the top first and ring the bell. A girl opens the door, and she smiles past me, at Troy.

Inside, I check out the surroundings. On a rustic window ledge is a collection of polished brass objects. Laura Ashley floral paper lines the walls. The woodwork is freshly glossed, and it is a house like most of the houses on the outside. Each time I go to these parties, I notice there are mums, dads, children, curtains, cushions and settees, fridges filled with food, wardrobes with clothes. It's different to my life, and I am desperate to fit in. These homes do not need to be explained to visitors and potential members. It is odd, when you think about it, to be taught as a child to describe your 'way of life'.

In the living room are the girls from my class. 'Let me take a photo of you.' I grab my camera from my bag. Inside the viewfinder, I frame a line of fourteen-year-old girls. Flicked hair is sprayed in layered waves. Baby-blue plastic earrings dangle from ears. Matching bangles clunk. Skirts, shirts and heels coordinate. The girls are immaculate. Click. I take the photo, and Charlotte grabs my camera. 'Let me take a picture of you!' And I try to run away but she snaps a shot. Click. In the photo, I am holding a small boy in a headlock. He holds a plate of crisps and looks concerned.

Troy says, 'Put some music on.'

'But not too loud!' The birthday girl is anxious. Her parents are next door, having dinner with the neighbours. We have been warned we must behave. She puts on 'Like a Virgin'. We pile our handbags into a pyramid, dancing to Madonna. Feet and hands synchronize. On the sofa, the boys hold a peanut fight. Before long, couples form. Troy is with the birthday girl, and I know that they will only snog. There are parents next door. Things can only go so far. This is not the community. I've been to parties before, but this evening I feel like an outsider, a tourist in another world. I lift my camera and click.

As the evening moves on, I don't know where to go or who to talk to. After what happened this summer, I can't be in the same room as Troy. Someone puts on 'Careless Whisper'. Lights are dimmed. People start to slow-dance. Hands drift from the waist, go slowly from First to Second Base. All I can think about is the Mattress Room. Leaving the living room, I walk into the kitchen, out through the door into the night. In the garden, leaves crunch beneath my feet, and above, stars glow. Boys in oversized sweatshirts are smoking, even if the birthday girl said this was strictly banned. If the maths boys were here, I think, we could look at the stars. But they don't go to parties.

Instead, by a fence, a boy swigs from a bottle. 'I made a cocktail from my dad's drinks cabinet. Put in a little bit of everything. It's wicked. Want to try?'

I gulp down a mouthful and pass the bottle back. The boy swigs again, and hands it back to me. Soon, other boys come and join us. None of the girls are there but I say, 'It's fucking good,' and I like this dizzy feeling, the rush, the dazzling glow. We drink until the bottle is empty. No one tries to kiss me, or hold my hand. But I think this is where I should be, getting drunk with the bad boys. Later, Thomas comes to pick up Troy and me. At the door, I tell the birthday girl's mum, 'Thanks so much for having me.' I try to be polite, but slur, 'They said it will be sunny tomorrow.' Then, I burp loudly, and the mum gives me The Look. Afterwards, in the car, I think I will be sick.

When we arrive at the house, Troy goes inside, and I vomit by the air-raid shelter. In my Unit, all night, I run along the glass corridor, get to the toilet, am sick and return. No one sees or hears me, and this will become a habit – the drinking, the dazzling and the vomiting.

The next morning, I tell Alison I have the flu, and miss school because I cannot face the class. Most weeks, I miss a day at school. It's not difficult to negotiate. During the following weeks, a strange thing happens. I take a book from my shelf, a small hardback leather volume. I do not remember the title for I do not read it. Instead, I bring the volume crashing down onto my arm. I don't know where I get the idea, but I call this 'growing bruises'. It seems to equate to something, and I don't know what the sum is, but I sit in my room and grow the bruises like plums all over my arms.

The bruises are part of my armour. This protective layer corresponds to my new understanding of the community ideology: as I grow up I must drink, be hard-talking, tough and wild. The kind of gal who can survive the Wild West. I begin to have a hard outer shell like my little black ball, I am a bit of space debris that got nudged out of orbit and burnt while crossing the atmosphere.

Later, when I work with adolescents in psychiatric units, or adults talk to me in sessions about their troubled teenage years, I often think that what is extraordinary is that these people, like the little rocks, survived their journey to earth. Most meteoroids come from the asteroid belt, a kind of scrap-metal junkyard filled with the remains of planets formed 4.5 billion years ago. They travelled at speeds of up to 160,000 miles per hour, got through the seven layers of the atmosphere. Meteorites are intriguing, as they start their existence in a cosmic trash can and become sacred objects to be revered.

In the spring, I decide to change my hair. Lizzie's mum cuts and Lizzie dyes. Mia comes to watch, standing in ripped Levi's and a black skintight top. Lizzie's mum slides buzzing clippers up the nape of my neck, snips until my short hair is even shorter. When she leaves, Lizzie holds out a brown lump wrapped in layers of cling film. Mia says, 'Where did you get the *black*?'

Lizzie says, 'My aunt buys my dope,' then chucks the dope at Mia. 'Roll a joint.' Lizzie paints bleach on my hair. The acrid smell mixes with the scent of burning dope.

Flipping through magazines, I see photos of Leigh Bowery, the performance artist, red paint trickling down his moon-round face. Mia passes the joint. 'I knew someone who once used toilet bleach to dye their hair. It went a brilliant white, but it all fell out.'

We laugh and begin talking about magic mushrooms, and I think of the 'nice girls' at school who sip Babycham. In dyeing my hair, I am leaving that world behind, saying goodbye to fitting in at school. Thirty minutes later, Lizzie rinses out the dye. In her mirror, my hair is yellow and tangerine. I was aiming for a sharp peroxide-white. Lizzie promises, 'We'll do it again.'

But Lizzie is going to London. So I buy a bleach kit and do it alone. I ignore the fact that she told me to wait a week, until the dirt builds up so the bleach eats through grease before it hits your scalp. For nearly two hours, I leave the bleach on, waiting, until I get burn marks, blisters round my ears.

That evening, Alison sees me in our Unit corridor. 'You look appalling. Absolutely dreadful. And you do realize that the dye can go into your brain!'

But I don't care. My hair is Marilyn white. My body is a war ground, but I lead the battles now, and I start to wear bright red lipstick and white foundation, and give up on dressing like a casual. At school, I begin to wear two-piece vintage tweed suits, leopard-skin tights and Doc Martens shoes that are too big. I stuff the toes with newspaper. At junk markets, I sift through piles of mildewed clothes, find a three-quarter-length cream mac, a man's pinstriped suit, a pair of crocheted flares, and begin a collection of 1950s cocktail dresses. My favourite one is ruched and olive green.

While all the girls in my class are perfecting their Lady Diana flicks, I practise drawing giant black Betty Boop eyes. I am very erratic about removing the make-up. In Shared Time that year at school, we study Youth Culture and look at pictures of mods and rockers on the Brighton beaches. Charlotte dresses in jeans and a white cable-knit jumper. I wear a navy-and-white spotted fitted sixties top, a miniskirt, black tights and blue suede creepers. A boy turns to me, saying, 'You know, Susie, you've got a cracking personality, but your clothes taste is down the drain.'

At school, I am regularly bullied now. Outside the art classroom, where we are learning about colour symbolism in medieval painting, a girl pushes me. Yellow is for betrayal, the colour of Judas. My back bangs against the wall. The girl starts to grab and hit me daily. I am perfect prey. The idea of self-defence is beyond my comprehension. In the community, the Adults refused to intervene with bullying among the Kids. No one has ever defended me or told me bullying is unacceptable. So, I retreat, terrified. She spits on me. 'You fucking freak.'

Slowly I transform into this freak. There are only a handful of us in our school. Freaks are the bastard children of the punks. But, unlike punks, the freaks don't choose their name. It is thrown at them, implying abnormality. Nevertheless, I adore dressing-up even if in the community dressing-up is looked down on: as researcher Melford Spiro observed of the Israeli kibbutz, socialist clothing must be utilitarian. For me, every day becomes a carnival, and I meet Mia and Lizzie's punk friends and the women dance, spit and laugh. Spiked, made-up and free.

It becomes an act of resistance to put my body inside a make-up mask of red, purple and cobalt blue, a worn leopard-skin cap, a gold leather skirt and a Victorian velvet jacket. There is something mysterious in dressing-up, and the word 'mystery' is linked to the Greek *myein*, 'to close, shut', perhaps referring to closed lips or shut eyes. Mystery keeps things safe.

It is much later that I read Diane Arbus's words: 'There's a quality of legend about freaks. Like a person in a fairy tale who stops you and demands that you answer a riddle. Most people go through life dreading they'll have a traumatic experience. Freaks were born with their trauma. They've already passed their test in life. They're aristocrats.'

The French philosopher Nicolas de Condorcet wrote that clothing is one of the things that distinguishes us from other mammals. It is a form of non-verbal communication, and when I work in hospitals clothes allow us to differentiate nurse from doctor, patient from member of staff. In terms of fashion, punk clothing and that of the freaks was DIY and inventive. It embodied the anarchic spirit of art movements like Dadaism. Punk musician Judy Nylon acknowledges punk was about shapeshifting. My freak fashion gave me what Nylon calls the 'widest possible wingspan'.

Today, partly because of my professional life, I am often smartly and neutrally dressed. If you cross paths with me in the street, I look like a slim, tall, blond-haired, white, middle-class cisgender woman. My partner, rebelling against his own upbringing, is often casually dressed and has a ponytail. When we meet people, and particularly liberal hippies, they always assume he's the wild child and I am the straight guy. Our books are judged by their covers.

We often laugh about this – how when people first see us, they make assumptions about our present, but also our past. We share the awareness that our clothes protect us, they allow us to pass from one world to another.

My middle daughter says, 'Maman.' In our French kitchen, she stumbles with her words, suddenly awkward. She is nearly eleven, 'Mum, can I buy a bra top? Because all the other girls in my class have bra tops.' Smiling, I say, 'Of course we can.' She gulps, 'I am so happy.' We hug and I think about my own lingerie.

Over a decade ago, I decided to stop buying plain cotton underwear and threw it all away. Privately, I wanted to indulge my femininity, and I set myself the rule only to cover my skin in lace. The words for underwear in French are taut, soft and sensual: *culotte*, *broderie*, *soutien-gorge*, *décolleté*. Velvet ribbons and gauze. Holes and threads. This lingerie collection has developed into a personal and political choice, a reclaiming of my female body, an experiment. It has become another point of resistance.

In France, I've learnt a cultural sense of the body linked to pleasure, and sensuality. My body can be serious, beautiful and engaged. It is a complex argument, as Second Wave feminism opened the path for the Third Wave feminists, and my daughters say, 'We can be feminists and beautiful. Have hairy legs and wear miniskirts.' Neither they nor I began the revolution or fought the first fights, but that does not mean we cannot ask questions.

When we go to the shops to buy my daughter her first bra, I want her to feel indulged, for the awkward terror of adolescence to be held by pleasure. Writer Iris Murdoch thought the best life was made of 'continuous small treats', and as our daughters become young adults, I call out to the sky to bring them good fortune for their different journeys.

Upstairs in my office, I open my desk drawer and hold my meteorite in my hand. The small dark stone has travelled through so much, so fast. It survived turning from a meteoroid into a meteorite, transitioning from the cosmos outside to inside our atmosphere. The plump boy in my class called them 'micro-miracles', and perhaps the metaphor for meteorites should not be about speed, for it takes meteorites hundreds and thousands of years to get to earth. Instead we could think of meteorites as epic travellers, Homeric space stones. For when we crack open these black stars, their insides tell us about the entire history of the solar system, a story from the very earliest moments, when solid material formed in the solar nebula. Meteorites, like teenagers, can tell us about where we start.

14. The Part of the House That Can Tell the Most Things About You

'Everything in here was clean and bright, warm and cosy. What a joy it is in life when you happen to have a clean, warm kitchen.'

Olga Tokarczuk, *Drive Your Plow Over the Bones of the Dead*

'The kitchen is a theatre for many emotions.'

Bobby Baker, *Redeeming Features of Daily Life*

Mao said the Chinese Revolution allowed the people to 'grasp the essence of the thing'. In any utopian experiment, inhabitants seek unprecedented authenticity, the space to be themselves. But over the years, in the community, what is seen as authentic and true shifts alongside changes in the world. In the mid-eighties, the New Right philosophy – Thatcherism in Britain and Reaganism in the US – leads to free-market victory over social justice. Liberal instead of social democracy. With the end of the miners' strike, the hard left has lost political favour in the UK. Inside our house, collective life becomes less important. More people have employment outside the community. The house becomes whiter, more British and less international. The new members enter and exit the house with private vehicles, driving to jobs as graphic designers, therapists and part-time teachers. The community enables their income to be small because our living costs are cheap. No one spends much money because people still look at what you buy and wear. It's still important not to care about fashion. The cows have gone because only Alison was milking them, and our milk is now delivered in small glass bottles. House maintenance, gardening, and cooking meals are still communal, but the Adults pursue more individual dreams, the agrarian fantasy replaced by self-development.

We're in the Breakfast Room, next to the Kitchen. In the world outside the community, Swedish home retailer IKEA will soon open its first British store. Crowds will flock to buy home decor, revamp bedrooms, bathrooms and, most importantly, the kitchen. Italo Calvino wrote that 'the kitchen is the part of the house that can tell the most things about you.' In our Kitchen, flies buzz over unwashed plates, but the sticky papers that once hung from the ceiling have gone. Instead a machine crackles as ultraviolet rays attract flies, and a high-voltage power grid kills them instantly. I ask Sasha, 'Do you want some bread? David made it, so it's edible!' I laugh too loudly. Sasha has just moved in, with her mum. She is sixteen, wears thick glasses and wants to be a doctor. Sasha is quiet, and I would like her to be my friend. Twisting my bleached blond hair, I regret having put on red lipstick.

'Where's the bread kept?' Sasha's eyes glance anxiously around the room. They alight on the dirty plates in the sink with blemished rims, the cutlery coated with oily smears, the soggy breadcrumbs and spiderwebs. The fly machine crackles again.

The Breakfast Room is the old TV Room. The Adults demolished the wall, and the new room opens into the Kitchen. On one side of the Breakfast Room, a raised platform has been built with fitted seating around a metal woodstove. As we are still mostly self-sufficient, the Adults made the Breakfast Room – cut, sawed, installed and painted. Opposite the raised platform is a line of pine tables and benches, also made by members, and a tea and coffee area. It is cosy, yet the space is torpid. It is easy to get stuck here, read the paper and let the hours pass.

In her recent book *A Little Give*, Marina Benjamin described the kitchen as the heart of the house, 'the place that pumps love through its different chambers, lifeblood of our domestic operations'. A recent study shows that in most Western homes, the kitchen is the room we spend most money on. Purchasing new ovens, fridges, worktops and white appliances, we lavish money on this room. Yet, historically and politically, the kitchen is also a place of female oppression, where women are expected to carry the burden of domestic work, 'chained to the kitchen sink'.

In most utopian experiments, the kitchen is a focal point. In the early twentieth century, architect Alice Constance Austin dreamt of collective housekeeping and liberating kitchens from houses. In *The Grand Domestic Revolution: A History of Feminist Designs for American Homes, Neighborhoods, and Cities*, historian and architecture professor Dolores Hayden describes how Austin planned for homes where food arrived 'from the central kitchens to be eaten in the dining patio'. The dirty dishes 'were then to be returned to the central kitchen for washing by machine'.

'Oh, the bread is always in here,' I answer Sasha, pointing to an old enamel bin. 'BREAD' is stamped into off-white, the word indented in navy blue. The bin has an arched lid with a curved handle. Every time you open or close the bin, it clangs.

'Just check who made the bread before you try to cut it.' I joke, reaching inside to remove a fresh loaf. Our bread is always rectangular. Pillows of raw dough are cooked in metal tins. The edges of the bread are rough and grainy.

Throughout my childhood I eat this bread, and as an adult, in our French kitchen, I relish it. Heavy wholemeal bread – detested by my partner and daughters – is my Proustian madeleine. Oddly, I only realized recently that this bread is the closest thing I possess to a favourite childhood dish. For all my meals were eaten collectively.

'What are you laughing about?' Claire says. She's sat on the new bench, flicking through *NME* magazine. Next month, Claire is going to London to a David Bowie video shoot. A guy from the community is a cameraman, and he's filming the video for 'Let's Dance'. Behind the counter, I take the breadknife and start to cut two doorstops of bread, hacking through the heavy dark wholemeal crust. There is the fermented smell of yeast, the tang of salt. 'Do you want it toasted?' I ask Sasha.

*

In our Breton house our kitchen is a warm, unrenovated, rustic French affair. The cupboards are too small for our jumble of saucepans. Forty different spices, oils and sauces crash together on a shelf. Sticky cookbooks are piled up alongside notes from schools, a teapot collection, bills and vitamin pills. A and I cook in here, and bicker over stirred saucepans of (my) chickpea stew, (his) grilled meat and (our) homemade flatbreads, Passover biscuits, glasses of wine and mugs of lime-flower tea.

There are family arguments, hugs and dancing. A and I whisper secrets here, forgetting our eldest daughter can hear everything upstairs in her bedroom, through the uninsulated floor. We also argue. 'Stop messing with my food,' I snap, when he micromanages my cooking, adding extra seasoning. 'Chill out,' my daughters moan, when I nag them about clothes, washing and every subject under the sun. Kitchens are nourishing but also claustrophobic, dangerous places. A kitchen provides food but is full of knives and hot oil.

Peter, Mia's brother, comes into the Breakfast Room. Peter is dribbling a ball. He is a wiry, dark-haired, half-Italian boy. 'I'm skill. I'm skill,' he shouts at the top of his voice. 'Spurs are on their way to Wembley.' Peter dashes from the Breakfast Room into the Kitchen. Ball on foot, toe pointed. Ball in. Ball out. 'Tottenham's gonna do it again.'

On the raised platform area, Gabriel skulks by the woodstove. Back hunched, he's reading *Jonathan Livingston Seagull* and sipping a mug of herbal tea. Gabriel used to work as a flute teacher, but is taking a break, trying to 'visualize my future', and is training to be a co-counsellor. He's been in the Breakfast Room for a couple of hours. Tense and undirected, he pulls at his corduroy jacket, whistles operatic tunes. There are moments like this in any home: the domestic frustration of nothing happening, nothing changing.

'I'm gonna score,' Peter shrieks, kicking the ball. 'I'm gonna SCORE.'

Peter darts round the kitchen, where Jim, the therapist, makes lentil casserole. He's following a recipe from the ring-bound *Whole Earth Cook Book* but has added peanut butter and dried apricots. 'Just to make it crunchy and sweet.' Jim has red eyes from peeling twenty-five onions, but he is happy about this, because crying means that he is expressing his emotions. He calls it 'letting his stuff out'. When his daughter Sally cries and wets her bed, he also calls this 'letting her stuff out'.

Jim is about to stir his onions when behind him Peter skids past the sink. It is full of chopping boards and dirty pans. 'Get out of here,' Jim yells at Peter. 'I'm trying to cook dinner.' The ball leaves the room. Peter follows. The phone rings in the Post Room and someone picks up, and then yells loudly, 'Jim, it's for you, some guy from the co-counsellors.' Jim disappears to take his call.

Later I will read articles about co-counselling as a therapeutic technique, and how the lack of any theoretical foundations, and the reliance on group work, encourages a cult-like conformity. The movement is linked to Scientology and reeks of charlatanism, chat and prattle, whistles and bells. The boundaries that exist between a client and a therapist do not apply in our community. We live with the co-counsellors and, as Kids, we are the fodder for their experiments. Jim is Australian and believes in open relationships. 'Hello,' he says, into the receiver.

In our French kitchen, we start our days over cereal and yogurt, and we finish them in the same room at night. Some days, we cook cheap frozen food, and on others glaze local scallops, moving between trash food and gourmet cuisine. Our middle daughter rustles up ramen soup, and the eldest posh cheese on toast. The youngest has just learnt how to make pancakes.

This room is a place we come back to throughout the day, unloading and loading the dishwasher. It is a place of return, and the word comes from 'turn', meaning both to revolve and to transform on a lathe. Our kitchen pulls us back to ourselves and our rough edges are rubbed smooth again.

In the Breakfast Room, the toast pops up. Smiling at Sasha, I grab the industrial tub of peanut butter. 'That's disgusting.' Sasha points at the lid glued to the pot with a thick, dried crust. Inside, natural peanut butter floats in a swamp of oil. The shelf beneath the breadboard is lined with crumbs. The sink behind us is coated in grease. Inwardly, I laugh at Sasha's reaction to the dirt. Cleanliness is unnecessary. It is like tan tights, net curtains, and mattresses. My hard body can sleep on the floor.

Peter skips back into the Breakfast Room, leaps. 'I'm gonna score.' Nothing can stop him. He picks up his ball, throws and catches. 'Let's play Piggy in the Middle. Claire. Sasha. Who wants to play?'

Claire raises her eyes from an article she is reading on Morrissey and the post-punk band The Smiths. Morrissey dresses like a granddad in oversized cardigans, and twirls like a melancholic crow. In the eighties Morrissey is seen as alternative but later he will express support for the far right.

Peter shouts, 'Come on, who wants to PLAY?' Everyone ignores him. I am buttering the toast.

On the platform Gabriel snaps and throws his book down. 'Please shut up, Peter.'

No one hears because no one is listening. Gabriel picks up a newspaper, but it's clear he can't concentrate because the ball is bouncing, and he frowns. In the Kitchen, there is a sizzling sound. Jim's onions are burning. The fly machine crackles as another insect is exterminated. Claire is singing a Morrissey song.

Gabriel stands up. Suddenly, he shouts, 'Peter, stop playing with that bloody ball!'

I put the peanut-butter knife down, glance at Sasha. I see Peter turning towards Gabriel. Peter stops moving. He throws the ball to one side. But Gabriel is charging at him. He rushes from the raised platform, pushing pine furniture out of his way. Chairs tumble to the floor. Gabriel dashes forward and grabs the ball in one hand, and Peter in the other, shouting, 'You stupid bloody little boy!'

Gabriel's eyes protrude from their sockets. His anger shuts him inside himself. Gabriel is like a nervous horse in a narrow corridor, galloping forward, his metal bit pulled tight. Gabriel whips himself. Nobody can stop him. He has Peter now, between his hands, and he shakes him.

Gabriel's rage pours into Peter's body. Peter says nothing. Gabriel screams, 'It's unacceptable. All I want is peace and quiet.' He pushes the ball into Peter's face.

Everyone has stopped moving, and I hold the peanut-butter knife, my finger near the sticky blade. I look at Sasha, at Claire. In the Kitchen, the onions turn black. Claire stands up. She rushes over and pulls Gabriel off Peter. Peter slumps to the ground and Gabriel and Claire are opposite each other. The gap between them could be measured with a shift of silk. He's over forty. She's sixteen.

Without warning, he slaps her around the face. She hits him back. And, quickly, they are slapping and pulling at each other. And then, he hits her face, and I stand by the bread bin, furious, and begin to cry. The tears are hot and warm. The fight, the dispute, the brawl, the argument, the attack, it seems to last for an eternity. I am shocked, Claire is shocked, Peter is shocked, and so is Sasha.

One day, as an adult, I attend a clinical conference about shock. A psychiatrist explains that the word 'shock' comes from the Old French *choquer*, meaning 'to strike against' or the violent encounter of a pair of warriors. It implies a degree of suddenness and severity. There are two different clinical shock syndromes: physiological and psychological. The first is physical, involving a dramatic reduction of blood flow, while the second happens after a traumatic physical or emotional experience, impacting the victim's state of mind.

Psychological shock impacts hormones, cognition and emotions. When people experience a traumatic or shocking event, the body goes into 'fight or flight', releasing two major stress hormones: adrenaline and cortisol. High levels shoot through the body and brain, disconnecting reason from emotion, impacting memory. This is why, I explain to health staff, when giving a difficult prognosis, information should be repeated several times, clearly and slowly, as if patients (in a state of shock) won't understand or remember important details.

Shell shock, first recognized in World War I, produced mutism, anxiety, paralysis, nightmares and depression. In Vienna, Sigmund Freud testified as an expert witness for the state, stating military psychiatrists had 'acted like machine guns behind the front' and were therefore the 'immediate cause of all war neurosis'. Freud refocused the responsibility for war trauma from individual failure to a systemic issue.

In the Breakfast Room, we are shocked, and then, all at once, the room is filled with people. Kids and Adults enter and depart. Voices are raised, and others speak in soothing tones. Gabriel is nowhere to be found. The gas under the burnt onions is turned off and Jim scrapes them into the compost bin. He comes and stands close to me, looks at me without blinking or smiling. 'Tell me. How are you feeling?' He stares like he can see into my insides and all I want to do is punch him in the face.

Suddenly, Alison is in the Breakfast Room. She rounds us up, holding our arms, saying, 'Come on, come with me,' and other people arrive. I put the loaf back in the bread bin and replace the enamel lid. Bill once told me that enamel is made from crushing glass and fusing it inside a furnace. An enamelled object is scorched, but the outer shell gleams. Suddenly, we are enamelled. Alison is looking after us and takes us upstairs.

That night, I write in my diary, 'I want to kill Gabriel. I want to kill him.'

A week later, there is a meeting about what has happened. Gabriel is not there. He has gone to stay with his mother in the Cotswolds. People say in quiet voices, 'Whenever he entered the room, it was as though there was something strange in the air.' There are understanding sighs. Outraged faces.

They say, 'It isn't the first time he has been difficult.'

Jim says, 'He struggles being around the Kids. It's a pattern.'

People listen, and then another man, who is also a therapist, adds, 'We mustn't forget we are all essentially good. We can all be forgiven.' Someone nods a head in compassion, because one by one the Adults seem to agree it is difficult being around the Kids. Everybody knows the Kids are now difficult. All the co-counselling therapists who have been on weekend courses, and qualified in two days, have something to say about the Kids, about the patterns we are in.

A new language has invaded the community at this time, a kind of psychobabble, a precursor to the misuse of the words 'trigger' and 'trauma'. The language itself is not questionable but rather who uses it, where, when and how. Therapeutic language is a delicate thing. Constructed between therapist and client, it is rarely formulaic. In the community, the co-counselling use of language is miasmal. It envelops us in a poisonous cloud, in the way that psychobabble not only weaponizes therapeutic language, using expert terms to control, but also removes the space for authenticity.

After the incident in the Breakfast Room, we sit for hours talking. Before the meeting is over, Jim turns to me and says, 'You know, no one is ever to blame, because we are all damaged.'

That night, I write in my diary that the conversation made me feel: 'So shitty. It was horrible. I now feel like I can't live my own life. I don't know what to do.'

In the meeting, there is agreement things have gone too far. But this is the fault of society and not individuals or the community. Possibly, it is the fault of the Kids because we are out of control. Yet, despite what is said in the first meeting, over the following days there is a general feeling something must be done. During more meetings and discussions, a decision is taken: Gabriel will be asked to leave, but whenever it suits him. He comes back to live in the house and hangs around for weeks and months. Finally, he moves back in with his mother.

A few years later, Claire is at university and Peter no longer lives at the community. I am in sixth form. Sasha is studying to be a doctor. Most of the Kids and Adults have left, and new people have arrived. One Sunday, I walk into the Kitchen to see Gabriel, in a tweed jacket, talking to a new female member.

He says, 'Hello, Susie.'

'Gabriel's moving back in,' the new woman says.

Rage scrambles through my veins. It careers up and down. I stare at him, and I do not know what to do. My breath disappears and my voice has gone. Gabriel repeats, 'Hello, Susie.' He grins again, and there is something like triumph in his smile. In the Kitchen, I look past him, through him, and decide he does not exist. Nodding at the woman, I walk slowly out of the Kitchen and go back up to my Unit. On my bed, I hug my knees to my chest.

This is not what our utopia was intended to be, and as I write this, Foucault's words come to me: 'People know what they do; frequently they know why they do what they do; but what they don't know is what what they do does.' In the community, despite good intentions, the institution adopted a lenient ethical code, either ignoring what was happening or hiding behind the moral relativism as though everything could be forgiven and forgotten. For years I struggled with this, secretly convinced there must be a right and a wrong. In the book *Anthropologies of Revolution: Forging Time, People, and Worlds* by Igor Cherstich, Martin Holbraad and Nico Tassi, a chapter on 'Revolutions, pretence and belief' explores how, in the USSR, people behaved in ways that meant they formally accepted reinforced ideology while not holding a sincere belief in the content. They did not practise what they preached. In the community, behaviour betrayed beliefs. The bad days undid the good.

Now, when I work with MA students on interculturality, I talk about the vital importance of tolerance and ethno-relativism, but also keeping a steely eye on the limits. 'We all want to get on with every colleague coming from every culture in the world, but we must recognize our limits. What won't you accept? Gun carrying? Homophobic behaviour? Misogyny?'

When I look back at the community, most of the hopeful, funny, left-wing, idealistic members were not individually or intrinsically 'bad people'. Susan Sontag, in a 2003 TV interview, gave her understanding of human beings' moral sways: 'Maybe 10 per cent of people in the world are really cruel . . . and about 10 per cent are truly good . . . and then the other 80 per cent can go either way.' She described her own frustration with people's constant surprise at atrocities, because we are all capable of such things. The work of Primo Levi echoes this viewpoint: 'Monsters exist, but . . . more dangerous are the common men, the functionaries ready to believe and to act without asking questions.'

What I appreciate in these standpoints is their humility, the lack of self-righteousness. Jacqueline Rose adopts a similar position in *Women in Dark Times* when she states, 'The sole way for the revolution – for any revolution – to usher in a genuine spirit of democratic freedom . . . is to recognize the fallibility at the heart of the revolutionary moment itself.' When we want to implement change *and* look after each other, all these thinkers advise us to adopt a to-and-fro between what is happening and what we think, between our ideals and our humanly messy realities.

For the following few years in the Breakfast Room, the Dining Room, on the stairs, in the woods, by the vegetable plot, in the car park, on the drive, on weekdays, weekends and during all four seasons, I bump into Gabriel and refuse to speak to him. At first, he laughs at me, and then it irritates him, and he tries to get me to speak.

'Hello,' he says loudly, when he sees me. 'HELLO!'

But I will not acknowledge him. It is an unspoken promise I make to my sister, and a line I draw in the sand. Even when the tide rises and my mark disappears, I return and dig my line again. I look through Gabriel. He does not exist.

Years later, I tell Claire that I refused to speak to him. 'For all those years?' She looks at me with wide, acknowledging eyes. I nod my head. I won't forget.

Throughout our childhood, Claire was my witness, and I was hers. As adults, our conversations about the community provide statements of proof. Over the years, we faced silence from other people, the many things that were left unsaid, a rubbing-out of everything. Over the years, we told each other frequently, 'Yes, you are not crazy. It happened. I was there with you.' To bear witness is to offer testimony, a presence. It is impossible to do this alone. Recognition is an act that allows partial repossession. It is only when I've left the community, when I am in my twenties and thirties and talk to Claire, that I begin to question what happened inside our home, and ask why and how. When I take decisions for my own children, I realize their care comes before politics – or perhaps care, in all its shapes and forms, is one of the most fundamental forms of political activity.

15. Where the Wild Things Are

'It is true, we shall be monsters, cut off from all the world; but on that account we shall be more attached to one another.'
Mary Shelley, *Frankenstein*

'What would an ocean be without a monster lurking in the dark? It would be like sleep without dreams.'
Beowulf on Film: Adaptations and Variations, attributed to Werner Herzog

It's nearly the end of 1986 and Claire and I are in the shopping centre. Sat on a bench, we're sharing a prawn cocktail sandwich. We didn't have enough money to buy one each because we're saving our cash for the winter sales. She's looking for a jumper, and I want gold ankle boots.

Yesterday was a bad day at the community. Claire found out I had borrowed her skirt – without asking – and she needed it for her Saturday job. She ripped the cover off my favourite book, *Fame*, and I screamed, 'Get out of my life.' *Fame* is the novel of the film about the High School of Performing Arts in New York. All the artistic students are different, burnt and beautiful, and I dream of going somewhere like this. As we're growing up in the community, our longings and dreams are like tentacles. These elongated limbs are creeping out through the windows, our hopes for the future are opening doors. We're growing up and out of our home.

But inside, the Adults sniff at us, and outside we don't fit in. We know we can't live in suburban houses; they are filled with Thatcherite monsters. Where do you go to from utopia?

Adolescence is often depicted as a 'monstrous' age. Between acne, hair and hormones, we experience metamorphosis, turn from a child into something else. In her book *Managing Monsters*, Marina Warner highlights the past century's struggle with what she describes as 'the nostalgic worship of childhood innocence'. She cites mythical figures such as Peter Pan, examples of our culture's devotion to a utopian prepubescent state. Warner explains how this notion of a pure beginning has consequences, as it implies that in growing up we might become monsters. In the utopian community, this pressure is great, for if we grow up badly we are evidence the utopia has failed, that our blueprint didn't lead to paradise.

When our model was designed, children were to embody two countercultures: a hippy childlike state of wonder and simplicity, and the New Left's liberated, political Kid. In becoming teenagers we betray our beautiful childhood where we ran free as noble savages, true and pure. As we put make-up on our teenage faces, we betray feminism. When we crave McDonald's we betray Marx and ecology. As we gossip obsessively about school, music, magazines and fashion, we betray everything. The Kids become the fallout from the dream. But how to parent us now, when right from the beginning we have been told we should bring ourselves up?

'Who do you think did it?' Claire says. We're walking past shop windows, mannequins in crop tops, leg warmers and headbands, leather and power suits. Claire insists, 'Tell me who you think did it!'

She's talking about a scandal at the community. A while ago, Violet and a couple of the therapists decided all the Kids should do something artistic as a group. In the Kids' Room, where we have never played, they decided we should paint a mural on a dirty white wall. Violet gave us old tubes of oils and tins of gloss paint. Twenty of us started daubing paint, and Sunshine and I painted hills and a cottage, Brandy added a rainbow, and Claire painted a horse. But, after a few sessions, we forgot to clean the brushes, or couldn't be bothered and everyone got bored. We wanted to play computer games, watch the new soap opera *EastEnders*, or go into the woods, smoke joints and swig something Lizzie calls 'scrumpy', a strong cider that makes you puke.

For a few weeks, the mural stayed unfinished on the wall, badly done. But one morning Violet found out someone had painted a bright red swastika in the middle. It was a scandal. A shock. The Adults called a meeting because the symbol dripped in red, and it is against everything we stand for. They said it was a sign the Kids are tipping over the edge, because it is a Nazi symbol from the Holocaust. 'It's used by the far right,' Violet shouted, and we were silent because Violet is Jewish and we knew it was bad. But nobody would admit to doing it. The Adults made us paint over the swastika in white.

'It's ridiculous,' Claire says. 'We'll never know who did it.'

'I know,' I answer. In the Kids' Room all you can see now is a faint geometrical form. It glows red through the white.

In the shopping centre, Claire finishes her sandwich. 'They're stupid fucking hippies anyway.' She redoes her lip gloss. I shift uncomfortably as I know that she's right, some of the Adults are stupid. But they are also left-wing, and against sexism and racism. They are trying to change the world, and that is amazing. We're lucky, is what I still think.

Inside the community Claire is more rebellious than me, but outside I am more rebellious than her. I hate school, and now, on my school report, even though I get good marks, the teachers say I am 'too critical'. Every day, I complain about the education system and inequality. Sometimes the teachers listen, and sometimes they sigh. Claire says I should shut up.

In the past year, I seem to be becoming a bad girl. My clothes are getting more outlandish. My hair is short, bleached. I shaved the sides, and got my nose pierced. From one nostril dangles a silver ring. Claire got her long hair permed, and wears jumpers and jeans. She is starting to get good marks at school. She is sixteen and I am fourteen and we're growing apart. We both feel like outsiders but are reacting in different ways. However, what we always do together is our pretending game.

*

We go into Topshop. My favourite lipsticks come from here: deep reds, and bright, matte orange. I head to the make-up stand, and Claire prods me, starts wiggling her hips, doing the dance from *The Rocky Horror Picture Show*. In *Fame*, the students see this cult movie in New York, dress up in stockings and suspenders. Men in make-up, girls as boys. In the shop, Claire and me whisper, 'We're on planet Transsexual.' As she flips through dresses, Claire, who is studying English A-level, tells me these monsters are like Frankenstein's creature, 'the product of someone's warped experiment'. But inside their castle they revel in their difference – enough to drive them insane. In *Rocky Horror* a 'normal' couple are corrupted by the monsters. But the monsters are the heroes of the tale. As Claire grabs some Topshop clothes, we mime the choreography for 'Time Warp', laughing hysterically.

'Let's try stuff on,' she tells me, and I follow her into the changing room. As she opens a cubicle, she chats to another girl, saying she's a journalist and I am an actress, getting stuff for a photo shoot. I am wearing a vintage fifties suit with a miniskirt. Claire is dressed in black. People often think we're much older than we are. The girl is trying on a crushed silk, bright blue all-in-one jumpsuit, with a high ruffled neck and matching belt. She looks at herself in the shop mirror. 'What do you think?'

Claire mouths at me, 'Hideous.'

'You look wicked,' I tell the girl.

'Yeah. It's the kind of outfit you could dress up or down,' Claire says.

'That's exactly what I thought.' The girl grins.

I butt in, eager to continue the 'pretending'. 'You could

wear the belt around your middle or as a scarf around your neck.'

'Exactly.' The girl glows.

Or you could wear it round your head, I think of saying, but decide this is taking the joke too far. The girl leaves, and Claire and I collapse in laughter on the changing room floor.

Claire and I often play this pretending game, becoming different people with different lives. We play our game with strangers or with family. Recently, we saw our grandma Mutti again, tidied ourselves up, and said our life was 'normal'. She said, 'Goodness, you are nice. You might have turned out like awful hippies or something,' and afterwards we laughed at our prowess. Over the holidays, we played it with a dour cousin. Single, plump, and suffering from bad knees, he owns what they call 'stocks and shares' but has a reputation for counting his slices of bread. Over lunch, Claire kicked me under the table, saying, 'We met this really strange person recently. Can you imagine, he was always complaining but he had everything.'

I kicked her back. 'Yes. It was completely weird, because he was so lucky, but had no idea.'

'He was in a bubble like he would float into the sky.'

'Oh, fancy that,' the cousin said, and Claire and I continued, wanting to giggle so hard our bodies convulsed.

'Oh yes. He was really strange.'

Pretending to be someone else is fun, and doing it with Claire is wicked. When we're outside of the community, we pretend we're students, actors, cousins or friends, or whatever we need to be. When we're in the North, we're studying in Liverpool. In the South, we're from Brighton. We're eighteen, nineteen, twenty. We're rarely ourselves. Being ourselves is too weird.

All teenagers pretend as part of the learning process. I see this with my own children, and the young people I've worked with over the years. Yet our pretending game was extreme because we were so rarely authentic in our own lives. As Akash Kapur describes in his memoir *Better to Have Gone*, about growing up in the Auroville commune, all children of utopian communities are exiles. Even now, as an adult, when I see *Stranger Things* I relate to the character Eleven, and the freakish feeling of being an experiment.

For Claire and me, our pretending game gave us agency. We felt in control when we put the masks on ourselves. When we lied to strangers, invented fake personas, pretended to be *Rocky Horror* monsters, or told people outside the community that things were normal, we regained power over our lives. We took the reins and called the shots, became the puppet masters. We felt beautiful, wild and free. Later, when I went to university and my friends got in sticky situations, I would ring their banks' managers or their landladies, pretending to be an outraged mother. Pretending gave me strength.

Yet the downside to this pretending is that fake monsters were born from these 'false selves'. Research by psychologist Susan Harter shows that, for teenagers, being able to be authentic and share their opinions is associated with a higher level of perceived self-worth. Similarly, adolescents' suppression of personal voice and self-expression is linked with depressive symptoms. For me, the powerful feeling of pretending was in part rebellion but in part a trap, and I got lost in all the costumes, scripts and characters. Finding my real self became difficult, the mask got stuck to my face.

As I write this, I also realize our pretending only happened outside the community. I wonder if it was because Claire and I carried secrets from inside. We never mentioned to anyone what had happened in India or the Mattress Room, with Lionel or Gabriel. No one outside the community knew these things. They had been whitewashed by the Adults (or ignored), painted over like the mural on the wall with layer after layer of paint. Perhaps as Claire and I were fiendishly pretending, our dark secrets from inside utopia were the real monsters we were running from.

Back at the community, I am in Lizzie's room. She's rolling a joint. 'Guess what I just heard? The Adults decided at the Friday Meeting to ban Kids' mixed sleeping. We can't sleep together in the Yoga Room, in our bedrooms, or anywhere else.'

'What do the Adults take us for?' I am furious. Since we were little, the Kids from different Units have slept in the same room together. We're not like other people and the Adults never cared about this before. Lizzie raises an eyebrow. But I can see she isn't bothered. She's leaving the house next year anyway. There are rumblings that other people are leaving soon too. Lizzie examines her reflection. Her mirror is decorated with pictures of Blondie and The Cure, ripped paper, men with smashed black make-up.

'It's totally stupid,' I rage. 'We should bring it up at the Friday Meeting. I don't understand why they can't talk about these things openly?' Even though, deep down, I know everything is hidden and nothing ever brought into the light. Lizzie outlines her lips in glistening red, wipes a spot of lipstick from the corner of her smile. The Sleeping Ban news flies over her head. Lizzie has only been here for two years. But this house has always been my home.

Outraged, that night I write in my diary, 'Do they think we're little girls?' I don't understand the Adults' trying to take control. For years, they have told us to be autonomous. Throughout our childhood, they avoided all rules. After what happened to me in the Mattress Room, the ban seems ridiculous. We can, I am convinced, look after ourselves. The Sleeping Ban is a scandal, and the choice of the word 'ban' is telling. For a ban is a decree that is publicly proclaimed, and in the twelfth-century 'to ban' was to curse. The Sleeping Ban is the subject of much discussion. The Kids have been publicly named and cursed.

Later, Lizzie and I head downstairs for lunch. We eat leftovers and, when Max asks for help, Lizzie refuses to do the washing-up. All the other Kids shake their heads. 'Please participate,' Eagle begs as she carries plates to the Kitchen, but we disobey. Our chimera is multiplying heads and limbs; the haystack creature swells out of control. By this point there are twenty teenagers in the community. Eva frowns. Max sighs. It is a Kids vs Adults battle. We are a painting that has gone beyond the paper, and now we have been banned. The Adults are attempting belated parenting, and implying we're unsightly, unbelievable. Ed barks, 'Fucking kids. Thank god I never had them.' Barbara snaps, 'We're a collective! But the Kids don't pull their fucking weight.' Charles mutters, 'These Kids are impossible.'

Moon Unit Zappa, daughter of musician Frank Zappa, wrote in the foreword to the book *Wild Child: Girlhoods in the Counterculture* that the lack of boundaries in her communal house gave her an 'awful floating feeling'. Noa Maxwell, who grew up in an ashram, reflected in the *Guardian*, 'If you have no boundaries in your life the world is quite scary.' As I follow Lizzie upstairs to her room, I feel guilty for not helping the Adults, and aware of our monstrous capacities. The therapists and co-counsellors have told us, 'You must manage your inner dialogue. You are in a pattern, blocked.' I say nothing to Lizzie, but it is a terrible feeling, to know we are responsible. Outside, snow falls and settles. Later, in the woods, I smoke a damp cigarette. Sat on a fallen tree, I ask myself question after question, until I am shivering, desperate and confused. The winter days pass, and I long for a vessel to hold my impossible self.

At the start of 1987, in my diary, aged fourteen I make an assessment of the previous year. 'In some ways I've changed for the bad but I've grown up a lot.' The good list includes kissing a boy at a party, going to camp with Isa, getting on better with Sunshine. On the bad list, I note that 'I am still smoking and drinking' and another bad point is my stealing, which I think is out of control. Coins buy me make-up and cigarettes, and I steal from everyone except

Alison. Since I was little, I've known our monthly budget. To steal from her would be unfair. Finally, I write that the worst thing that has happened in the past two years is 'the incident with Troy, which is still an unmentionable subject with Claire'. I add that recently Troy sent me another note, asking me to go to the Mattress Room. But I didn't. I hate him. Part of me still floats beyond the Kármán line, and that part of me cannot find a way home.

But I conclude the assessment by writing, 'Praying helps, praying helps.' Between the ages of thirteen and sixteen, even though I have no memory of this ever happening, I often write in my diary, 'I pray daily.'

Two weeks later, I leave to go on a school trip to Northern India. The trip has been proposed to stop my boredom at school, because for months, to anyone who will listen, I complain, 'I hate school.' The work is too easy and I don't know if I should hang out with the maths boys, the 'nice girls' or Charlotte. I can't really tell anyone about what is happening in the community. It is my secret.

Recently, I was tested, along with another girl, to see whether we should be put up a year. When we got the results, Alison met with the teachers, and returned with her face cracked into a smile. 'It's amazing. You aren't going to move up a class even though your results are excellent, particularly in Maths. Instead, you'll go to India in January. Normally the trip is for older children. It's such an opportunity.' It seems like changing classes would make me too different, too clever, and it's better to go away.

Word spreads around the community. In the Kitchen,

Eva is grilling pumpkin seeds to decorate nut loaves, 'Wow, India. It is such an opportunity.' Jim joins in, 'It will be such a positive experience. A change!' When I bump into Thomas, in the garden, wrapped in an old duffel coat, he looks almost jealous and exclaims, 'You are so lucky.'

I write in my diary, 'I am pretty nervous. Why do they all keep saying it is an opportunity?' Yet I never make the connection with what happened in India with Claire.

This is the dichotomy of the community:

India good. Grammar school and moving up a class bad.
Commune family good. Nuclear family bad.
Helping others good. Ambition and helping yourself bad.
Running wild good. Overparenting bad.
Poverty good. Materialism bad.
Intervention outside the house good (as in criticizing the system). Intervention inside the house bad (except for mixed sleeping).
Bare face good. Make-up bad.
Innocent noble savage children good. Teenagers and mixed sleeping BANNED!

Before leaving for India, I take a photo through my bedroom window. The landscape is bathed in thick white. Tree branches bereft of everything. For the trip, I have been given a photocopied pamphlet; on the front of it is written 'Images of India, Our Changing World'. Inside are chapters including 'A Biography of an Indian Village', and instructions on 'How to Put On a Sari'. That day, I roll my strength into a ball, and Alison drives me to meet the airport coach. Among the crowd of parents and children, we share a rare hug. She says, 'Have a lovely time.'

The trip changes me. It is a watershed, as though I have been searching for where I can grow outside of utopia, and I am given an answer when I board the plane to Delhi. Nearly all the other pupils on the trip are aged sixteen or seventeen. As I walk along the aisle, I seek out the unfamiliar, and an older girl beckons to me with naughty, bright blue eyes. 'Come and sit next to me.' She looks like she would try to make the sun run. As we fasten our seatbelts, she says, 'So, is it true you live in a hippy commune?' Nodding, I don't correct her and say it is a community. She says, 'Cool,' and I settle back into my seat. Natasha gives me the answer to how I can grow up.

By the time we've landed in Delhi I have learnt many facts about Natasha. She is terrified of flying – she is sick into two paper bags. She's nearly seventeen, but her boyfriend is twenty-two. She smokes, and is obsessed with Paula Yates because she looks like a glamorous murderess. Natasha loves being thin and is invincible on the topics of music and suicide. She has no brothers or sisters, had a 'bad time' as a child. She lives with an aunt and is a highly sarcastic vegetarian who takes photos of her hipbones. I have made a friend.

That night, in the dormitory, I write: 'It is strange here, but I met a girl called Natasha. She is ace.' During the month in India, I keep two diaries – my own private diary, and the official trip diary for school. The latter must be written daily and will be checked and handed into the teachers. They are two entirely different records, but I am used to compartmentalizing. Over the following weeks, I write in my official diary about visits to a rubber factory, a sugar mill and a bicycle factory, drinking chilled bottles of Campa Cola, and sucking sugar cane. There is a day trip to Delhi, visiting the National Museum – where I admire the paintings – and the Indira Gandhi Memorial. I write, 'The place was so lovely. They had a tall iron pole and if you could get your arms to touch around the back of it then you had a wish.'

The other diary details my friendship with Natasha, a boy, and two Indian girls. I describe a fainting fit after smoking Indian beedi cigarettes with Natasha, writing, 'Apparently, I had a few convulsions . . . I got up and afterwards I didn't feel too bad, but I had a massive lump on my head.' When I see the teachers, I say, 'It must have been the food.' I don't mention the smoking because, as I write in my diary, 'They'd make out I was an innocent, and Natasha was corrupting my mind.'

The month in India is relentless. I write, 'Every day, I am so tired, so knackered.' I barely eat, and have food poisoning as we travel around the Golden Triangle to the Pink City, the Red Fort, and work in a rural village. In the official diary, I describe meeting the regional president of Haryana, being solemnly presented with an engraved metal tray. We participate in the school debate and watch a censored version of *The Sound of Music*. In my personal diary, I write about 'the other men', lingering in museums, behind street kiosks. A stranger strokes my bum, another squeezes my breasts, one runs a hand inside my top – and I am very scared. I write they are 'perverts'. But I say nothing to the teachers.

In my personal diary, I write, 'I am a weirdo now', but I also feel liberated, because, for the first time, I have told an outsider about the community – what Natasha calls, provocatively, 'the hippy commune'. When she hears about the Sleeping Ban, she laughs and laughs, saying 'Bloody hippies!' It's like I have found a shape where I can be myself, or at least where my secrets can be told.

During our last week, we return to Delhi. Natasha and I explore alone, walking through streets that, at fourteen, I love and fear. Following this trip, I'll develop a lifelong love for India, and will return to work and travel there. For now, Natasha and I jump in the back of a yellow and black rickshaw. As we screech through the streets, we slip and slide. We are alive, crackling with electricity, swinging between wonder and vulnerability. Tomorrow, we're going home.

Back at the community, the Adults ask, 'How was India?' Exhausted, I don't know what to say. For months, I have been flickering from one form to another. Now, I find myself making choices recklessly. When I get back from India, something bursts into life, and I become Natasha's friend. I am fourteen, she's seventeen. We are divided by light-years, what a nerdy maths boy in my class calls 'globular clusters'. But I do not recognize our age difference because, since I was six, I have been friends with Adults and older Kids. In my diary, I write, 'I am smoking beedis, I miss Natasha. I feel really crazy, weird.'

Natasha and I begin to write to each other daily. In the

Post Room at the community, I receive hundreds of letters from her. We write about clothes, films, the general election, and Margaret Thatcher becoming prime minister for the third time. Each of her letters to me is addressed to the 'Hippy Commune', and alongside the address she writes 'Diet Pepsi is the Opium of the Masses' and 'I'm wearing fur pyjamas and leopard skin underwear' and later 'School can't be that bad Soozie it just can't'.

Returning to the classroom, I sit with Charlotte. At breaktime, the maths boys tell me about new stars and black holes. But, at lunchtime, I now disappear to the Sixth Form Common Room. I tell Charlotte, 'I'm off to see Natasha.' Charlotte shrugs her shoulders as I walk away. In the Common Room, Claire is furious when she sees me walking in. I am trespassing in her space.

Another day, in French class, I explain to the teacher, 'I've got a meeting about the India exchange.' I bunk off school and catch a bus to Natasha's, as she has no classes that day. I begin to do this a few times a week, or more. Either I go to the Sixth Form Common Room, or I bunk off, and nobody seems to notice.

When I arrive, Natasha is in the kitchen. She is dressed in jeans and a plain white T-shirt, her long, dark hair combed back from her face. The kettle is on. 'Want some vodka in your tea?' When I nod, she pours the transparent liquid into our mugs.

In the living room, we perch on the leather settee, being careful of the cream fitted carpet. Natasha is particular about these things. She puts a heavy glass ashtray on the coffee table, opens the window. 'Want a fag?' We smoke, sipping hot vodka tea. 'I'm corrupting you. Don't tell your mum,' she says. But I laugh, because I think I am already corrupted, have bought the T-shirt and seen the film. Alison trusts me to look after myself.

During our tea and vodka sessions, Natasha plays me Velvet Underground songs on repeat, drawn-out lyrics about cutting and dying. I cry, and she looks at me, and says, 'Let's have toast. I *am* corrupting you.' We talk about how one person a day in Britain is now reported to be dying of AIDS. Another day, she shows me the film *Christiane F.*, about a thirteen-year-old becoming a heroin addict in Berlin.

One night, Natasha, her boyfriend and I have a *Rocky Horror* evening. Her aunt is away. Before watching the film, Natasha pours us large glasses of vodka. We have red painted lips, black eye make-up, fishnet tights, and Natasha's boyfriend strokes my thighs. He says, 'Having fun?' Afterwards, I write in my diary, 'I go mad every time I've seen Natasha. I go mad.' Yet Natasha shows me art where people are beautiful monsters, outsiders: Mrs Robinson in *The Graduate*, the rebellious gay couple in *My Beautiful Laundrette*, the priest in the film *Lamb*, played by Liam Neeson. The priest helps a young pupil escape from an abusive Catholic reform school and tries to create a new life for them both, but ends up drowning the boy.

These films and many others we watch focus on violent, rebellious coming-of-age stories. It is as though before I met Natasha, I didn't know where I fitted, and our friendship and her iconoclastic vision have given me a home. I feel free drinking vodka, listening to 'Walk on the Wild Side'.

Yet it is only years later that I see how hard this new world was for me, because I was a seedling in comparison to Natasha's sapling. If she was a yearling, I was a foal. Despite thinking I was grown-up, as we ventured into unknown territories I was too young, too gullible and too unformed.

'I don't like Natasha. She's too old for you.' In her bedroom Claire puts a postcard on her noticeboard: Siouxsie Sioux. Then, sticking a drawing pin through a leaflet for the local Rape Crisis Centre, she adds: 'And her best friend is weird. You should keep away from him.' Natasha's best friend makes lamps with dollies hanging themselves. They dangle, ropes around pink plastic necks. Now, I spend every lunchtime with him and Natasha in the Sixth Form Common Room. Even if I am only fourteen, I get invited to the same parties as Claire and dance with her friends. I walk out of her room, slam the door.

In my bedroom, I open my schoolbag. Inside is a small black metal tin, picked up at a market, along with tinted 1920s floral photographs. In the box are paracetamol pills, and I count them because I need ten. This is the number it takes to die. Natasha and I read it in a book. Every day I ask, 'Should I die, or stay alive?' The box is in my bag, and I will ask this question for months and years. I act in plays, take drama exams, sleep at friends' houses, drink, smoke, sleep at the community, go to Dad's house, then punk clubs and mosh in the pit. In the small metal tin, I also place razor blades. Self-harm replaces what words cannot say.

I don't tell anyone what is happening, not even Claire. In my diary, I write and rip pages out, but others I leave, where

I scrawl 'I thought I'd do it I did, but now I am happy.' I have built my own government, and this is my system of defence. Secretly, I long for someone to stop me, look at my scars, sit me down and ask what is wrong. But Natasha is the shaky island on which I've planted my flag, and she has her own problems. She thinks she's going to leave the sixth form, might fail her exams. Sometimes, when I am at school, I stare at the teachers hoping they will see what is happening to me. I am burning, running, that is all I know, steaming into a wild world.

When my two eldest daughters were small, their dad made them a book called *Monsters Don't Wear Jumpers*. It was based on a series of jokes, a kind of game they'd play, describing the different things that monsters did or didn't do. On each page was the same group of monsters: hairy and short, tall and bony. The monsters were purple, green, black and brown, had five eyes, or one, or tentacles. At the top of each page was a sentence:

Monsters don't wear jumpers.
Monsters don't eat soup.
Monsters don't like dancing.

Then, at the bottom, was written 'Yes they do', and in the picture the monsters would be wearing jumpers, eating soup, or dancing. They were doing the ordinary things everyone does.

I think the point of the book *Monsters Don't Wear Jumpers* was about understanding that monsters are considered as outsiders, things that are radically different to us. Yet monsters are also normal. Etymologically, 'monster' entered the English vocabulary in the early fourteenth century, and referred to a 'malformed animal or human, afflicted with a birth defect'. The word came to us via the Latin *monstrum*, a 'divine omen, especially one indicating misfortune'. But *monstrum* derives from *monere*, 'to remind, instruct, or teach', because we have so much to learn from looking at what we think are wild monsters.

When I work with clients, I always find it useful to unpack their monsters, take off the frightening masks, see what people are really scared of – the real monster hiding behind the mask. Recently, I was chatting to A about the community and monsters. He started talking about what had given birth to our utopian dream. He mentioned the monsters that had haunted my parents' generation and the Adults in the community: World War II, the lack of food during rationing, corporal punishment at school, their difficult experiences of being evacuated or estranged from their absent parents, repressive discrimination in terms of gender, class and race, the trauma of the Holocaust. Utopias, I reminded him, are always born from dark times, an attempt to make something better. As we spoke, I wondered how many of the boomer generation's hidden monsters we were channelling in the community, carrying a kind of epigenetic dread.

'Come on.' Claire is pulling my arm. We're heading down a corridor towards the Yoga Room. It's pouring outside. A gale is blowing. It's mid-afternoon, but strangely dark outside. I have begged various Adults for a lift to see Natasha, but no one will take us anywhere. We're stuck thirty minutes' drive from everywhere. It is often like this.

The other Kids arrive: Troy, Saskia, Brandy, Michael, Karl, Mia, Lizzie, Jason, Tina, Sasha and Ophelia. It's one of the last times we'll all be together. 'It's just the right moment to move out,' the Adults explain. By the Dining Room, we walk past Charles. 'Where are you off to, Karl?' he asks nervously. 'You know there's going to be a storm?'

Karl says nothing. He doesn't like living here, and refuses to speak to Charles. Lizzie doesn't talk to her dad either, because he found LSD in her bag, and Tina has fallen out with Walker as she slapped a girl at school. Charles looks at me.

'We're going to the Yoga Room,' I say.

'Remember, no mixed sleeping there. It's BANNED!' Charles says. The thirteen of us ignore him and march off. We file along the corridor, move as one.

In the Yoga Room, we put ourselves in a circle. Troy sits opposite Lizzie. He fancies her. Everyone knows. She is beautiful, a Mediterranean punk princess. But Lizzie has a twenty-year-old boyfriend who plays in a punk band. Troy smiles at Lizzie, and I watch. Inside me everything hurts.

I turn and smile at Sasha. But she's edging close to Michael. He's going to university soon. Sunshine told me Sasha fancies Michael but Michael fancies Mia now. There is a sudden crash. It comes from outside.

'Let's look.' Lizzie pulls open the shutters. On the lawn, the world swirls in dangerous spins. Even in the darkness we can see bushes and trees being dragged from roots, hear threatening creaks, as though our woods will tumble. We all stand for a moment, looking into the storm, until Troy announces, 'Let's play.' We return to the circle.

The rules for our game are as follows:

1. Players sit in a circle.
2. One player is nominated as High Priest. The player to his/her immediate left is Little John. The player to Little John's immediate left is Number One, etc.
3. The objective of the game is to reach and keep the position of High Priest.
4. The High Priest always begins the game.
5. The High Priest chooses another player, saying, for example, 'High Priest to Number Two'. Player Number Two must immediately respond, choosing another player; saying, for example, 'Number Two to Little John'. Little John must immediately respond choosing another player, and so on.
6. Any hesitation in replying, stuttering, laughing, or mistakes in pronunciation result in the player concerned being relegated to the last number.

Troy is the first High Priest. He begins, 'High Priest to Number Three.'

Mia grins. 'Number Three to Number One.'

'Number Two to . . .' Ophelia stumbles with her words. We all laugh as she is confined to Number Eleven. Everyone moves up. The hierarchy changes. From the woods we hear cracking, a whine, a roar. The wind howls. Troy starts again. This time, he chooses Lizzie.

'High Priest to Number Three,' he says. I'd like to slap his face.

'Number Three to Number Seven,' she says. I am Number Seven. I throw it back.

'High Priest –' Lizzie collapses into laughter and is relegated to Number Eleven. Everyone moves up again.

For hours, we carry on. It gets darker and we have school the next day. The wind blows stronger. It is a warm, southerly gale. Air from Hurricane Floyd has flowed across the Atlantic Ocean and is heading towards Northern Europe. 'High Priest to Number Two.' 'Number Two to Number Eight.' Again, the High Priest Troy begins a round. Again, Little John and the eleven players answer. Winds rush through the vegetable garden, the orchard, the woods and across fields. There are seventy-knot gusts, rumbles of thunder. Flashes of lightning clear the sky. Up and down the circle we move, losing and gaining power. Troy has been High Priest for a long time. No one can usurp him, even though I want him to fall, to watch him suffer. We bombard him until he falters, stuttering 'High Priest to – to . . .' and that is when it happens.

A bolt of freak lightning hits a very old, perfectly shaped oak tree in the middle of our field. The tree explodes. It is a huge ball of glowing red and orange flames. No one moves or speaks. Then, as one, we run outside into the pouring rain: Troy, Saskia, Brandy, Sasha, Michael, Karl, Mia, Lizzie, Jason, Claire, Tina, Ophelia and me. In the future, we will become different things: advisers, horse whisperers, entrepreneurs, fashion designers, marketing managers, academics, artists and more. Our life in utopia will be forgotten or remembered, a horrific memory or a beautiful, nostalgic dream. But for now, in the glow of the burning tree, blown by the wind, we run on the front lawn, in the torrential rain, through the path of branches and debris. Soaked to the skin, we shriek and scream like wild things, monster Kid gods.

In traditional fairy tales, monsters are often interpreted as symbols enabling us to confront our fears. When children play with their fear of monsters in a story, for example in 'Little Red Riding Hood' or 'Beauty and the Beast', this means they learn to manage the monsters in real life. In the children's book *Where the Wild Things Are*, the child Max leaves the boredom of his home and travels across the sea to become an island monster and a King. He takes part in a wild and wonderful dance, a kind of teenage party. At the end of the story, Max gets tired and decides that he needs to get back, and he leaves the island and the Wild Things. Max goes home.

In the community, being a Kid monster is different, for we never chose to be considered as outsiders or freaks. Like a Frankenstein's monster, at the start we were assembled from ideological scraps, a quack's elixir and boomer dreams. As teenagers, when we played at being monsters, becoming the haystack chimera, taking drugs in the light of the moon, arguing with the Adults, when bad things happened, it was inside our home. The traditional monster story requires boundaries to function, a wild world and a safe one. Unlike Max, we could not leave the wild things behind us, get on a boat, sail away and return to our bedrooms. Children of utopian communities are exiled; we cannot ever go home from here.

16. The Only Way Is Up

'Never has our future been more unpredictable . . . It is as though mankind had divided itself between those who believe in human omnipotence (who think that everything is possible if one knows how to organize masses for it) and those for whom powerlessness has become the major experience of their lives.'

Hannah Arendt, *The Origins of Totalitarianism*

'What does the artist do? He draws connections. He ties the invisible threads between things. He dives into history, be it the history of mankind, the geological history of the earth or the beginning and end of the manifest cosmos . . . History speaks to artists.'

Anselm Kiefer,
from a speech at the Tel Aviv Museum of Art

When I wake up, a dream lingers on the cusp of my mind. It's teetering, almost here, almost gone. In the dream, I am writing this book, and reach into the back drawer of my granddad's desk. Among his sermon notes, and family letters, I find a necklace and think I must keep this for my daughters. When I hold the necklace up, a pearl dangles at the centre. Against the black wooden desk, it turns like a star. Then a blanket brushes, rough, on my face. I am awake in my house. The dream slips from my grasp. In my bedroom, the dense darkness unsettles me, and I flip on the light.

Close by, our youngest daughter shouts out, 'Maman,' and I now remember my deadline. I must finish writing, let this book go into other homes. Beside me, a tangled mass escapes from under covers. A's hair. He is snoring. For nearly three decades, we've woken together; he is bad at mornings and me at evenings. It is my turn to be the parenting early bird. More feet thud on the staircase. 'Maman. Papa.' It is our middle daughter. Her voice clear and bright.

I say 'Yes' and 'Open the door, babe'. She comes into the room, and I whisper, 'Let's get your sister.' Together, we go downstairs. On the kitchen table is a buttery knife, a crumb-strewn plate. Our eldest daughter has already left for school. As I am completing this book our youngest daughter is close to the age I was when I arrived at the community, our middle daughter is a teenager, and the eldest is about to leave home. As she approached sixteen, seventeen and then eighteen, our eldest daughter prepared for young-adult life. We had discussions about dreams, jobs, studies, and her future.

In the kitchen, I put the kettle on, green tea in the teapot, coffee in the machine, get out feta, flatbread, za'atar, cereal and milk, and turn the radio on. On France Culture, there's a programme about Saint Augustine and his *Confessions*. A voice is saying, 'My soul is like a house.' The kettle boils. I pour water onto the tea leaves, and I think about houses and souls, trinkets and rooms, realities and blueprints, monsters and utopian dreams, necklaces strung with meteorites and pearls. Sipping tea, I say to my middle daughter, 'I had such an odd and beautiful dream. All about my book, you three, and a pearl.'

It is July 1988. London. A trippy pop tune bounces on hot tarmac. In shops, it dashes through racks of psychedelic clothes, around velvet scrunchies and neon bangles: 'The Only Way Is Up'. Yazz, a tall Jamaican British woman with cropped bleached hair, pulls us up the ladder. She sings that even if we get evicted, we can still dance, because we're ascending, rising out of the gloom. Plans are being unveiled for Europe's tallest skyscraper to be built at Canary Wharf. Margaret Thatcher has become the longest-serving UK prime minister this century. Unemployment is down, and there are genuine bargains at unrepeatable prices. The streets are moving, car horns beeping, yuppies' padded power shoulders turn. Tony Blair, the future prime minister, is appointed to the shadow cabinet. He represents the 'soft left' and embarks on a serious political career. The SAS is cleared for gunning down unarmed IRA terrorists (but is later condemned for violating human rights). Dulux offers square deals for masonry paint. You can transform the façade of your home, make the outside fresh and new. Even if inside things are falling apart, I am sixteen and the only way is up.

In Isa's South London townhouse, at 9 a.m., I sit on a bedroom floor, fenced in by adolescent debris: half-drunk cups of tea, audiotapes, books and dirty clothes. Rizla papers in hand, I am rolling a joint, surrounded by teenage city girls. Except for Isa, I barely know them. The girls wear ripped Levi's 501 jeans and boys' boxer shorts. Their hair intimidates me. It trickles like honey.

Sneaking a look at the girls, I turn flimsy cigarette papers, praying my joint will not disintegrate. Isa says, 'We'd better go.' She glances at me. 'It'll take us twenty minutes to get to the agencies.' She asks the other girls, 'What are you doing?'

'Have to see a Docklands exhibition, Freeze, with my mum,' one sighs.

Another says, 'Going to the Docklands thing.'

As I light my joint, I picture the Docklands exhibition. Apparently it's organized by a guy called Damien Hirst. For my A-levels, I want to do Art, but I am more interested in artists like Tracey Emin. Her confessional work puts ugly things into light, and I also love Frida Kahlo: naked limbs, blood, flamboyant dresses, suits and myth. This is art where things and people meet, in piles of rubbish, beauty and artefacts. Walter Benjamin wrote 'living means leaving traces', and even to Isa's house I have brought knickknacks: a china dog, and its little carpet. Before I go to sleep, I lay my house gods down. My stuff is a nest, as though in the absence of history and home, I have built my own. Tracey Emin will soon exhibit a squashed cigarette packet belonging to an uncle killed in a car crash. She draws scratchy pictures of people having sex entitled *Everybodies been there*. Later, this autobiographical work leads me to artists like Charlotte Salomon, narrating her personal and Holocaust story through seven hundred paintings. Salomon asks:

'What makes you shape and reshape yourselves so brightly from so much pain and suffering? Who gave you the right?' This is pain made beautiful. Flowers and bodies claiming the right.

Isa interrupts my thoughts. 'I said I'd ring my parents today.' For two weeks, we've got free run of her house. Isa's two younger brothers are away with her parents. Her mum and dad – according to her – have allowed me to stay, as they know I get good marks. Whenever I see them, I make an effort.

The house is a home from home, a regular stomping ground. I like Isa's parents, and their organized fridge shelves. The breadknife is sharp, and their kitchen swept clean. Isa's mum often makes us moussaka. We eat around a scrubbed pine table: Isa, her family and me. Isa's dad serves us, and we have normal conversations and my fork slices through potatoes, tomato sauce, mince and aubergine. But, sometimes, I wonder if I sound like a robot, as though someone has programmed me to speak. 'I am fine, fine. Thanks for having me to stay.'

'What do you think?' Isa pulls her hair into a ponytail. It twitches dangerously from side to side. She wears a tight black T-shirt. Her breasts squeezed together by a Wonderbra. Isa crackles like a pylon with electricity. 'Do you think I'll pass for eighteen at the agency?'

'Oh yeah.' I don't ask whether I can fake my age. Everyone thinks I am older than I am.

'Susie lives in a commune,' Isa often announces to her friends. Suddenly, my upbringing is my golden ticket, and I conform to the look of a commune Kid: piercings, bleached hair, cat eyes, wild clothes. For a brief few years, the commune gives me street cred, a nod of acceptance into certain crowds. At this time, I begin to call the house a 'commune', as I realize the word 'community' doesn't mean anything outside. With 'commune' I hold my own with left-wing university lecturers, gallery owners, drug dealers and Hare Krishna kids. For once, I feel like I fit in.

The city enters my blood. In my small town, there are yuppies, casuals and freaks, but here there are punks, skinheads who like ska, mods, New Romantics, rockabillies, early ravers. Anyone can become any of these things. When I stay at Isa's house, we get stoned and drift along the South Bank, listening to Bruce Springsteen on her Walkman, 'Dancing in the Dark'.

We emerge from the underground and walk along Tottenham Court Road, past the Scientology Church and shops selling knock-off hi-fis. To temp, you must be eighteen, but we have forged the papers. The agency woman looks us up and down, 'Do you have experience in catering?' I nod. Since I was thirteen, I have cooked and served food at festivals where rich hippies eat salads from Tibetan bowls.

'You'll start tomorrow.' The woman turns to me. 'Your job is in a hospital.' Then she says to Isa, 'Yours is at breakfast TV.' We walk out grinning. Isa's going to put her money towards Interrailing, travelling around Europe with the girls. I will use mine for clothes, train fares, and petrol for my new moped. I need money to get around and get out.

The next morning, in a London hospital kitchen, when I push open the doors a plump black woman with purple lipstick hands me an apron. 'You are peeling potatoes, my dear. You must fill the machine every day.' She points towards a cylindrical metal machine. Every five minutes, I must empty heavy sacks of potatoes into a spinning hole. Then, a man collects them to roast, boil, mash and fry. 'There are five hundred people to feed.' The woman's voice is warm, her smile like spreading butter. At the bottom of the machine mush forms, the rot of old potatoes left to ferment. This must be scooped out. 'If not, we'll be killing the patients,' the woman giggles. I laugh too. In this kitchen, everyone laughs. The cylinder vibrates, and every morning my feet trample on the pavements. The cylinder turns, and I forget about the community. Sun hits the pavement cracks, and I spread my wings.

Despite his criticism of hope in *The Myth of Sisyphus*, Albert Camus stated that it is (nearly) impossible to live without it; and that summer, hope feeds me. It is food in my body, vitamins for my soul. In London, everything opens like a pop-up book and makes the future seem possible.

Before leaving Isa's house, I write in my diary: 'It has been nearly three months of moving, travelling. I cannot imagine the smells and sounds of home.' In *Erewhon*, Samuel Butler's novel, the hero leaves utopia in a hot-air balloon, floats through the clouds and into his future. In 1988, I am filled with dreams. Yet, despite all my efforts to get out of the gloom, when I return to my utopia, the hope evaporates, I fall down from my cloud, everything has changed.

When I get back to the community, all the Kids have left. Every single one. There are no Kids slumping around the woodstove in the Breakfast Room, no insults flying round the Dining Room. The Yoga Room is bare of all adolescent hormones, and our sleepovers are a faint echo on the varnished floor. No Kids roam the woods. They've moved out with their parents, the Adults. Since the start of the year, people have been leaving, and I knew that they were going. Sunshine, Mia and I promised we'd stay in touch 'forever'. When Troy left I didn't say goodbye. I waved at Brandy and Tina's removal van. Sasha and her mum just seemed to arrive and then disappeared, and others moved out while I was away. Brandy and Tina have gone to Holland with Walker and Thomas. Jason and Rainbow left with Barbara for New York. Michael and Saskia are both living in London with Violet. Ophelia left her gerbils behind and went with her mum to California. Sunshine and Troy are in India with Eagle, who has decided to train in Ayurvedic medicine. Karl returned to his showers and private school. Lizzie went to Ireland to become a traveller, living in a renovated van. Mia and Peter didn't stay for long. In September, Claire is going to university, and she's spending the summer staying with friends. She's working in a department store and her bedroom is bare. Only my brother and I are left.

However hard I try to resist, there is a feeling of amputation. A limb has been torn off. Things are missing from our home. The absence and change are a shock. We were neighbours, best friends, enemies, cousins, family, brothers and sisters. We have gone from twenty-three Kids to two. I will never see most of the Kids or Adults again.

*

When my children have changed schools, or we've moved house, I've always tried to build bridges between our past and present lives. The first summer after we arrived in our Breton home, I organized an open house, and old and new friends turned up. As the house was a tip and I had a three-month-old baby, we ate sandwiches and Lidl salads off camping tables, served on my newly acquired porcelain plates. The children ran round the garden, and connections were made between our old and new existences.

All lives and societies undergo transitions, involving significant changes in roles, responsibilities and routines, requiring humans to adapt. To live through these evolutions, I think, requires joining up the dots, ritualizing departures and new starts, providing ceremony. To head into the future, set foot on a path, we need to be in the present and recognize the past.

That summer, my brother and I joke with Alison that we are the only Founding Members left in the house. We are the oldest members of the community. This gives us a kind of status and a prestige, as we're finally at the top. But we're at the top of nowhere. During those August days, I cry constantly. A dam has cracked and I can't stop the flow. The sadness invades everything. In my diary, I write, 'I don't want people to know I feel so fucking helpless. Maybe that's why I keep wanting to go away. All I want to do is keep on moving.' I miss the other Kids terribly, but I think about the Adults in a different way.

Recently, I told a friend on the phone, 'One of the hardest things about having grown up there, aside from the traumatic events, is the thought that all these Adults were part of my childhood, tickled my preteen body, told me their life stories, gave me advice. People I would never see again, people who did or didn't care. There was no sense of boundaries or continuity.' It sometimes feels like I was a prop in the Adults' utopian dream.

When I look back, the sheer number of people who I grew up with means I also now often think about group sizes, questioning what the right number of people is for different groups. But also, how long should these groups exist?

In hospitals, when we form clinical closed art-therapy groups (meaning the same people stay for the therapy cycle), these usually involve five clients. When I work supervising hospital teams, the number of monthly participants is between fifteen and ten. In Robin Dunbar's renowned research on the human social world, he states that human social networks have a distinct fractal structure, like that observed with other primates. He claims our current personal social worlds still reflect our evolutionary history and a need for small-scale groups, with 1.5 intimates, 5 close friends, 15 best friends, 50 good friends and 150 friends. According to Dunbar, it is not possible to be intimate with a crowd of fifty ever-changing people. In the community, our big group was dehumanizing. Its fluctuating nature, with people coming and going, meant there was equally no sense of having a past that was shared.

That summer, I struggle with the new, mainly Adult community. In the Dining Room there are empty chairs. It's like the Adults and Kids who lived in the house didn't exist, and in the next few weeks we mention them for a while and then stop. 'It's lovely and quiet,' someone remarks. The community, like most utopian thought, has always relied heavily on the future. The past is rejected as everything can be remade. Growing up, I have understood history as something to be freed from. Marx wrote, 'The tradition of all dead generations weighs like a nightmare on the brains of the living.' Yet no human society or individual exists without a relationship to its past. It is strange to be raised in this territory, like having foundations built on shifting, treacherous sands. As Golda Meir once said, 'One cannot and must not try to erase the past merely because it does not fit the present.' When I look back, the community's lack of acknowledgement of its past was like living in a family home without photographs or with no stories told by the same people around the same table. It was like inhabiting a train station, buzzing with strangers.

Before going back to school, in mid-August, I act in the Brecht play *Mother Courage*. The director, a teacher from my alternative school, goes braless, and tosses words like knives in the air. I am opinionated, burning bright, tearful and furious. But all my anger is directed towards the world outside. At school, I get good marks but I am not shy about correcting the teachers. The language and politics of the community are mine, and I use them freely, saying 'fuck' and 'shit'. During a rehearsal, laughing, the teacher tells me, 'Some teachers at this school really don't like you. They think you are precocious!'

Humiliated, I decide I will leave school. Despite all my bravado, I am a hurt child, reasoning that Natasha did not finish sixth form and Charlotte is going to work in a pub. Other friends have started work at the Honda factory. All my life, books, learning, thinking and writing have been floating in the atmosphere around me. It seems better to abandon them now. In the last weeks of summer, I tell Alison over dinner that I won't be going to the sixth form. She says that I should do whatever I feel is right, because this is what Adults say. In the community, we get to invent our lives. It is like things are made from fairy dust, and fingers can be clicked and castles built. It is as though we don't need guidance to grow.

Later, Claire is back for the weekend. In her bedroom, I blurt out what the teacher told me, adding, 'So, I am going to leave school. There is no point.' Unexpectedly, she shouts at me. 'That teacher is totally irresponsible. She's in a position of power and abused it. You must do your A-levels and go to university!'

Slamming her door, I run outside. By the sequoias, I gaze at the sky. Thin, wispy cirrus clouds drift over the redwoods, strands of atmospheric possibility. These clouds are travelling elsewhere, and I slump to the ground and run dried pine needles through my fingers, tipping the soft bits from hand to hand. Many commune Kids I know left school before their A-levels, but Claire's words echo in my mind. She is a bossy big sister, but sometimes right, and in the following weeks she persuades me to stay on at school, saying, 'Susie, you don't have a choice!' That September, Claire leaves the community and I hate her for moving out but can't wait for her to go. As a going-away present I make her a clock from a vinyl LP. At its centre is a collaged flower, and the petals reach outwards, scraps torn from magazines. The night before she leaves, Claire tells me, 'I can't wait to get out of here.'

Claire's bedroom becomes mine. I decorate it with old mirrors, fragments of shop dummies, broken Lloyd Loom furniture from charity shops, plastic pineapples, snow globes, seaside souvenirs, beaded 1930s jewellery, punk posters and gloomy self-portraits. Inside these four walls, I use car paint to revamp lamps, draw and learn the foreshortening technique, read *The Women's Room* (again), practise lines for plays, learn songs for musicals, write terrible poetry, sip on bottles of whisky, put on eye make-up, and house my expanding collection of vintage clothes, caps for raving and hats for dressing-up, books, boxes of buttons, and old magazines. The elephants are on my dressing table, and my secret box is under the bed. There are files filled with old letters, and on my bookshelves are novels, plays and poetry. A day doesn't pass without me reading, and the objects jostle around me.

My bedroom is like a nest. The word 'room' comes from the Old English *rum*, meaning 'space'. It is a space in extent or time; scope, opportunity. The original sense remains to make room or 'clear space for oneself'. Like many teenage rooms, my space is sealed, I never open the windows or the curtains. The word 'window' comes from the Old English for 'eye-hole', and also an Old Frisian term meaning 'breath-hole'. But this room is dark, smelly and dusty. It is more like a space for hiding and hibernating, and perhaps this is what we do in teenage rooms – build our chrysalis and hope that one day from inside these stuffy, strange spaces, we will become butterflies.

From here, I begin the sixth form. It is another beginning, and I step inside. There is no Natasha or Charlotte, and I make new friends with dyed hair, shaved sides, handmade and vintage clothes. Suddenly, I am not so much of an outsider. At school, I must choose three subjects. Initially, I choose five. Only very bright pupils choose five subjects, hard-working oddballs and girls in knee-length skirts. I begin A-levels in Maths, Theatre Studies, English, Sociology and Fine Art. Quickly, I drop Maths, because I don't work hard enough, and when I turn up to the class in my Doc Martens, pink fishnet tights and fake Persian lamb-fur coat, all the serious Indian boys and bespectacled girls stare.

But my dad sighs when he hears my choices. 'Why can't you do some academic subjects?'

As I get older, I see less of him, my stepmother and my four little half-brothers and -sisters. My father has seven children now; an eighth will soon arrive. Despite my love for my siblings, our visits to their home are often an ordeal. They involve changing nappies, rows, indifference, wine, sneaked cigarettes and Nickelodeon TV. My school reports gather dust and are left unread. There are too many children here and I don't belong. When she comes back to the community, Claire rows with our mum, and when we're staying at his house, I snap at my dad. We're both fighting to fit in somewhere.

But in 1989, the world is on the road to peace. Half a million people gather in East Berlin in a mass protest, and the Berlin Wall dividing communist East Germany from West Germany falls. It is not a big event in the community, as all the Marxists have gone. Discussions about socialism can no longer be heard. But there are unprecedented press conferences between US president George Bush and his Soviet counterpart Mikhail Gorbachev. In the 1988 TV documentary *Back in the USSR*, Jerry Schecter described Gorbachev's attempt to revive a society and people, brought up under communism, completely numbed by a relentless totalitarian rule.

At school, a sixth-form teacher asks me, 'Do you want to prepare for the Oxbridge entrance exams?' These are the required tests for both Oxford and Cambridge University. Raising my eyebrows, I laugh, 'No way.' My future is a map. I will travel the world, never get married, own seventeen cats and have lovers across the globe. I want to unite punk and the fritillary petals from our woods. Art is my new home. I will paint the flowers and stroke pigment onto canvas. Everything ends with flowers.

The community becomes different, calmer. New members arrive: a wood sculptor, a graphic designer, a plumber, a smattering of science teachers. Nobody with children moves in, and there is an unspoken rule that children moving in should be avoided after what happened with the Kids. Suddenly members start saying we're an 'intentional community' because members have intentions, whatever that means. Friday Meetings are less heated, and I no longer attend. When I was a child, they were a way to spend time with the Adults. But my fascination has dimmed for the voices droning in the Lounge. During discussions on permaculture, a man with a large forehead earnestly shows pictures of worms. Outside, members drag bales of hay and discuss the merits of mud.

People are kind but nobody is particularly inspiring until a couple, a woman and her partner, move in. She is heavily pregnant and organizes arts events; he is a painter. They become my new Adult friends. Early mornings, I knock on my new friends' door – I do knock now, as I recently walked in on a different couple having sex, and the man shouted, 'Susie. Fuck off!' But my new friends are kind, they make me treacle-thick black coffee, and we sip it as their baby plays on the floor. We talk about art, and I tell them I want to get plastic surgery 'to cut a hole in the palm of my hand so I can see through myself'. Often, I mention how people always think I am a boy.

And it's true that as a young woman, when I don't wear make-up, I am often mistaken for a young man. My hair is very short and I am built like a boy. When I visit Claire at university, our favourite thing is to get dressed up, get drunk and dance at the gay disco. My love of dressing up extends to drag queen culture, and I spray my body silver and put on gold hot pants. Even now, decades later, I love the exaggerated femininity of drag. I was a girl and then I felt like a boy and then became a woman, learning and choosing to be feminine. There is a nostalgia for something lost and found.

At sixteen, I have my first serious boyfriend. When I am with him, in the street people think we're two men. My boyfriend is five years older than me; like Natasha, we are separated by light-years. He is an underground skateboarder. Much later, I will realize he always dated much younger girls, and was too old for me. But Alison and the people in the community like him. He does yoga in his underpants, standing on one leg, and says, 'I hope we'll stay together forever, my soul sister.' He fits the values of the community. I say to him, 'Why the fuck are they all asking me to take those Oxbridge exams?' He replies, 'Susie, you don't have to go to Oxford. You can be free.'

We begin having sex. It is what I said in the Mattress Room – that I would wait until I was sixteen – and I am determined to get this over with. When we have sex for the first time, it is not unpleasant nor exciting, but I have reached my determined date. Vicky, a goth from my school, who ties patent leather boots onto her army surplus bag – and has had sex with one of the teachers – tells me that when she lost her virginity all she could think of was the soundtrack to *Black Beauty*.

There is a fast harshness to these years. As I move on and up, the messages from *Spare Rib*, rational language, cold baths, David, what happened with Lionel and Troy, mean my body is finally hard; I have a thick outer shell. I've developed the embodied conviction that as a liberated woman, I must be tough. It is, of course, a misreading of feminism. Sometimes, I imagine my skin covered in small spikes. I should be able to handle anything, battle with reality, the real.

Jacques Lacan, the French psychiatrist and psychoanalyst, theorized that 'the real' is related to 'that which is strictly unthinkable', unspeakable, including the horrors of life. As Kids in the community, 'the real' was unavoidable, as there was no application of child development theory, nor safety belts provided for the knowledge that 'the real' is a tunnel that has no end.

When I am sixteen, I will sleep on any floor, drink anyone under the table. Thinking I can confront everything, I work and play hard without exception.

But having a boyfriend confuses me. Each morning, as a mantra, I tell myself: I am going to leave him because intimacy terrifies me. When I stay overnight, despite his benign character, I am convinced he will do me harm. Yet instead of splitting up with him, because I think I am grown-up, I commit. It is a paradoxical position, but I believe I must have a serious relationship, be old before I have been young, be a responsible adult in a couple, having never been a dependent child. Later, I will see many young people who have experienced forms of parentification adopting this behaviour. Anxiety rises inside me. It is a spiralling fear and I stay at his house two or three times a week, too often for my own good.

'Invite your boyfriend round,' Natasha says, 'We can drink vodka and talk about India!' 'Bring him to London,' Isa tells me. Lizzie invites us to Ireland. 'Come and hang out with the travellers.' But I crave my solitude. My worlds must not collide. So I rarely introduce my boyfriend to my friends, cannot connect my worlds, connect the past to the present or to the future. The 'false self' compartments I began when I was a child continue, and my life and time are divided into parts. I rarely introduce my friends to each other. My habit of division is too ingrained.

On weekdays, when I leave my boyfriend's place, I walk alone to the sixth-form college, my homework in my bag. Inside houses, people open curtains. In kitchens, they make toast and tea. Glancing in, somehow, I feel part of their mornings, and I stop at the local bakery, buy a breakfast of a custard tart and milk. Walking along the pavement, biting through pastry and nutmeg-studded custard, it feels like freedom. Yet this solitary liberty is a double-edged sword, because I am outside the houses looking in. From the street, I enjoy cosy breakfast scenes, but I cannot enter, do not know how to unlock the door and do not have the key. I cannot get inside a home.

Daily, I read and write. They are my practices, and I never stop. In my bag, there is always a book and a notebook. Life is unimaginable without these things. *The Women's Room* is still on my shelf, but has been joined by Seamus Heaney, Jane Austen, Dostoevsky, Leonora Carrington and Jeanette Winterson. The razors and pills have been discarded as I have grown older and moved on to other things. Instead, I am an avid smoker, a winebibber, a whisky drinker and a drug taker. With Isa in London, I tip down pints paired with Jack Daniel's chasers. Natasha, her boyfriend and I gulp vodka, and smoke Marlboro cigarettes. Alone in my bedroom, I roll joints. Often, I take Cora's tins of buttons, tip them over my bed, and sort them into colours: maroon, sea green, gold and pearl.

All my addictive habits are regulated by rules. It is like I am a doctor and prescribe my own medicine. Unusually for someone of my age, I regularly consume drugs and alcohol alone. They are forms, I would say now, of self-medication, to numb my deep distress. But it is like juggling slippery plates. On occasion, I notice friends looking shocked as I offer them an afternoon swig from my whisky.

Yet I will not let my habits stop me from moving on. When I am sixteen, seventeen and eighteen, I still write the timetables, things to be done. 'Theatre Studies: notes on Anarchist Dario Fo. Art: finish batiks. English: write essay plan. Sociology: revise.' There is a private balance between pleasure and survival, the thrill of risk and annihilation, between passing my exams and passing out. Regularly, I faint, as though my body cannot cope with the strain because I sleep in three or four different houses every week. Years later, my archaeologist friend sends me Plutarch's explanation of how certain Egyptian kings, before the reign of Psamtik, would not drink wine, as they believed grape vines grew on battlegrounds where men had fought and lost against the gods. The deceased's blood mingled with the earth. The kings thought drunkenness drove men senseless, as they were filled with the deadly fluids of the past.

Finally, when I am eighteen, I do not take the Oxbridge exams but I apply to and am selected for a competitive Drama course. I leave the community to go to university, as Claire said I should. By this point, I am running so fast through life that, when I leave home, I barely notice the change. Alison drives me to university, and I arrive with tomatoes from the greenhouse, and a huge bag of cashew nuts. I take a ton of stuff from my bedroom and put a poster David gave me of Route 66 on my wall. In the hall of residence, I own my first keys, and I have to learn to lock and unlock a door. For years, and even now, I will struggle with doors and keys, and I am always obsessively shutting things.

On my first day at university, a dark-haired woman asks, 'Don't I know you?' We discover that for over six years – as children – we entered the same drama festival. While I sat at the back wearing Sunshine's dress, she was one of the girls in black leotards I longed to be. To my astonishment she says, 'Oh Susie, you always looked so pretty, in your flowery dresses. We were so jealous.'

All I remember of the drama festivals is the feeling of being an outsider. Later, even Isa tells me that her London friends were envious of my freedom and cool clothes. As time passes, I begin to understand that The Look is a filter through which *I* have perceived the world; my deep sentiment of shame. It turns out that sometimes the others – the mothers at the gate, the aunts and uncles, the teachers and girls – were simply sending interest or compassion my way. But I didn't know how to see it or feel it.

As I begin my new life, unlike other students I know how to do my washing, cooking, and manage my money, and I am not afraid to speak my mind. At university, a handful of us come from state comprehensives, but most of the students come from private schools. From one side of my mouth, I explain my dad and Grandma Bella's heritage, and from the other I talk politics and skateboarding. In

Bourdieu's terms I own a smattering of cultural capital, but community life has left me highly self-confident yet inept and emotionally reckless. Natasha comes to visit, and is scandalized that after months I've never wiped my sink, and she buys me cleaning products. I don't know how to look after myself, physically or mentally.

I run through the next three years, write short stories, make films, organize midnight cabarets, interview Maya Angelou, sing in a folk band, perform one hundred plays, have a disastrous love affair with another older man, work in Romania in an orphanage, busk in Scottish streets, and return to India. At university, I am outspoken with lecturers, defending my friends and any social cause. I burn academic bridges to protect the underdog. It is the song I learnt from Tripti, Lawrence and all the Adults: the collective first. Overworked, I also become Women's Officer for the Student Union. Following meetings, for which I write agendas, I set up a programme providing free rape alarms, and question reading lists for gender balance. I fight for women's rights and never stop.

Pushing myself to the limit, I work for months as an artist's model, pose naked just to prove I can. On weekends, I protest against fox hunts, and one day get badly beaten up by a gang of men with baseball bats. I am so impacted by this that I lose my voice for several weeks, and literally cannot speak. But I protest again because I read *Survive the Savage Sea*, and the combination of parentification and the post-traumatic 'forcing' described by Leguil means I am in total denial of my limits, in cognitive dissonance with myself. I can survive but cannot be.

There is a cacophony of actions; I electrify, translate the molten lava that is flowing through my veins. I work and party until my batteries are flat. After my first year at university, when I am nineteen and back in the community for the summer, we move into one final Unit: the Unit where I was sexually abused. There is the bedroom where Lionel gave me the massage, and our living room is where I slept that night. The day we move, boxes in my arms, I hate the thought that I am going to live there. But I tell myself I am being overly sensitive. It is ridiculous to make a fuss, and I say nothing as I walk up the stairs.

Secretly, regularly, I fall into black moods. They are barren moorlands and stretch out endlessly. Discreetly, I enrol for sessions with a student counsellor. It is nothing like being with the co-counsellors. She is soft-spoken and kind, and we begin by putting my life events in order. On a chair in her office, I cry, and talk about dreams where, in the background, there are always ancient wars. I know that there are things wrong with me and I think it is to do with my past. But I don't tell her everything because I am stuffed full of secrets: the early secrets of a child survivor from the wall, secrets from utopia. Years of secrets fill my insides. Sometimes, it feels like they have replaced me.

At the age of twenty, I use words to talk about politics, theatre, literature and women's rights. When I speak, I avoid euphemisms and, like I was taught by Barbara, I say it straight. But when it comes to talking about my utopian childhood, the language stops. I am lost for words. No one can understand 'Unit', 'income sharing', growing up with

Kids who are not your family. I cut conversations short, give small details, or, like Claire, I make jokes about the hippies. Strangely, I can't look back to a place that had no past.

Yet being able to narrate our lives is part of living. In *The Good Story*, J. M. Coetzee discusses with psychotherapist Arabella Kurtz how we talk about our pasts, as individuals and postcolonial societies. Kurtz says, 'The more determinedly a society feels the need to look upon itself as having risen above the past and being free and distinct from it, the more likely it is it will be in history's unconscious sway.' As I enter adult life, I am constantly influenced by a past I do not know how to face.

In *Memory, History, Forgetting*, French philosopher Paul Ricoeur writes about human relationships to the past. Psychoanalysis, he maintains, makes it apparent that a good life necessitates being reconciled with our history, and the pain any life inevitably entails. Failure to face the past leads to trauma in the individual, and it is the same for society.

My sister and I give one last radio interview to a journalist, where I say that my childhood in the commune was 'mixed'. Sat next to me, Claire speaks into the microphone. 'It was rubbish,' she says. And I am furious with her, because I am still trying to protect our home. Following the interview, I never talk to a journalist about my childhood again. It seems that in every film, programme and article, the community is portrayed as either heaven or hell. My life is reduced to a predetermined agenda. Later, I will read Nigerian writer Chimamanda Ngozi Adichie's essay on 'The Danger of the Single Story' and the use of power to determine identity. The problem with the single story is that it creates stereotypes and these are incomplete. In the documentaries on communities, there are drugs, chanting, and swaying hippies. People dig in fields and children run wild. But no journalist investigates what it means to grow up in a group, a crowd, a pack, an institutional life, or the dehumanizing lack of intimacy. No one really asks what happens to young bodies and minds brought up in communal experiments.

After years of being a documentary subject, I no longer want to talk. As I turn twenty and become an Adult, the words to describe my childhood are alien to me. They are out of reach.

In the year I turn nineteen, Mum tells us she and Bill are going to live in Africa. I know I will miss them terribly. Months later, they pack up their things, and I pack up my things. Claire has already gone to live with her boyfriend and is working in marketing. All our rooms are stripped bare. Bill and Alison fly across the world. A member of the community helps my brother move to university. A five-minute phone call costs twenty pounds and we ring each other once a year.

I hold a sale and discard most of my belongings. It is strange, as my eldest daughter approaches the age when I left, to picture her selling off her things, having nowhere to land between adventures.

As my brother, sister and I have never had a room at my dad's, when Alison leaves we have nowhere else to go. At twenty, I sell off family heirlooms and my childhood bed.

I throw out five bin bags of my letters and keep one hundred in a cardboard box. There are no more fields, woods, buildings, gardens, Kids, Adults, bread, signing in or signing out, no more meetings, no monsters, no Christmases with five turkeys and fifty people. We leave a place that has engulfed us completely, shaping our bodies and minds. It was a separate planet, a cosmos. A universe. Alfredo taught us, right from the start, that everything could be remade.

One year later, I graduate and turn down a high-profile job in Japan. Against all logic and reason, I blindly follow my new boyfriend, A – who I have just met – to come and live in France. I cut off all ties with the community and those that connect me to my former life. It is as though I disappear, vanish in smoke, and begin again. It is another start. A new home. I say, '*Je m'appelle Susanna.*'

Epilogue: Home Is Where We Start

'It is very difficult for people to recognize that the essential of a democracy really does lie with the ordinary man and woman and the ordinary common-place home.'

Donald Winnicott, *The Family and Individual Development*

'I was also searching for a house in which I could live and work and make a world at my own pace, but even in my imagination this home was blurred, undefined . . . It was as if the search for home was the point . . .'

Deborah Levy, *Real Estate*

When I move to France, people ask where I come from, and when I answer 'Great Britain' they always ask *where* in Great Britain. Often, I am lost for words because I cannot identify a place or a home, and I change the subject. Regularly, when I ask the question in return, the French person identifies their ancestral village, referring to *mon pays*, my country, or for North Africans *mon bled*. They describe a hamlet, or a scrap of land, where for generations their family worked, ate, and laid their heads. Their home.

Initially, this puzzles me, then I understand that as the Industrial Revolution happened later in France, the culture is still rooted in the earth. As months and years pass, I enter intergenerational family homes, become friends with people who have never caught a plane, and work in psychiatric hospitals where extended families have been both patients and staff. From my utopian upbringing, with an exploded nuclear family, I end up spending most of my adult life among a people with a traditional sense of home. I bang up against this shared, rooted culture, admiring and disliking it. For while I appreciate the depth of shared history, I can never, nor do I aspire to, recreate a past that is not my own.

Recently, I've come to accept a transhumanist kind of movement suits me, a regular wandering from my main home to part-time homes. These new homes – hotel rooms, rentals, friends' spare bedrooms – are always created in translation. As Iris Murdoch wrote in *Under the Net*, 'I just enjoy translating, it's like opening one's mouth and hearing someone else's voice emerge.' In these different places, with my family or alone, I find I can be different and the same: myself.

I have only been back to the community once. Around a decade ago, I visited with my two daughters (the third wasn't born yet), made my way down the drive and climbed the sweep of steps to the double doors. A took a photograph.

I have a baby on my hip, a five-year-old holds my hand. My eldest daughter says, 'It's beautiful here, Maman,' and I smile because I also thought the house was magical when I first came, but I do not elaborate. I have decided to show my daughters the house, so they can anchor themselves in their family history, my start. I do not want my past to be a blank page.

When we enter the community, I barely know anyone. A friendly woman with dreads shows me around. It feels slow, peaceful and dreary. There is none of the excitement, nor the madness from those early utopian days. As I walk through the house, I photograph the Dining Room and the Post Room where I received hundreds of letters. In the Kitchen, my viewfinder frames the mixer and the notice-board. On the board my name is written in chalk because I am a visitor, alongside 'A list of jobs to be done', 'Notes for the meeting' and 'PLEASE TURN YOGA ROOM LIGHTS OFF!' But, above all, I take pictures of the dense woods, the green place where I felt free.

On that day, I am a journalist, and I document. Before I leave, I explain to the woman the dates that I lived in the house. She pulls a face. 'Oh! You were here when there were too many teenagers. Everyone knows about the time when there were too many teenagers. They never let it happen again.'

When we leave, I wonder at her statement, for in the story the community has been telling itself it seems like the teenagers were to blame, were 'out of control', and I feel furious.

As an adult, I rarely mention my upbringing, attempting to tame these fifteen years of my life. Make them normal, just like everyone else. But it is difficult to run from the house, the woods, the Kids and Adults. When people ask about my childhood, I beg my wild beasts: shut up and behave. I invent organizational systems and train the annals of my past. I change the subject, time passes and the dust grows thick. When the subject cannot be avoided, I cast off the line, 'Oh, it was a little rock and roll.'

After several years, Bill and Alison return from Africa and buy a small house in the UK. For a while, we paste our family back together, and it appears we have turned the page. We celebrate Christmas and birthdays, sometimes with my dad. He divorces and remarries and we set up our own homes. Children are born and Claire and I share pregnancy tales. Alison begins to call herself 'Mum'. The word slowly re-emerges on birthday cards, and Claire and I notice this and feel awkward, but we say nothing to her because she *is* our mum. We try to accept that, with our parents, we have moved on, that life requires living and loving. But when all of us are together, no one mentions the community. There are eerie absences, topics of conversation we avoid.

As I read, study and write, work as a therapist, and have children of my own, the statues from my childhood start to tumble. Some fall, and others I push down of my own accord. In clinical meetings, I hear of damaged children whose stories echo my own. In my mind, 'revolution', 'change' and 'utopia' become potentially hollow words. Sometimes it is as though wild horses enter my living room. There are tight tendons in their necks and terrified hooves clatter on the ground. These horses can get frantic, out of control.

When my third daughter is born, the five of us move to the Breton house. Earlier that same year, Claire died, leaving behind her a beloved husband and three children. My dad and mum bear an awful, second tragic loss. My half-siblings, my brother and I lose a second sister.

When Claire made the playlist for her funeral, she chose 'If I Die Young' by The Band Perry. Before the funeral, heavily pregnant, I listened to it on Spotify. The song advises mourners about how when you're dead, people can start listening. After the funeral, for months, alone on the train, in aeroplanes, I put headphones on and play the song on repeat.

The same lyric always sticks in my head, and I wonder what it is that I need to hear, what Claire would want me to listen to. When we arrived at the community, she was eight and I was six. Often, I question whether, as she was older and had lived outside longer, she was less malleable than me. She rebelled while I conformed. Yet it seems what we shared, despite having friends, was an inner ache of loneliness. Sometimes, after Claire dies, it feels like I have only two choices: to advance blindly again, or to turn around and, like an archaeologist, look at the past in the present light. For a long time, I left the snow globe of our childhood on an attic shelf. When I take it in my hand, the past rushes in.

Each inch of the community is inscribed in my flesh, and the faded scars rise from my skin. The house is haughty and proud, ready to pull me back inside, and soon I am pushing open each door. There is a banging Gong, the balmy scent of rising bread. Plunging my fingers into an industrial sack, a cascade of black beans trickles like bottled rain. I hear the violence in the Adults' dissenting voices, the Friday Meeting fury, the elation at Christmas, and a summer picnic lunch. We are sprawled, forty of us, on the rolling fresh-cut lawn. Potatoes coated in warm basil dressing, sun, and cloudy homemade apple juice. A sharp sweetness, thinly sliced. The Adults play football, and drink beer. I play on a swing, veering forwards and backwards over the pastoral scene. Babies nuzzle at breasts. It is a Bacchanalian ecstasy. Everywhere there is hope for change, for the chosen ones. I swing higher and higher. Then, later, I stick a knife into a plug socket. There is the thud of electricity. A bolt aims for the beat of my heart. Everything returns: the cold baths, Lionel, the haystack, and the Mattress Room. I am a Kid alone in a utopian crowd.

After Claire dies and our third daughter arrives, the home I make with A and the girls becomes another kind of start. Grey stone is overlaid with an ivy sprawl. In the garden are old roses and a wooden gate. There is a fig tree and hydrangeas. Along an old moss-covered wall, white and yellow ox-eye daisies grow. Their heads turn towards the sun.

I unpack boxes and discover dozens of unfinished texts, computer files, paragraphs in notebooks, in which I have begun this book – pages dating from when I was fourteen, sixteen, nineteen, twenty-five, thirty years old and more. Strung out over my past is a longing to write, to go back to the utopia and open the doors and try to understand what it means to be the product of a social experiment, a freak.

There is always mention in my writing of how to tell the

truth. As Lea Ypi asks in *Free*, her book about growing up in communist Albania, how do I differentiate between what I've been told to say to the outside world, and the story I want to tell? I grew up with a trained tongue, linguistic enculturation shaped my speaking muscles, and I need to find my own words.

Paradoxically, my upbringing provides me with part of the solution: to frame my childhood in a rethinking of the everyday, an unpacking of the 'personal as political', a micro-story in a macro-world, a critical analysis of our utopia. By my desk, a stack of books and articles grows, a Greek chorus of thinkers. Modern and old practices. Research across time. In Greek theatre, the chorus is the voice of the city, providing a different perspective on the action onstage. Yet, I begin to realize, dry theory is not enough. Throughout my childhood, theory became ideology when no one noticed what was happening. As I write this book, life must accompany theory, and beauty tries to edge its way onto the page: the thoughts are felt.

When we moved into the stone house, the idea of home intrigued me, because as a family we were starting again as five. Our first homes, spaces and places form much of our future lives. We begin within a shelter with other people; they enter and exit in specific ways, wear certain clothes, eat certain foods, and tell different stories that reflect their beliefs.

I begin to wonder what I have used, discarded and kept from my first utopian home. There are silver linings to the cloud: I grew up with powerful women around me and am an unabashed feminist. Witnessing breastfeeding and natural childbirth means I have not only been at ease with these parts of motherhood, but enjoyed having babies. Having grown up in an institution founded on collective values, many things I do involve groups because I hold a deep faith in human gatherings. Yet I want to do things differently from the community; to make the groups safe, open-minded *and* egalitarian. Training hospital teams, supervising Covid units, running drama-therapy workshops or collaborating with artists, I love the thrill of alliances, and the unpredictable, rich power of the multitude. All the groups we frequent throughout our lives have the potential to become temporary homes, and we can start things and flourish inside.

I realize there will always be things I don't understand about my start, for part of the self is always unknown to us. If we imagine ourselves as a house, we can never be in all the rooms at the same time. If we're in the attic, a cat may be prowling in the cellar. While we fry eggs in the kitchen, a silk dress might fall from a hanger upstairs. Even if we step outside of the house, we can never see the roof, the front and the back simultaneously. This is one of the flaws of the myth of utopia, of clean political living – the idea that somehow, we can consciously and politically control ourselves, erase anomalies. There is something unobtainable about utopias, and I think that is why they are doomed to fail.

The problem is not the desire for change, feminism or equality, for these are my own battle cries. But when people withdraw from society, the revolutionary stance becomes inward-looking and almost stilled, because it is hermetically sealed. In utopias it seems like something often becomes trapped in the attempt for perfection, because we are not living next to neighbours or working with people who challenge our ways. The limits of Enlightenment thinking are here, as in utopias messy unreason can be driven away. Homes become ideological institutions, dehumanizing in the drive for success. Margaret Thatcher once said, 'Utopia never comes, because we know we should not like it if it did.' But she was squashing people's desire for equality and social justice. I strongly disagree with her, believing instead in radical hope, a concept developed by philosopher Jonathan Lear for situations which seem impossible. What makes his hope radical is that it is directed towards a future goodness and it anticipates good. But those who have this hope accept that – for now – they lack the concepts with which to understand this future. It is an imperfect, hopeful hope.

Ultimately, utopia makes me think of beauty: it is something we should want. When I work with clients in art-therapy sessions and they fear drawing badly or dislike their work, I say, 'Beauty is what we aim for, an ideal. We all have a perfect image in our mind of a perfect work of art. We need this aim, it's our drive. But there is always a difference between what we imagined and what happens. And that is the best bit' – I pause – 'because it means we keep on making art.' Then I tell them the story of my Spanish photographer friend, who when asked which his favourite of his photographs was, answered, 'The next one.'

*

In France, I finish the first draft of this book on a hot July day in my office. My room is as dusty and messy as my teenage den, crammed with hundreds of books and heaps of art supplies. On the walls are notes for collaborative writing projects with people in India and America, ideas for art therapy, and cards from artists and friends. There is a picture of my sister Claire on my wall, and I touch her face each time I walk through the door. Beneath her is a picture my archaeologist friend sent me of a statue of Telesphorus, a protector of children and one of the Greek healing gods. He symbolized recovery from illness, but his name also means 'bringer of completion'.

Inside my home, a blood family lives, and our parents, their partners, cousins, aunts and uncles, and other relatives come to stay. But a wider family also sits in our kitchen and breaks our homemade bread. This chosen family is intergenerational, international, made of believers, anarchists and atheists, fabricated from people, values, drawings and words. It includes the living and the dead. Yet it is consciously small, for there is little respite when you live in a pack. If we believe in the trope that it takes a village to raise a child, how that village is organized – and who the villagers are inside – becomes crucial to the child's development. Our chosen family resists various forms of oppression, but without the loss of intimacy and care.

There are many places in my life that I have felt at home – alone, or in a crowd of strangers. On trains, in stations or airports. There is something about the unknown that always means there can be a new start. I feel at home in hospitals and institutions that look after people, and my other home is art. Home is being with patients and staff, and at literary festivals, or Zooming with my Indian translator friend. There is a gap, a huge hole in my heart, the hollow nowhere of utopia. But I continue to return to the snow globe of my childhood, hoping to fathom something new. The Fates and Furies whisper and hiss on the rooftop, but they are calmer now, have settled down, are taming my wild horses.

Austrian novelist Stefan Zweig wrote that 'only he who lives his life as a mystery is truly alive'. Inside a home, we can aim for love and a constant rewilding, a place for retreat and shelter, for being as opposed to just surviving. Our stone house, our current home, also contains contradictions. We flip between Foucault and manga, can be gorgeous nail-varnish-wearing militant feminists, navigate between intention and impact. But this embracing of the sweet taste of paradox and complexity goes beyond the political. It is also holding the unknown of ourselves in our home, to offer our children and ourselves a quiet space for dreaming.

Author's Note

All parts of this book that refer to clients in my clinical art-therapy work or participants in lectures have been anonymized: individuals have been blended, dialogue fictionalized, and names, places and dates changed.

In writing this book, in attempting to understand my own story, I've placed it within a larger perspective, historically, anthropologically, sociologically and philosophically. As Svetlana Alexievich writes, 'I believe that in each of us there is a small piece of history.' To situate events, I undertook extensive research, particularly at the British Library, reading through contemporary archive documents, newspapers, books and magazines.

However, this memoir is *my* story of a childhood in a utopian community, and that in itself is a choice. As I grew up believing the collective took precedence over the individual, it felt important to try to recount my own experiences, to find my own language to explain.

Much energy and time was devoted to protecting the identities of the people in the book who I grew up with. All names, dates, identifying characteristics and places have been changed. All the events took place, but dialogue and characters have been blended. This was very important to me, as the book is an exploration of a system and the utopian movements which have been inspiring humans for centuries. In writing my memoir I have tried to be compassionate and fair.

To paraphrase André Gide, it is not the corks floating in the sea that interest me, but the currents that carry them. I wanted to ask questions about the intentions of social experiments and how these can impact adults and children.

Finally, my memoir is, of course, based on my memories, and these, by nature, are ever-changing and fallible.

Acknowledgements

A book is written by one person, but many people are involved in its making. On its journey to publication, *Home Is Where We Start* has crossed paths with some extraordinary individuals.

Firstly, Helen Garnons-Williams, the first time we met there was a crackling of electricity, and I knew I wanted you to edit this book. My sincere thanks to you and Ella Harold for your sharp minds, sense of humour, sensitivity, and for being all-round brilliant people.

Jessica Craig, my wonderful agent, I am very grateful for your literary conviction, belief in my work, and your powerful vision for this book. Gracias.

Many thanks to all the Fig Tree team, particularly Annie and Natalie for your ongoing work. Applause to Sophy Hollington for your extraordinary cover design. Gemma Wain, huge gratitude for your excellent copy-editing.

Early versions were read by many writers and friends. Particular thanks to Nick Flynn, Lara Pawson, Seraphina Madsen, Mien Wong, Marion Michell, Luanne Rice and Frouke Arns for your encouragement and thoughts. Marina Benjamin, very warm thanks for commissioning and editing my Aeon essay 'The Utopian Machine', in which I discovered the voice for this book.

David Collard, merci for the discussion in your kitchen about why I should write this book!

Thanks to Sam Mills for commissioning my clown essay for the anthology *Trauma* (Dodo Ink, 2021) which is partly reproduced in this book.

Home Is Where We Start began – and the proposal was written – during a Fellowship at Hawthornden Castle, in the excellent company of writers Frouke Arns, Lucy McKeon, Ryan D. Matthews, Morgan Thomas and Rachel Cantor. Much gratitude to Hamish Robinson and the excellent team for looking after us and providing writing time and space.

Thanks also to the Brooklyn Institute for Social Research, for the scholarship in 2023 which allowed me to attend the course 'Hannah Arendt: The Life of the Mind', and much gratitude to Samantha Rose Hill for your excellent classes, taking us into the world of Arendt.

During my extensive research, the team at the British Library were incredibly helpful. In France, the Lirici team have always provided a great welcome. Libraries are my soul food.

Many thanks to the students, patients, colleagues and hospital staff with whom I've shared profound, moving and enlightening times.

To my friends, *mes amies*, who have supported me through the hard and joyful moments of writing this book and welcomed me into their homes. I am very grateful to have you in my life. And to all the artists, writers, musicians, film-makers and people who bravely keep making work that challenges the world and tells the complicated stories. Power to you!

ACKNOWLEDGEMENTS

Many thanks to my parents for supporting me in the writing of this book.

My thoughts also turn to those who are no longer with us, and my eternal gratitude to my amazing sister (in the book, Claire).

And last but not least, my biggest thanks and love to A, my rock, and our three extraordinary daughters. Sharing, making and imagining a home with you is a wild and wonderful privilege. Merci.

Permissions

p. vii – extract from 'Four Quartets' by T. S. Eliot, published by Faber and Faber Ltd. Copyright © T. S. Eliot, 1943. Reprinted by permission of Faber and Faber Ltd

p. 11 – extract from 'Levitas', *The Concept of Utopia* by Ernst Bloch

p. 12 – extract from *Asylums: Essays on the Social Situation of Mental Patients and Other Inmates* by Erving Goffman

p. 16 – extract from *The Utopians: Six Attempts to Build the Perfect Society* by Anna Neima

p. 17 – extract from *Burger's Daughter* by Nadine Gordimer

p. 17 – extract from *The Poetics of Space* by Gaston Bachelard

p. 36 – extract from *Literature and Revolution* by Leon Trotsky

p. 42 – extract from *A Runaway World* by Edmund Leach

p. 43 – extract from *On Revolution* by Hannah Arendt

p. 43 – extract from 'Reality Demands' by Wislawa Szymborska, translated by Stanislaw Baranczak and Clare Cavanagh

p. 69 – extract from *Notes on the Management of Spoiled Identity* by Erving Goffman

p. 76 – extract from *Parole de Femme* by Annie Leclerc

p. 78 – extract from *Utopian Body* by Foucault, published by MIT Press, 2006

p. 83 – extract from *The Children of the Dream* by Bruno Bettelheim

p. 92 – extract from 'Social Education', Vol. 23, National Council for the Social Studies, American Historical Association, ed. Erling Messer Hunt

p. 96 – extract from an article by Mary Catherine Starr in the *Huffington Post*: www.huffpost.com/entry/parenting-double-standards_l_61f03176e4b0061af2569c00

p. 109 – extract from *The Open and Closed Mind: Investigations into the Nature of Belief Systems and Personality Systems* by Milton Rokeach, New York: Basic Books, 1960
p. 110 – extract from 'Ode on a Grecian Urn' by John Keats
p. 121 – extract from *Ignorance* by Milan Kundera
p. 126 – extract from 'On Whiteness and the Racial Imaginary' in *Writers on Race in the Life of the Mind* by Claudia Rankine and Beth Loffreda, Fence Books, 2015
p. 129 – extract from 'Terminator vs. Avatar: Notes on Accelerationism', presented by Mark Fisher at the Acceleration Symposium, Goldsmiths, September 2010
p. 135 – extract from *Double-Tracking* by Rosanna McLaughlin
p. 144 – extract from *The Lemonade Ocean & Modern Times* by Hakim Bey
p. 145 – extract from *The Writing Life* by Annie Dillard
p. 146 – extract from *The Bacchae*, Euripides, translated by Michael Cacoyannis, Meridian, 1987
p. 148 – extract from 'Why Utopian Communities Fail: The Shortcomings of the World and the Impossibility of Change' by Ewan Morrison, *Aeon* magazine, 2018
p. 150 – extract from *The Concept of Utopia* by Ruth Levitas
p. 151 – extract from *La fabrique du rêve* by Paul Valéry, translation by Susanna Crossman
p. 166 – extract from *To look at the sea is to become what one is* by Etel Adnan
p. 169 – extract from *Anthropologies of Revolution*, ed. Igor Cherstich and Martin Holbraad
p. 170 – extract from an interview with Sarah Kane by Dan Rebellato, Royal Holloway, University of London, November 1998, via intranet.royalholloway.ac.uk/dramaandtheatre/documents/pdf/skane1998.pdf
p. 172 – extract from *Slouching Towards Bethlehem* by Joan Didion
p. 176 – extract from *Qui je fus* by Henri Michaux, translation by Susanna Crossman
p. 177 – extract from *The Unbearable Lightness of Being* by Milan Kundera
p. 179 – extract from *Crowds and Power* by Canetti

p. 180 – extract from *Une histoire mondiale du communisme* by Thierry Wolton, translation by Susanna Crossman

p. 187 – extract from *The Non-Expressible Part of Thinking*: *Talking to Etel Adnan* by Andy Fitch

p. 199 – extract from 'Of Courage and Resistance', in *At the Same Time*: *Essays and Speeches* by Susan Sontag

p. 201 – extract from John Berger's 1972 documentary 'Ways of Seeing', via BBC

p. 202 – extract from *L'air et les songes* by José Corti, translation by Susanna Crossman

p. 211 – extract from *Pol Pot*: *Anatomy of a Nightmare*, Philip Short. Short references interviews with Long Visalo (a Khmer expatriate who returned to Cambodia after the Khmer Rouge victory) on November 26, 2001, and December 8, 2001

p. 216 – extract from *Historic Notes of Life and Letters in New England* by Ralph Waldo Emerson

p. 216 – extract from *The Utopians: Six Attempts to Build the Perfect Society* by Anna Neima

p. 216 – extract from 'Thoreau', Virginia Woolf, in the *Times Literary Supplement*, 12 July 1917

p. 241 – extract from *Frankisstein* by Jeanette Winterson

p. 253 – extract from *Eros the Bittersweet* by Anne Carson

p. 253 – extract from *Thésée* by André Gide, translation by Susanna Crossman

p. 255 – extract from 'An Enraptured Male' by Kathleen Jamie in the *London Review of Books*

p. 260 and p.273 – extracts from *Wandering*: *Notes and Sketches* by Herman Hesse

p. 269 – extract from *Metaphysics as a Guide to Mortals* by Iris Murdoch

p. 275 – extract from *The Letters of Virginia Woolf* : *Volume 3*, 1923–1928

p. 287 – extract from *The Letters of Emily Dickinson*, ed. Thomas H. Johnson

p. 298 – extract from *An Aperture Monograph* by Diane Arbus, ed. Doon Arbus and Marvin Israel

p. 301 – extract from *A Single Spark Can Start a Prairie Fire* by Mao Tse-Tsung, quoted in https://www.marxists.org/reference/archive/mao/selected-works/volume-1/mswv1_6.htm

p. 302 – extract from *If on a Winter's Night a Traveller* by Italo Calvino

p. 310 – extract from 'Trauma and the state with Sigmund Freud as witness' by Elizabeth Ann Danto, *International Journal of Law and Psychiatry*, vol. 48

p. 313 – extract from *Madness and Civilisation: A History of Insanity in the Age of Reason* by Foucault

p. 314 – extract from an interview with Susan Sontag via C-Span: https://www.c-span.org/video/?172991-1/depth-susan-sontag

p. 314 – extract from *If This is a Man* by Primo Levi

p. 325 – extract from the *Guardian*, April 2018: www.theguardian.com/tv-and-radio/2018/apr/24/wild-wild-country-netflix-cult-sex-noa-maxwell-bhagwan-shree-rajneesh-commune-childhood

p. 341 – extract from a speech by Anselm Kiefer at the Tel Aviv Museum of Art, via www.theartnewspaper.com/2011/12/01/speech-by-nir-barkat-anselm-kiefer-on-jerusalem-and-the-kabbalah

p. 344 – extract from *Paris: Capital of the Nineteenth Century* by Walter Benjamin

p. 345 – extract from *Life? Or Theatre?* by Charlotte Salomon

p. 352 – extract from *The Eighteenth Brumaire of Louis Bonaparte* by Karl Marx

p. 352 – extract from *My Life* by Golda Meir

p. 379 – extract from *The Unwomanly Face of War: An Oral History of Women in World War II* by Svetlana Alexeivich

Sources

Houses and homes

Gaston Bachelard, *The Poetics of Space*, translated by Maria Jolas (Penguin, 2014)

Bobby Baker, *Redeeming Features of Daily Life* (Routledge, 2007)

Marina Benjamin, *A Little Give: The Unsung, Unseen, Undone Work of Women* (Scribe UK, 2023)

Pascal Dibie, *Ethnologie de la porte: Des passages et des seuils* (Poche, 2012)

Sherry Turkle, *Evocative Objects: Things We Can Think With* (MIT Press, 2007)

Memoir and auto-fiction

Svetlana Alexievich, *The Unwomanly Face of War*, translated by Richard Pevear (Penguin, 2018)

J. M. Coetzee and Arabella Kurtz, *The Good Story: Exchanges on Truth, Fiction and Psychotherapy* (Vintage, 2016)

Lily Dunn, *Sins of My Father: A Daughter, a Cult, a Wild Unravelling* (Weidenfeld & Nicolson, 2023)

Annie Ernaux, *The Years*, translated by Alison L. Strayer (Fitzcarraldo Editions, 2022)

Deborah Levy, *Living Autobiography* (Penguin Books): Book 1, *Things I Don't Want to Know* (2018); Book 2, *The Cost of Living* (2019); Book 3, *Real Estate* (2022)

Édouard Louis, *The End of Eddy*, translated by Michael Lucey (Penguin, 2018)

Ali Millar, *The Last Days: A Memoir of Faith, Desire and Freedom* (Ebury Press, 2022)
Charlotte Salomon, *Charlotte, Life or Theater?* (Allen Lane, 1981)
Lea Ypi, Free: *Coming of Age at the End of History* (Penguin, 2022)

Groups, family, childhood

Pragya Agarwal, *(M)otherhood: On the Choices of Being a Woman* (Canongate Books, 2022)
Elias Canetti, *Crowds and Power*, translated by Carol Stewart (Farrar, Strauss & Giroux, 1984)
Erving Goffman, *Asylums: Essays on the Social Situation of Mental Patients and Other Inmates* (Penguin Classics, 2022)
J. E. Goldthorpe, *Family Life in Western Societies: A Historical Sociology of Family Relationships in Britain and North America* (Cambridge University Press, 2010)
Julia Samuel, *Every Family Has a Story: How to Grow and Move Forward Together* (Penguin Life, 2023)
Marina Warner, *Managing Monsters: Six Myths of Our Time* (Vintage, 1994)
Donald Winnicott, *Play and Reality* (Routledge Classics, 2005)

Trauma and bodies

Melissa Febos, *Body Work: The Radical Power of Personal Narrative* (Manchester University Press, 2022)
Olivia Laing, *Everybody: A Book about Freedom* (W. W. Norton, 2021)
Clotilde Leguil, *Céder n'est pas consentir: Une approche clinique et politique du consentement* (PUF, 2021)
Jacqueline Rose, *Women in Dark Times* (Bloomsbury, 2015)
Maria Tumarkin, *Axiomatic* (Fitzcarraldo, 2019)

Revolutions, utopias, philosophy

Hannah Arendt, *The Life of the Mind* (Harvest/HBJ Book, 1981)

Albert Camus, *The Rebel*, translated by Anthony Bower (Penguin Modern Classics, 2000)

Igor Cherstich, Martin Holbraad and Nico Tassi, *Anthropologies of Revolutions: Forging Time, People and Worlds* (UC Press, 2020)

Andrew Gallix and Richard Cabut (eds), *Punk Is Dead: Modernity Killed Every Night* (Zero Books, 2017)

Carlo Ginzburg, *Threads and Traces: True False Fictive* (UC Press, 2012)

Pierre Hadot, *What Is Ancient Philosophy?*, translated by Michael Chase (Belknap Press, 2004)

Homer, *The Odyssey*, translated by Emily Wilson (W. W. Norton, 2018)

Milan Kundera, *The Unbearable Lightness of Being*, translated by Michael H. Heim (Faber & Faber, 2000)

Anna Neima, *The Utopians: Six Attempts to Build the Perfect Society* (Picador, 2022)